Faith&Courage

Praying with Mandela

Thabo Makgoba
Archbishop of Cape Town

Library of Congress Cataloging-in-Publication Control Number : 2019018171

Photos:
Cover photo: African News Agency (ANA)
Pages 19, 28: Photo courtesy of Polokwane Municipality (Polokwane
        Museums).
Page 157: Trevor Slade
Page 196: [CC BY-SA 3.0 (https://creativecommons.org/licenses/by-sa/3.0)]
Page 200: South Africa The Good News/www.sagoodnews.co.za
        [CC BY 2.0 (https://creativecommons.org/licenses/by/2.0)]
Page 212: Gallo Images/Die Burger/Nasief Manie
Pages 142, 214, 226: Anglican Communion News Service
Page 220: John Allen

ISBN: 978-0-88028-470-7

North American printer and distributor: Forward Movement, 412 Sycamore Street, Cincinnati, Ohio 45202

First North American edition, 2019

Printed in the USA

www.forwardmovement.org

Faith&Courage

Praying with Mandela

Thabo Makgoba
Archbishop of Cape Town

Forward Movement
Cincinnati, Ohio

To my ancestor, Kgoši Mamphoku Makgoba
To my parents, Masilo and Kedibone Makgoba
To my dear family, Lungi, Nyakallo, and Paballo Makgoba

Table of Contents

Foreword by Graça Machel ix

Preface xi

Chapter 1   Makgoba's Kloof 15

Chapter 2   Alexandra 33

Chapter 3   Soweto 55

Chapter 4   Science, Politics, or Theology? 69

Chapter 5   Into a Boiling Pot 95

Chapter 6   Hard Graft and Gunfire 111

Chapter 7   Bishopscourt 137

Chapter 8   "Religion is in our Blood" 145

Chapter 9   The Quietening Years 155

Chapter 10   Facing the Setting Sun 177

Chapter 11   Go Forth, Revolutionary and Loving Soul 195

Chapter 12   Madiba's Legacy 211

Afterword   A Young Palestinian on a Donkey 229

Appendix A   Mandela Day Pledge at the Human Chain 247

Appendix B   Celebrating Madiba's Legacy and Its Lasting Impact
             Around the Globe 249

Appendix C   Prayer at the National Memorial Service for
             Nelson Mandela 255

Appendix D   Valedictory Service at the Home of Nelson Rolihlahla
             Mandela 259

Appendix E   Address to a "Procession of Witness" to Parliament 265

Appendix F   Sermon for the Easter Vigil at St. George's Cathedral ... 271

Acknowledgments 279

About Forward Movement 281

Foreword
by Graça Machel

These prayers are part of Arch's spiritual journey with Madiba, my husband, Nelson Mandela, over the years, from our home in Bishopscourt, Cape Town, where they shared quality time over long afternoons of bonding, always ending with a prayer.

As Madiba became frail, they met sometimes in Houghton, Johannesburg, and at other times in Qunu in the Eastern Cape, where Arch was regular company. He was always a comforting presence, especially in the last three years of Madiba's life.

I remember countless times in the hospital in Pretoria when Arch reached out to me with an evening prayer over the telephone, or even a kind message. He was a constant, caring presence.

How I learned to value those messages, alone in my corner whilst watching over my husband, aware of his slow departure yet unable to do anything except hold his hand.

Thank you, Arch! Your support during those times was invaluable.

God bless you!

Preface

The writing of this book began with a decision on whether to publish the prayers I shared with Nelson Mandela and his wife, Graça Machel, when visiting them during the last years of Madiba's life.[1] When I told one friend what I was considering, he asked, "Do you really want to put that on paper?" Others questioned how it would affect my pastoral ministry in the future. But yet others, including some members of the Mandela family, urged me to go ahead on the grounds that reflecting something of Madiba's spirituality would be beneficial to the country, the church, and the world.

The book has since developed into a personal memoir relating how I—the son of a pastor of the Zion Christian Church, with roots in our nation's nineteenth-century resistance struggle, first interested in a career in science rather than a vocation to the priesthood—came to minister to the most respected icon of justice and reconciliation of our time. After introducing you, the reader, to my journey of faith, I turn in the concluding chapters to an account of my exchanges with Madiba and Me Graça, selecting and placing in their context some of the prayers I shared with them.

I and my wife, Lungi, shared deeply with the Mandelas during this ministry. However, I do not disclose some of our interactions, whether on the phone, in the short text messages we shared or in person—for I think those were personal and publishing the details would go against what a cleric should reveal. So I beg your indulgence as I balance the need for pastoral confidentiality with sharing a story that will help people understand the important role faith played in Madiba's life and how this impacted the spirituality of South Africa.

---

1   Madiba is Nelson Mandela's clan name, by which he is popularly known in South Africa.

Prayer for Madiba
offered by Archbishop Thabo Makgoba during a pastoral visit

Blessed are you O Lord our God, creator of the universe;
by your breath we were created,
and by your will we have our being.

You have kindled in us a fire that never dies away.
In our darkest night when the flames of hope began to burn low,
you raised up your servant Nelson Mandela
to stoke the flames of our imagination
so that we could have a foretaste of the dream of God.

In him, the fullness of your love was pleased to dwell.
You have blessed him with longevity
and a resilient spirit that has allowed him to carry on his shoulders
the dreams, hopes, and fears of a nation.

We bless and praise you for all that he has meant to us,
the embodiment of all that is beautiful,
all that is good,
all that is true,
and we ask your blessing on him at this time.

As he turns to face the setting sun,
comfort and help him in his time of need,
look upon him with eyes of mercy,
hide him in the shadow of your wings.

Brood over him like a mother hen broods over her chicks
So that this time may be a time of rest and quietness,
free from pain and anxiety.

May he continue to lead the rest of his life
in the radiance of your glory,
and mark him as your own, forever.

This we ask in the name of Jesus Christ,
Our only mediator and advocate. Amen.

Chapter 1

Makgoba's Kloof

My ancestral home lies in South Africa's northernmost province, Limpopo, in a place we call Makgoba's Kloof. Afrikaans-English dictionaries translate "kloof" as a "gulf" or "ravine" but Makgoba's Kloof is far more than that—it is a huge slash cutting through the Great Escarpment separating our high-lying interior plateau, the Highveld, from the plains below, the Lowveld. It is best known to travelers by the name "Magoebaskloof," a distortion of our name by the settlers who dispossessed us of our land in the nineteenth century.[2] It's been more than twenty years since our liberation, yet the official geographic names database still calls the area Magoebaskloof. We have approached the South African Geographical Names Council to correct that formally.

Makgoba's Kloof is a land of mountains, valleys, and rivers falling down the escarpment before they merge with the Great Letaba River, which—after it runs in turn into the Olifants River (the Rio dos Elefantes in Mozambique)—empties into the Indian Ocean. It's a land of thick, lush riverine vegetation and of what geographers call Afromontane forests. And it's a land of mists: Afrikaners call a nearby mountain Wolkberg (Cloudy Mountain) and travel books call the kloof Valley of the Mists or Land of the Silver Mists, which is how the local tourist industry now

---

2   Afrikaans is the language developed from Dutch by early settlers, whose descendants now form the Afrikaner community.

markets the area. For travelers today, says *Getaway* magazine, the
"Magoebaskloof Pass," which plunges 558 vertical meters over 6.5
kilometers, is "reminiscent of a funfair ride, the series of twisting
S-bends and hairpins…offering plenty of thrills for motorbikers as
well as drivers."

For me, Makgoba's Kloof is a land of great joy, but also of great
pain. The joy comes not only from its beauty but also upon
reflecting on our heritage. We Makgobas speak Sepedi, the
country's third biggest indigenous language after isiZulu and
isiXhosa. But we don't draw our primary ancestral identity
from the baPedi polity or its powerful nineteenth-century king,
Sekhukhune, famed for his resistance to colonial occupation. If
you ask me to describe my identity, my reply is that I am South
African first and a member of the Tlou clan second. We baTlou,
who consider ourselves as quite distinct from baPedi, are named
after our totem, which in English means elephant.[3] We say that
we are from Bolepye, the land in the Letaba Basin where the great
elephants roam peacefully. I see myself as moPedi third and as a
Makgoba after that.[4] The Makgobas have a praise poem, which
goes like this:

> *Ke Makgoba a sefara,* (Makgoba of the shoot)
>
> *A Sefara sa molapong.* (The shoot of the valley)
>
> *Ke Tlou,* (Elephant)
>
> *Tloukgolo ditswa Bolepye* (Great elephants from Bolepye)
>
> *Bolopye Ba tlhaku di a liwa* (Bolepye where there is abundance)
>
> *A gee Tlou!* (Hail Elephants!)

---

3   Strictly speaking grammatically, we should not be called baTlou (or diTlou) but rather ba bina
Tlou, since when someone asks what is my token or clan, they ask "u binang?" (what do you sing?)
and I reply, "ke bina Tlou."
4   In English, people call us the Pedi. One of us is moPedi, many of us are baPedi and we speak
Sepedi.

The baTlou intermingled with baTlhalerwa (whose totem is variously described as a wild dog or a leopard), so in the African way we also identify ourselves as being part of this clan too. As happens across the world, identities in our parts are often contested, and some people—notably one of our local historians, Tlou Setumu—use baTlhalerwa as the principal clan name for our most famous ancestor.[5] We are also occasionally called part of baKolobe, said in some accounts once to have belonged to baLobedu ba gaModjadji—the Lobedu people of the fabled nineteenth-century rain queens, all named Modjadji, who lived in seclusion in an area to the northeast of us, and whose magical powers and rain-making abilities were revered by kings across southern Africa. A moLobedu historian says we once owed our allegiance to baLobedu and paid tribute to them.[6] For those interested in British imperial history, popular legend has it that the writer Rider Haggard based the mysterious white African queen in his classic novel *She*, or "She-who-must-be-obeyed," on the second rain queen, Masalanabo Modjadji II. But a recent paper by a British historian seems to debunk this; Haggard is reported to have said he had never heard of the Lobedu when he wrote his book.[7]

Early colonial records say that in the 1750s baTlou were living about 20 kilometers from Makgoba's Kloof, over the mountains to the northwest, but that we moved to the kloof in about 1800.[8] Going

---

5   Tlou Setumu (2005), *Kgoši Makgoba* of the *Batlhalerwa* (Polokwane: J.P. Publishers)

6   PJ Mampeule (2000). *A Short History of the Lobedu, Their Contact with Missionaries and the Origin and Development of the Christian Faith in Bolobedu 1600-1981* (Polokwane: University of Limpopo), 5. Quoted by Professor Louis Changuion in *A Report on the Potential Impact of Ndowana's Prospecting Activities on Items of Historical Significance in Haenertsburg and its Surroundings*, 2008, 8. Accessed November 2015 at: https://makhudutraditionalauthority.files.wordpress.com/2013/12/historical-specialist-report.pdf

7   Julia Reid (2015). 'She-who-must-be-obeyed': Anthropology and Matriarchy in H. Rider Haggard's She, *Journal of Victorian Culture*, 20:3, 364

8   Tlou Setumu (2001). *Official Records Pertaining to Blacks in the Transvaal, 1902-1907*, Master's thesis, University of Pretoria, 93. Setumu points out that although there are "numerous flaws and limitations" in colonial records about black South Africans, a result of prejudice, bias and cultural differences, "they are still important sources of information."

back in time beyond the eighteenth century, a DNA test tells me
that I also have Zanzibari and even East European ancestry. This is
explained by our clan's oral history, which says that over perhaps
hundreds of years our forebears gradually migrated south from
East Africa, through Mozambique, Zimbabwe, and Botswana,
and finally to South Africa. Secondly, the European genes could
well be from missionaries—local folklore is that apart from trying
to convert us, some missionaries were also creating fair-skinned
Makgobas, and it is true that some of us are lighter in complexion
than others.

Our best-known ancestor is my great-grandfather, Kgoši (King)
Mamphoku Makgoba. We have no record of exactly when he was
born, but he was living in the kloof in the 1860s and 1870s when
the first whites arrived in the area as woodcutters and prospectors
for gold.[9] Although the first Boer[10] trekkers had come north from
the Cape to Limpopo and the surrounding provinces in the first
half of the century and established their whites-only republic,
the Zuid-Afrikaansche Republiek (ZAR), in 1852, they were for
decades a tiny minority in our area.[11] It was only after the British
annexed the ZAR in 1877 that Sekhukhune, the most powerful
ruler in our part of South Africa, was crushed—with the help of
8,000 Swazi allies. And the Boer republicans began to win control
over our territory only after defeating the British in an armed
rebellion in 1881.[12] The pain of Makgoba's Kloof begins then.
The re-established government of the ZAR in the capital, Pretoria,
wanted to attract more white settlers and promulgated a law
whose name is translated as "The Occupation Act for State Land."
This allocated land free to farmers, provided they occupied it

9   Changuion (2008), 12
10 Settlers of Dutch descent identified themselves as "Boers," literally "farmers."
11 Louis Changuion (1999). *Makgoba (Magoeba) and the war of 1895* (Polokwane: Review
Printers), 1
12 Hermann Giliomee (2004). *The Afrikaners: Biography of a Nation* (Cape Town: Tafelberg),
183; Peter Delius (1984). *The Land Belongs to Us* (London: Heinemann), 243

permanently and were willing to be conscripted for part-time duty as military commandos.[13] A year later, a proclamation established the Woodbush Goldfields in the district. Although the gold rush was short-lived, the seizure of land for "occupation farms" and the building of a village for the miners at the top of the kloof opened the way to expanded white settlement.[14]

Kgoši Makgoba's resistance to these incursions began in 1888, when beacons were erected to demarcate land for settler use on his territory[15] and the ZAR levied taxes on him.[16] He ordered his people to destroy the beacons and resisted paying the taxes. A fine was imposed. He refused to pay that too, and the local "native commissioner," a Danish settler, jailed

Picture courtesy of the Polokwane Municipality (Polokwane Museums)

The unusual portable iron fort from which my great-grandfather, Kgoši Mamphoku Makgoba, escaped in the late 1880s.

him in an "iron fort" on his farm 60 kilometers away. An unusual portable contraption designed by an Austrian-born artillery officer, the fort had walls and a roof made up of armored plates.[17] But it was placed on bare earth, so one night, Makgoba simply

13 Setumu (2005), 5; Changuion (1999), 1
14 Changuion (2008), 12, 15
15 Tim Couzens (2013). *South African Battles* (Cape Town: Jonathan Ball), 237; Setumu (2005), 7; Changuion (1999), 2
16 Louis Stephanus Kruger (1955). *Die Makgoba-(Magoeba) oorlog: 1894-1895* (Master's thesis, University of Pretoria), 27. Accessed November 2015: http://repository.up.ac.za/handle/2263/30534
17 *Scientia Militaria, South African Journal of Military Studies*, Vol 18, Nr 2, 1988, 50

dug his way out. When his jailers next came to see him, he was gone.

The war against Kgoši Makgoba was finally triggered, in the words of a current-day local historian, Louis Changuion, "when the government started applying forced removals in the 1890s."[18] An attempt by the ZAR to recruit more settlers in 1891 to boost the number of armed men to serve as commandos failed to attract more than about thirty men. Many of those were Germans, including one by the name of Heinrich Altenroxel. In response to petitions from the settlers, complaining that Pretoria was not offering them enough security, the ZAR tried to round up the people of about eight chiefdoms into what the government called "locations," a word that was used well into the twentieth century by both Boer and British colonizers for the areas to which they confined black South Africans. In 1892 a ZAR "location commission" told baTlou that our clan was too small to have our own location, and we must choose a bigger clan on whose land we would have to live. Makgoba refused, as did other local leaders facing similar ultimatums. In 1892 the chair of the commission said we should be driven out of Makgoba's Kloof, down to the lowveld and over the Great Letaba River. ZAR records show that one of Makgoba's brothers, whom they called "Januarie," appeared before the commission on August 5, 1892, to declare: "Makgoba has nothing more to say and he refuses to do what the Commission desires of him."[19]

With Makgoba and the baTlou playing a leading role, half a dozen local clans launched attacks on farms, Altenroxel's among them, driving many "occupation farmers" off the land. The ZAR seriously considered abandoning the district but after two years of skirmishes decided to send the chief of their army, Commandant-General Piet Joubert, a hero of the war that had expelled the

---

18 Changuion (2008), 16
19 Kruger, Ch 3

British in 1881.[20] Joubert sent Kgoši Makgoba an ultimatum on
March 1, 1894, telling him to leave the kloof and move across
the Letaba by April 1.[21] Makgoba refused. Soon afterward,
other leaders were given similar ultimatums. We won a short
respite when Joubert was sent far to the northwest to fight Kgoši
Mmalebôhô of baHananwa, who was accused of not paying taxes
to the ZAR and suffered a long siege in a mountain fastness. A
month after defeating and jailing Mmalebôhô, Joubert turned his
attention to our district.

Over the course of August and September 1894, Joubert raised
commandos against not only Makgoba but also against Modjadji
II and a number of the smaller chiefdoms: Mmamatlhola,
Maušuti, Mogoboya, Maupa, Tsolobolo and Maphita. He crushed
most of them relatively quickly, although Modjadji offered
considerable resistance and surrendered only after her home had
been surrounded. The commando that rallied against us was twice
delayed by rain but eventually reached Makgoba's headquarters
and razed the village after a fierce fight. But in the words of a
1950s government history, "this brave and intrepid chief managed
to escape in the thick forests." For months afterward, Makgoba
and his troops launched raids on farms, including a farm owned
by Altenroxel.[22]

Having failed to defeat us—and with the summer rains
beginning, the commandos needing to return home to plow, and
dissension rising in their ranks—Joubert had to find another
way of containing us. He embarked on a fort-building program,
beginning with two forts and eventually surrounding us with
six.[23] But, says Louis Changuion, although many attacks were

20 Setumu (2005), 7-10; Changuion (1999), 3-4
21 Kruger, Ch 4
22 *Archives Year Book for South African History* (1957) (Cape Town: Union Archives), 152-153;
Kruger, Ch 5; Couzens, 238; Changuion (1999), 4-6
23 Kruger, Ch 5; Couzens, 238; Changuion (1999), 6-8

repulsed, "the forts did not improve matters." In April 1895
Joubert convened a war council to plan a campaign against
Makgoba, who at this point is described by Changuion as the
"Lion of the Houtbosberg" (Woodbush Mountain). Commandos
from six districts right across the ZAR were called up. "Native
commissioners" from four districts were each instructed to raise
a corps of loyal African troops. The State Artillery from Pretoria,
made up of full-time professional soldiers as opposed to farmers
conscripted into the commandos, was summoned. It took nearly
three months, from April to June, to raise the force needed.[24] By
the time Joubert was fully mobilized, he had a force variously
estimated by historians as numbering between 800 and 1,000
commandos, supplemented by the State Artillery, and between
3,000 and 6,000 African auxiliaries conscripted under an 1876
ZAR law. A force therefore of at least 4,000 was judged necessary
to suppress a clan the ZAR authorities judged to number no
more than 500 families, including 250 troops.[25] Joubert told a
local missionary to warn other African leaders not to support
Makgoba and also to publicize an offer of thirty cattle, plus
expenses, to anyone who brought him in, dead or alive. He then
summoned representatives of local leaders—including Dikgosi[26]
Mmamatlhola and Maušuti—to a ZAR war council on May 29,
where he threatened to remove them from their land if they gave
Makgoba or his people any help. From the same war council,
Joubert sent Makgoba a final warning, saying if he did not give
himself up to be dealt with under the law, "no quarter or pardon
will be granted." The Dutch translation of what is recorded in
the ZAR archives as Makgoba's reply—written on the back of the
envelope carrying the ultimatum and received on May 30—reads:
"I have nothing to do with you. What have I done against you that
you want to trample me? Makgoba."[27]

---

24 Research paper by Henriette La Cointre-Potgieter, March 2017
25 Kruger, Ch 6; Changuion (2008), 9; Changuion (1999), 7
26 The plural of Kgosi.
27 Kruger, Ch 7

On Saturday, June 1, 1895, Joubert's war council decided to attack Makgoba's Kloof on the following Monday. Their first assault was disrupted by a counterattack in which Joubert's troops were caught off guard by a group of Makgoba's men who donned the white headbands worn by Joubert's auxiliaries and moved through the attackers' lines. One of Joubert's commanders, the German settler Bernhard Dicke, wrote afterward: "The native contingents drafted from different parts, not knowing one another and shot at from their rear, did not know who was a friend and who a foe. They started firing at one another and at anybody and everybody while Magoeba himself attacked from in front...Whites...tumbled off the heights as quickly as they could with the frenzied native fugitives jamming in between them." Dicke went on to describe the attackers as turning into an "avalanche of fleeing humanity that constituted part of the government forces—400 whites and 3,500 blacks who had lost their heads."[28]

Joubert ordered a new assault on Makgoba the next day, June 4. Struggling to penetrate the dense vegetation, the ZAR artillery managed to deploy only the two smaller of their three pieces but were still able to pound Makgoba's headquarters with shell-fire, then send in auxiliaries. ZAR records say five of Makgoba's troops and between one and three auxiliaries died in the encounter, but Makgoba and most of his forces had gone. Joubert's attackers burned the settlement to the ground. Three days later an attack on a reported Makgoba stronghold near a waterfall was postponed as a result of mist, rain and cold, and a third major assault was planned for the next day. But again, Makgoba and his forces were nowhere to be found.

Sunday, June 9, however, was to prove a fateful day for baTlou. Among the auxiliaries who fought on the side of the ZAR were an estimated 200 to 300 troops from neighboring Swaziland, who

---

28 AP Cartwright (1974). *By the Waters of the Letaba* (Cape Town: Purnell), 51; Kruger, Ch 8

had at various times during the previous half-century formed alliances with both the ZAR and the British against their fellow Africans. Their arrival was remarked upon later by Eliza Devenish, a resident of nearby Pietersburg[29] and an admirer of Joubert: "It was a rare sight," she wrote, "to see this large Impi (regiment) of Swazies [sic] in all their war paint, shields and assegais (spears) marching through the outskirts of the town on their way to the front."[30] On Sunday the Swazi troops came across a woman, supposedly one of Makgoba's wives, who was suffering from an injured foot. Under torture, she disclosed his whereabouts on the slopes of the Wolkberg. Joubert learned the news during a morning church service and immediately ordered all his troops and three artillery pieces to the area. But the Swazi auxiliaries found Makgoba first.

There are differing accounts of how Makgoba died but the most likely is that told by Bernhard Dicke, the commander who described the débâcle the previous Monday. On Dicke's version, when Kgoši Makgoba was confronted in the forest, he sent his wives and children away so that they could make their escape. Then he faced his adversaries alone on a forest path. He killed one with the first blast from his double-barreled weapon, but the second barrel misfired and he was shot dead. The Swazis beheaded him as proof they had killed him and took his head to one of Joubert's forts to collect their reward. Dicke and a ZAR officer went to identify him the following day. Dicke wrote later:

"From the expression on the chief's face one could still see that he had awaited the charging Swazis and his end with a scornfully sardonic smile. Even in death there was a proud smile on his countenance. Such a man was Maguba[sic]."

29 The principal local settler town, named after Joubert, now the Limpopo capital, Polokwane
30 Eliza Frances Devenish (1995). *Twenty Years in the Transvaal Republic*, published in PRETORIANA, Journal of the Pretoria Historical Association: Old Pretoria Society, No 107, November 1995, 41. Accessed November 2015 at: http://repository.up.ac.za/handle/2263/16072

Announcing the news to the ZAR government in Pretoria, Joubert ended his telegram: "The Lord reigns, and I am his servant."[31]

In follow-up attacks, Joubert's forces killed another nineteen baTlou and took one man and thirty women as prisoners. The following day they took another fifty prisoners. In the days that followed they rounded up not only baTlou but the followers of Mmamatlhola, Maušuti, and another leader, Selebulu, who were accused of giving Makgoba either "direct or indirect" support, probably by giving them refuge. By the time their deportation began, the numbers of those to be banished to a government farm in the Pretoria district had grown to between 4,000 and 5,000 people. Eliza Devenish saw them being sent into exile: "I shall never forget the sight of the poor native prisoners, men, women and children in such a pitiable state of starvation after the siege they had endured as they were marched through to Pretoria, driven on by mounted burghers,[32] whose anxiety to get back to their homes made them forgetful of the suffering of the poor creatures they were driving before them at so cruel a pace. Many fell behind and perished from cold and exposure. Such deplorable sufferings are often the unavoidable appendages of war."[33]

The final assault against my great-grandfather and our people was a short, seven-day affair, conducted against a small clan. But the extent of the Boer call-up needed to overcome us, the fact that we were among the last peoples in South Africa to be defeated, and Kgoši Makgoba's heroic but gruesome death have all combined to give our clan's struggle a prominence out of proportion to our numbers. After the British invaded the ZAR a second time during the Anglo-Boer War, establishing in its place a "Transvaal Colony"

---

31 Malegapuru William Makgoba (1997). *Mokoko, The Makgoba Affair: a reflection on transformation* (Florida Hills: Vivlia Publishers), 9; Bernard Dicke, *Die Dood van Maguba, Die Huisgenoot*, 22 December 1933; Cartwright, 52; Couzens, 239; Kruger, Chapter 8
32 Citizens
33 Devenish, 41

in 1902, the British War Office named us in a report assessing the
threat we posed as people who "rebelled against the Boers."[34]

In the historical fiction that glorified the British Empire, my
great-grandfather became a footnote. This happened soon after
the British defeated the ZAR, when they sent a young Scot named
John Buchan to help set up an administration for the colony. An
unknown civil servant then, he later became a famous English
author and the governor-general of Canada who once paraded
through the streets of Washington, D.C., with President Franklin
D. Roosevelt. Buchan's visit to Makgoba's Kloof made a lifelong
impression on him. In an account published in Edinburgh
Blackwood's Magazine and subsequently in a book, he admired
"this soft, rich, and fascinating garden-land...a place secret
and strange with a beauty so peculiar that the people who
tried to describe it were rarely believed," and where "mists and
cool rains abound, every hollow has its stream, and yet frost
is rarely known." He goes on to tell us of a visit to a farmer, a
Mr. Altenroxel, who "produces excellent pipe tobacco and a
respectable cigar." Leaving Altenroxel, Buchan heads up the kloof.
"Soon the hills closed in," he writes, "and we were in the long glen
of Machubi." He continues:

> Machubi was a Kaffir[35] chief with whom the Boers waged one
> of their many and most inglorious little wars. When his people
> were scattered he took refuge in the thick forest at the head of
> the river which bears his name. After my experience of that kind
> of forest I do not wonder that the Boers preferred not to fight a
> hand-to-hand battle in its tangled depths. So, after their fashion,
> they hired an impi of Swazis, who sat around the wood for three
> weeks, and ultimately slew the chief—not, however, before he
> had accounted in single-handed combat for three of his enemies.
> Mr. Altenroxel possesses the old warrior's skull, which, except

34 *The Native Tribes of the Transvaal* (1905). (London: British War Office), 51; Setumu, 101
35 A disparaging slur, the use of which is no longer acceptable, describing a black person.

for the great thickness at the crown of the head, is finely shaped, and all but Caucasian in its lines.[36]

Some years later, Kgoši Makgoba's skull re-emerges in an adventure novel that Buchan wrote and entitled *Prester John*, after the mythical Christian leader sought by Europeans in Asia and Africa over several hundred years. *Prester John*, says the present-day South African historian Bill Nasson, portrays the Transvaal as "an idealized white colony, governed by a strict racial order," one "steeped in an atmosphere of plottings and 'risings' by disgruntled black underdogs, manipulated by villainous men in touch with 'primitive' demonic forces."[37] Makgoba reappears in the following words:

> Machudi [sic] was a blackguard chief whom the Boers long ago smashed in one of their native wars. He was a fierce old warrior and had put up a good fight to the last, till a hired impi of Swazis had surrounded his hiding-place in the forest and destroyed him. A Boer farmer on the plateau had his skull, and used to drink whisky out of it when he was merry.[38]

Whether or not Altenroxel actually drank whisky out of my great-grandfather's skull, Buchan's accounts are the only written record we have found of its whereabouts. We have a photograph of his head, on which the name Altenroxel appears, apparently taken soon after his death by a Pietersburg photographer. Our clan's oral history tells us that it was first taken to the local landdrost (magistrate), GG Munnik, who had members of our royal council carry it to Pretoria as punishment. There Paul Kruger, the president of the ZAR, was furious over the beheading—because it had taken place on a Sunday. In a memoir published in Afrikaans

---

36 John Buchan (1903). *The African Colony: Studies in the Reconstruction* (Edinburgh: William Blackwood and Sons), 124

37 Bill Nasson (2002). John Buchan's South African visions, in *The John Buchan Journal*, No 26/Spring 2002. Excerpt published online, accessed November 2015 at: http://www.johnbuchansociety.co.uk/fiction/fpj.htm

38 John Buchan (1910). *Prester John* (Boston/New York: Houghton Mifflin), 180

in 1920, Munnik says nothing of the beheading.[39] However, in an expanded English edition of the memoir, published in the 1930s when he was a respected senator in what was by then a national South African parliament, he

My great-grandfather Kgoši Mamphoku Makgoba was beheaded by Swazi auxiliary troops that had formed an alliance with the ZAR.

makes what seems to be a new revelation, unrecorded in any of the other literature I have seen. When the circumstances of Makgoba's death were reported to Pretoria, says Munnik, the president of the ZAR, Paul Kruger, was "profoundly incensed and annoyed at the cutting off of Magoeba's head, as he said that it was inhuman, unchristian and uncivilised."[40] The person we now acknowledge as the reigning head of our clan, Kgoši Mokopa Geribold Makgoba, says that in the early part of the twentieth century, elders of the clan would go to a museum in Pretoria to pay homage to the head. But in the generations since, there has been no sign of it—until, just possibly, recently.

A few years ago, my wife, Lungi, our daughter Paballo, and I visited the National Cultural History Museum in Tshwane/Pretoria, which is built on the site of a prison and is part of our collection of national museums, the Ditsong museums of South Africa. Accompanied by my cousin, Jacob Makgoba, we were taken

39 GG Munnik (1920). *Kronieke van Noordelike Transvaal: die herinneringe van Senator G.G. Munnik*, Pretoria: Suid-Afrikaanse Boekwinkel
40 GG Munnik (1934). *Memoirs: covering eighty years of thrilling South African history, politics and war.* Cape Town: Maskew Miller

underground to a basement housing archaeological artifacts. Led through secure doors and gates, we saw the "pots of Makgoba"— large clay pots, big enough to hold a body, which were recovered from a cave around Makgoba's Kloof and in which the remains of our ancestors still lie. Finally, we got to "TM21," a skull classified as "Transvaal Museum 21" in the manner of a hominid fossil. We are not sure, and I hope we can do DNA testing one day, but museum researchers who have examined the skull suggest there is a good chance of it being that of Mamphoku Makgoba. Despite the uncertainty, it was for me a spiritual experience, a sacred moment of connection and the most memorable day in my life.

That is the story of my lineage. Expressed in the language of praise poetry, a singer would describe me by reciting the generic song that locates our clan as a whole—and which I recorded at the beginning of this chapter—and then elaborate on it to relate my personal ancestry in the following way:

"*Sa Bobedi rea aketja:* (We also add)

Ke Tlou, ke Madiye, Makhanyo (Elephant, Madiye, Makhanyo, my real Sepedi names)

Ke Ramaite wa ho loka (The gracious father of Maite)

MoThlabine (From Thlabine, in the Lowveld)

Mora Masilu (Son of Masilu, my father's name)

Setlogolo sa Makhanyo (grandson of Makhanyo, after whom I am named)

Setlogoloana sa Puledi (great son of Puledi)

Setlogotlogoloana sa Mpatele, Mamphoku! (Great-grandson of Mpatele, Mamphoku!)"

If we dig deep into my family history, it is not an uncomplicated one. When I try to piece together a family tree and become confused by the interlocking relationships, which hint that some of Makgoba's offspring must have been the fruit of an incestuous union, my family becomes upset and warns me off the subject. Despite some post-apartheid land restitution, baTlou have not prospered since our country's liberation in 1994 and that has generated tensions among us. Land seized in 1895 cannot be recovered, since under post-apartheid land reform laws only land taken after 1913 can be reclaimed. We lodged a successful claim for some of that land, but we have squandered this victory through dissension in our ranks, which resulted in some of South Africa's most productive tea estates lying derelict for years. To add to our troubles there are disagreements between the community trust that administers the land and Kgoši Mokopa Makgoba—and to make matters worse, some contest his kingship.

Driving through the district now, the white-owned land with its citrus farms, its avocado pear trees, and its commercial pine plantations smells to me of wealth, while the barren places to which baTlou were banished radiate the stench of poverty and dispossession. Sometimes I think the ghosts of Piet Joubert, of Judge Munnik, of Paul Kruger, and of H.F. Verwoerd, prime minister and "high priest" of grand apartheid in the 1950s and 1960s, must be resting peacefully, gently thumping their chests, celebrating that we still haven't figured out how to deal with what they did to us. Psychologically, Kgoši Mamphoku Makgoba's beheading has instilled in our clan a fear as well as a sense of reliance that someone out there ought to protect us. So we look to the state, and the state is happy to oblige, as long as we don't demand the restoration of the core of our identity, the kloof. This is because, we are told, South Africa needs social cohesion, which will lead to economic prosperity, and our turn will come. We are lulled into our own demise because somebody outside the valley needs our resources, and we must neither disturb their looting nor drive away foreign investment.

How, then, do we deal with this legacy? Returning to Kgoši Makgoba's severed head, I cannot escape my longing to resolve

the mystery of its whereabouts in my lifetime—a task which
the current Makgoba Royal Council has asked me to carry out.
It is not as if his death is ancient history. My father was born in
1910, only fifteen years after the beheading. My father's aunt,
Makgoba's young sister, died when I was sixteen, and we know
where her grave is, so surely we can achieve closure through
DNA testing? And since beginning the research and writing of
this book, another intriguing possibility has emerged: a German
website dedicated to uncovering the involvement of institutions
in the city of Freiburg in the country's colonial past records a
1908 letter from "a Mr. Altenroxel from Münster" offering various
items to collectors. Among them were two valuable war drums,
"spoils directly from the war of the Boers with Maleleo Magoeba ...
1894/95," "the hippo-whip of the fallen chief Magoeba"—and "1
Kaffernschädel, gratis" (1 kaffir skull, free).[41] The research for this
chapter shows that the story of colonial and settler occupation
involves more than Boer and Brit, but other Europeans too—
among them Germans, Austrians, and Danes. Perhaps further
study can help to bring answers and
healing not only to Makgoba's Kloof but also to people of other
nations as well.

But, using Makgoba's missing skull as a metaphor for the suffering
that not only our family and clan but also our nation has endured,
can there really be closure for us all? How do we as a clan deal
with the pain we feel when we see the descendants of settlers,
both British and Boer, prospering on our land? How do we look
upon the modern-day Swazi nation, given the role some of their
ancestors played in our defeat? How do we approach the role of
the missionaries, who were in some cases chased out of the kloof,
so unpopular did they become when they identified more with
the settlers than with us?

---

41 Website freiburg-postkolonial.de: http://www.freiburg-postkolonial.de/Seiten/Adelhauser-
Duerrenberger4.htm [Accessed 2 May 2017]

The pace at which we live and the circumstances of our living in
the modern world leave very little space for healing, but South
Africa's wounds are real, and we must own them. We must stand
in the gaps between feeling hopeless and hopeful, between being
helpless and helpful, between hurting and being healed. My own
spirituality has been nurtured and developed by the experience of
hearing of the pain, fear, anger, and resistance, but above all, the
faith and courage of my forebears. It has given me a determination
that wrongs must be righted, people must be treated with dignity,
and reconciliation needs to be achieved among the formerly
oppressed and the former oppressor. In these endeavors, I believe
the spirituality of Nelson Mandela, which I was privileged to
experience during the closing years of his life, can help us find
answers to these questions.

Chapter 2

Alexandra

Despite our clan's banishment from Makgoba's Kloof, some of us either escaped deportation or returned to the area. We are recorded by British colonial authorities a decade after Kgoši Makgoba's death as having settled on white farms in the district,[42] only later to be dumped in the Thlabine area of the Lowveld, near the area to which the Boers of the ZAR had tried to force Makgoba to move. That is where I was born in 1960, which is why, as well as identifying myself as among baTlou, I also identify as moThlabine of Tshaneng, which in English might be rendered as "a Thlabine of Tzaneen," the last-named place being how whites have referred to Tshaneng. However, my parents did not declare Thlabine as my birthplace to the government, and that had everything to do with apartheid.

In the early 1940s, my father, his brothers, and his cousins moved to Alexandra township, on the Jukskei River on the northeastern outskirts of Johannesburg, South Africa's commercial hub. Founded in 1912, two years after Afrikaners and English speakers joined forces to create the Union of South Africa, Alexandra, or "Alex" as we call it, began as a rarity—a freehold township in which black South Africans could buy land. It thus attracted sharecroppers and labor tenants who were being forced off white farms under a law that one of our most famous early authors, Sol Plaatje, described as turning a black South African

---

42 *The Native Tribes of the Transvaal*, 51

overnight into "not actually a slave, but a pariah in the land of his birth."[43] Those first residents of Alex were quite prosperous, and the most comprehensive history of the township says that they created a "bustling entrepreneurial community" on the edge of Johannesburg.[44]

My father, James Makgoba, on the left, who moved to Johannesburg's Alexandra township in the 1940s as part of a wave of rural people, including Nelson Mandela, drawn by the city's growth of industry during the war.

My father, James Masilo Makgoba, arrived during the first large-scale migration to Alex of Sepedi speakers from the north, which was itself part of the huge influx of rural people attracted to Johannesburg by the phenomenal growth of industry during World War II.[45]

Nelson Mandela arrived in the township at more or less the same time, after running away from home in the rural Transkei to escape an arranged marriage. He rented a room from the local Anglican priest, behind the local parish church, St. Michael and All Angels.[46] In a memoir written in prison and published in the collection, *Conversations With Myself*, he observed that Alex's freehold status meant that blacks could run their own affairs "free from the tyranny of municipal regulations" and that as a multi-ethnic community, its people were politically conscious

43 Sol T. Plaatje, 1916. *Native Life in South Africa, Before and Since the European War and the Boer Rebellion* (London: P.S. King and Son, Ltd.)

44 Philip Bonner and Noor Nieftagodien (2008). *ALEXandra: A History*. (Johannesburg: Wits University Press), Ch One

45 Bonner and Nieftagodien, 61

46 Anthony Sampson (1999). *Mandela: The Authorised Biography*. (Johannesburg: Jonathan Ball), 33

and articulate. But he added that by the 1940s, in spite of having "some beautiful buildings, it was a typical slum area— overcrowded and dirty, with undernourished children running about naked or in filthy rags" and teeming with "all kinds of religious sects, gangsters, and shebeens."[47] One of those "sects" was the Zion Christian Church (ZCC), now South Africa's biggest church of any sort, which has its headquarters at Zion City, Moria, a few kilometers away from the top of Makgoba's Kloof.

I think my father might originally have been an Anglican because he was in on the beginnings of the ZCC and the founding family of that church, the Lekganyanes, included Anglicans among their number, but it was as a ZCC pastor that he was sent to Alex. The area in which he and his cousins settled became like a little ZCC Makgoba outstation in an area designated by the local authority for Zulu speakers. From Alex, my father expanded his evangelizing to other parts of what is now Gauteng province, building new churches in Eastern Native township, better known as George Goch, on the edge of downtown Johannesburg, and in Sharpeville, to the south of Johannesburg near the Vaal River. In Sharpeville he met a ZCC colleague of about the same age, Noah Lekoane, and Noah's wife, Jane Ntsei. During his visits to Noah, as he popped in and out of their home for tea, a relationship developed between

My mother, Elizabeth Lekoane, far right, in Sharpeville in the 1950s. She was the daughter of a Zion Christian Church (ZCC) pastor and became my father's third wife.

47 Nelson Mandela (2010). *Conversations with Myself*. (London: Macmillan), 35-36

him and the couple's daughter. The fact that he was married
already was not a hindrance in the ZCC; the prohibition imposed
by European missionaries on the polygamy that was part of our
traditional way of life before they arrived was part of the reason
that African independent churches broke away and syncretized
Christian and traditional African ways of life. So it came about
that my mother, Elizabeth Kedibone Lekoane, twenty years
younger than my father, became his third wife and joined him in
Alexandra.

I suspect one of the reasons my father wanted me and my twin
sister, Nthabiseng, to be born in Thlabine was that even in those
days there were some weird beliefs about witchcraft and twins.
In centuries past, it's quite possible that either I, as the younger
child, or my sister, as a girl, would have had to be sacrificed
at birth, and I think my father wanted us to be born in a safer
place than Alex. But the main reason was that he wanted us to
be born on home soil, near Makgoba's Kloof and the place of our
ancestors. At the same time, he wanted to ensure that I would
have the right under what were called "the pass laws" to live and
work in Johannesburg when I grew up.

Pass laws to control the movement of black South Africans were
a feature of both the Boer republics and the British colonies
before union in 1910, but by the time I was born in 1960 they
had been codified in the Native Laws Amendment Act of 1952.
The notorious Section 10(1) of that act stipulated that "No native
shall remain for more than seventy-two hours in an urban area...
unless (a) he was born and permanently resides in such area; or
(b) he has worked continuously in such area for one employer
for a period of not less than ten years or has lawfully remained
continuously in such area for a period of not less than fifteen
years." If you didn't have "Section 10" rights, you were liable to be
arrested at any time and thrown into the back of a "kwela-kwela,"
which was what we called the blue police vans that roamed the

township looking for people who didn't carry the right passes. Then you could be deported to starve in one of the ethnically defined mini-states called Bantustans, which were designated under apartheid as the "homelands" of all black South Africans. My father must have been entitled to live in Johannesburg under Section 10(1)(b), but he wanted me to have the precious Section 10(1)(a) rights that allowed me to stay there permanently and move freely from job to job. So after Nthabiseng and I were born, our parents quietly brought us back to Johannesburg and registered our births at the Alexandra Clinic.

Although we hated the pass laws, I still recall the pride with which I carried the "dompas" (stupid pass), the green document that said that I was "Section 10(1)(a)." Once I became an adult I was liable to be arrested if I didn't carry it, so it always stayed in my back pocket, becoming very tatty.

That is how I, with roots in Makgoba's Kloof, came to grow up as an urban boy in a poor, crowded, filthy township during what some describe as the era of "high apartheid," when black South Africans were meant to be treated as "temporary sojourners" in the cities and on the white farms, preferably having left their families behind in the Bantustans. In Mandela's judgment, Alex, "despite its problems and flaws, gave the lie" to the argument "that Africans were by nature a rural people, ill-suited to city life."[48]

Alexandra township was unusual in that it was an area in which blacks had title to their property. To such a system this was anathema. More than that, we were becoming a nuisance to white Johannesburg as it grew northwards and encroached upon us. In the words of a government committee appointed to investigate our future the year after I was born, "prime residential areas" (for which read beautiful and expensive white suburbs) had grown

---

48 Nelson Mandela (1994). *Long Walk to Freedom*. (Johannesburg: Macdonald Purnell), 72

up around us, and we were "a cancerous tumor…[which] stunts
the growth of the surrounding parts of the body." The committee's
solution was to propose that families should be kicked out and
that such housing as there was should be replaced by what
became known as "locations in the sky"—huge, multi-story,
single-sex hostels, each housing up to 2,500 people, which would
accommodate 15,000 men and 5,000 women working for whites
in the northern suburbs of Johannesburg.[49] Of course I was not
aware of all of this as a child, nor did I have any idea of how it
would later turn our lives upside down.

We first lived in
a backyard shack
near the end of
19th Avenue,
not far from the
Jukskei River, but
when I was two,
my father began
to travel a lot,
and the church
headquarters felt
we needed to be
in a safer place.
We were moved
into the ZCC

*The one-roomed Zion Christian Church (ZCC) rectory to which
my family moved when I was two years old. It still stands and the
current leaders of the ZCC in Alex recently welcomed me to the
house, generously allowing me to refresh my childhood memories.*

rectory, a brick house nearby. There we lived in one room about
six meters long and five meters wide. The house still stands and
the current leaders of the ZCC in Alex recently welcomed me to
their premises and generously allowed me to refresh my memories
of childhood. When that house became too small for our growing
family, and the bishop's sister wanted a place to stay, we moved
to a rented municipal house at the other end of what was a very

---

49 Bonner and Nieftagodien, 182-186

long street, where it intersected with London Road, the street that now separates Alex from an industrial area. We were one of seven families sharing that house, and our family—my parents, my older sister, my twin sister, my younger sister, my younger brother and I—shared two rooms. One was the bedroom, where my parents slept behind a curtain and the rest us of shared beds with lumpy old coir mattresses, except for my brother, who slept on the floor. Our "beds" were frames mounted on big paint cans filled with concrete, high enough to create space for a "wardrobe" underneath, where we stored our clothes and our bed-clothes during the day.

The other room was the kitchen, dining room, and lounge, all in one, to which my older sister, Maite Mathapelo, whom we called "Mataps," moved when she was thirteen.[50] When we were young, my mother cooked, but after we moved from the rectory, she went out to work. This took her increasingly away from home so Mataps took over most of the cooking. Nthabiseng, whose nickname was "Tobi Tobi," did the washing, and my mother took care of the ironing

From the right, my older sister, Mataps, my twin sister, Nthabiseng, and myself with a neighbor in Alex in the early 1960s.

over the weekend. My role was to clean the primus stove and the enamel bucket for fetching water and to scrub the steel cooking pots with steel wool until they shone. I also kept a little vegetable patch where I grew lettuce, carrots and, later, broad beans.

---

50 "Maite" was the elder sister of the original Kgoši Makgoba and is an important figure in our clan when tracing our ancestry using the matrilineal line.

Alex was also known as "Dark City." Although we lived on the edges of the wealthiest suburbs of Africa's richest city, only a few houses in the township had electricity. The ZCC rectory did but not our rented house, so we had to use candles for lighting. To cope with Jo'burg's freezing winters, my mother boiled up candles, then mixed in a little paraffin to make a beautiful wax, which we smeared on our bodies just before going to sleep. You could build up a nice sweat under your pajamas, and if that wasn't enough to keep out the cold, I added a tracksuit and even a raincoat. You didn't need many blankets that way!

The families in the house, another adjoining house and in back yard rooms—say around twenty families in all—shared four "bucket" toilets outside. There was an unwritten rule that whether you were a boy or a girl, if you wanted to pass water, you didn't go to the toilet. You had to go somewhere else because the buckets filled so quickly and were emptied only once a week, on a Monday. I vividly recall as a child sitting on the stoop, (porch), daydreaming, smelling the unique Alex odor of stagnant water, dead dogs, and bucket toilets, and watching amaBhaca, men of a small ethnic group from the Eastern Cape, whose customary task it was to empty the buckets, as they went about their unpleasant job.

From our stoop, you could also hear the noises of the Jukskei— the frogs and the sound of junk and waste being washed along by the stream. Another smell was that of the blue soap we used for bathing, taking turns in a little metal bath, and for washing clothes. Apart from the primus stove, we had a black coal stove, and a gallon of water was constantly on the boil there, often filled with dishcloths or nappies. Another of my chores was to fetch water from the communal tap in the yard, which seemed to be running the whole day because the twenty families sharing rooms in the house and yard all had to have their turn to wash. Sometimes the water ran out. I hated the job. Anyone who wanted water, even from the street, had access to the tap, so it could be dangerous if the gangs were fighting, especially at night.

My paternal grandparents died before I was born, but during my childhood I came to know my maternal grandparents well. My grandfather, whom we called "Pa," was of baRolong and baKgatla descent, from Bapong, what is now the platinum mining belt in North West province. My grandmother, or "Gogo," was from the Thaise family in Lesotho, who were partly of Khoisan descent and had been forcibly removed, first from Koppies in the Free State and later from nearby Vereeniging. Gogo was a dominating matriarch in our family, so much so that although my mother counted Setswana as her home language, the family mostly spoke Sesotho at her mother's insistence.

We loved to travel by bus or train to Sharpeville to spend school holidays with Pa and Gogo during our school years—partly because they had a bathroom in their house—but my earliest memory as a child is of my grandmother in Alex. I must have been four or five when my mother contracted tuberculosis and had to spend six months being treated at the Rietfontein Infectious Diseases Hospital (now the Sizwe Tropical Diseases Hospital) in Edenvale. My grandmother came to Alex to look after us. One day, thinking that this poor old lady must be bored, I told her, "You know, Gogo, I can show you Magic Man!" Getting the go-ahead for my trick, I proceeded to stuff a tiny pebble wrapped in foil up my nose, hoping to recover it from my mouth. Of course it lodged itself up my nostril, and I was rushed to the Alex Clinic, then given a hiding with a whip.

Tobi Tobi and I started our education at a junior primary school called Emfundisweni, then moved to Ezenzeleni, a junior primary school for Zulu speakers. The Zulu children around us in that part of Alex used to mock us by singing that "God has created the baPedi by mistake." That wasn't the reason I rebelled against

Ezenzeleni, however. After four months the principal wanted
to promote me to a higher grade, separating me from my sister.
I protested vigorously. At first my father was unbending, so I
backed up my arguments by telling him that we had to pass

through the territory of the
Msomi and Mongol gangs
on our way to school. This
softened his heart, and
he allowed us to return to
Emfundisweni, where the
two of us could be in the
same class. From there we
went on to Pholosho Senior
Primary, whose teachers were
important mentors and role
models who provided me
with a structure that helped
me make the right life choices
as I was growing up. Former
president Kgalema Motlanthe

*At Pholosho Senior Primary School in Alex
with classmates, Elizabeth and Leta, ages about
thirteen.*

also attended the school, and we both keep in touch with it today,
raising money for it and sponsoring children with new uniforms.

One of my early recollections is of walking back from school
in shirt and tie, wearing long trousers and an old jacket but
without shoes. I had socks, which I wore secretly in class because
the cement floor was cold, but which I kept in my pockets at
playtime and when walking to and from school. If you weren't in
a classroom during school hours, you could expect to be picked
up by "thisa-abantwana," a blue van that would "collect" children
who should have been in school and take them to be locked up.
Ironically, the children who suffered that fate were those whose
parents could not afford to send them to school, and they could at
least get a meal while in detention.

It was also at school that I was first exposed to the Anglican Church. Emfundisweni had close ties with the church, as did Pholosho, which had actually been a church school called St. Michael's until the apartheid government seized control of black education in 1955. Entokozweni Daycare Center, where we could go after school to do our homework, suffered a similar fate; started by the church, it was taken over and re-named. Even after the government took over the schools, most of the staff continued to be Anglicans.

It was at Entokozweni that I first came to understand faith. At about the age of seven, I acted in a play there—it was probably Shakespeare in Sesotho, adapted to speak to Alex's conditions. I had to play a scary animal that looked like a pig with one eye, and I terrified the girls by shouting "Obe! Obe!" The teachers there were clever, however; they suggested I couldn't be involved without being baptized. Our background was quite ecumenical— my maternal grandmother had been Lutheran, my grandfather Dutch Reformed—and although my mother was loyal to my father's church, she was quite ambivalent about the ZCC when it came to us children. She encouraged us to join the churches associated with the schools that were thought to provide the best education. In that way my elder sister Mataps became a Catholic. My parents said if becoming Anglican would bring me a good education, I should go for it, and so I was baptized at St. Michael's.

As it turned out, despite going to Pholosho, Nthabiseng and I still had to negotiate territory crawling with gangsters both on our way to school and to church. Gangs weren't unique to Alex, of course. With their roots in the groups of street hoodlums called tsotsis, they had proliferated across Reef towns since the mid-

1940s. On the way to school, we had to pass the Spoilers, who at various times ran protection rackets and gained notoriety for gate-crashing parties and robbing guests.[51] Then there were the Msomis, the big ones, who terrified us. Named after an axe-killer who had been hanged in the 1950s for multiple murders, they had previously worked in league with corrupt policemen and ran their own kangaroo court on Sundays.[52] The Mongols, who had a distinctive swastika on their arms, also ruled by terror. As individuals, many of the gangsters were not bad people, but in groups they were dreadful. A gang leader living close by ensured a degree of protection. A Makgoba cousin named Poledi was second-in-command of the Msomi gang and was accordingly feared. Another gang leader, Themba, lived in our back yard in 19th Avenue. With a horrible-looking scar on his cheek as a result of a stabbing, he acquired the nickname "Killer." Without going too explicitly into issues concerning the sanctity of life, or lack thereof, his name meant exactly that.

Twelve years was the age of recruitment into these gangs. I was approached by one or two but refused to join. But I once made a big mistake that nearly cost me my life. Like many children of poorer families in Alex,[53] I earned money on the side by caddying at the Royal Johannesburg Golf Club. Tall but thin, I thought I could protect myself on the way to school by carrying a golf club, but one of the leaders of the Mongols, a short, well-built, and fierce-looking individual who felt he was being dethroned by Themba, decided he wanted to take my club from me. He overpowered me and hit me on the mouth with the golf club, cutting open my upper lip. I bled profusely but fought back and held onto the club. I was taken to Alex Clinic where my lip was stitched (and to this day I still carry the scar). The next

---

51 Bonner and Nieftagodien, 117-120
52 Op cit, 120-122
53 Bonner and Nieftagodien, 99-100

day he threatened me with an okapi—the gangster's knife of choice, sometimes called "the Saturday night special"—but was sent fleeing when my three sisters, Mataps, Nthabiseng, and my younger sister, Esther Matapala, hit back with shoes, bricks, and I don't know what else. The story quickly spread that we were the untouchables, giving us a measure of further protection. Tollman, the boss of another gang at 16th Avenue, thought I was going to rise to "fame" and came to school during the morning break to warn me that he was watching our movements. But I assured him, and anyone else who asked, that I didn't want anything to do with gangs, as long as they left my sisters alone—sometimes gangsters would look at a girl and say, "You're my girlfriend," giving them no choice.

How I managed to survive my school years, passing gangsters' homes with my sisters every day, is somewhat of a miracle. But there was a certain code of honor that protected young boys, especially if you weren't in a gang. If you were strong enough, you would meet a challenge by saying: "Fair go! No holding, no biting!" That meant you didn't want to fight with an okapi but were prepared to fight with fists. Then nobody would take out their knives. Most young boys in Alex would have been challenged to a fight like that at some stage or another, and I was defeated in one or two "fair goes."

Sophisticated gangs had firearms. These were mainly used for robberies or when the gang members were fighting with one another over big things such as cars or large stashes of cash. At night, they would fire the guns into the sky as they sought to instill fear in their enemies; you would stay inside and pray that no one in your family was hit by a stray bullet. Otherwise they used okapis and when they fought each other, it was terrible; they sometimes just stabbed each other to death. As in many townships, death in Alex was almost as normal as life. It was not unusual to come across a corpse in the street, especially on a

Saturday or Sunday morning. After checking to make sure it was
not that of a relative, people would shift it to the side of the road,
where open sewerage drains stank, so that it didn't get hit by cars
or trucks. Two or three people would then wait nearby to chase
dogs away until the police arrived. When I look back, I worry that
we were numbed to accept death too lightly, but at the time you
felt you had to move on—yes, you knew this place was dangerous
but if you reached fifteen and you hadn't been killed or joined
a gang, well then, hallelujah, it's wonderful, you have survived.
In local slang, this was "life in die township, life van clevers, nie
moegoes nie" (life in the township, where only the street-wise, and
not country bumpkins, survived).

Despite these conditions, I had no sense of deprivation during my
childhood; in fact I was relatively privileged, living in a solidly
built house. My father was the senior Makgoba in our area of
Alex, and I would hear a lot of talk in the community about our
Tlou heritage, our praise songs, and who each of us was in the
family line. My father inculcated in me a sense of my Makgoba
identity, and when I was about seven or eight, a ZCC pastor
who was regarded as a prophet told my father I was destined for
greatness. My mother was dismissive of such talk, however, and as
I grew up she discouraged me from ever going to Makgoba's Kloof.
She would say that not only were the Makgobas at odds with one
another but also the conflicts of the past were still palpable there.
"The Boers don't want to see you there," she warned me, "and if
they do, they will slit your throat and cut you to pieces." To back
up her warning, she would evoke the terror we felt every year on
December 16.

To explain this, we need to remember that the day that has been
re-purposed since our liberation as a national holiday called the
"Day of Reconciliation" was once called "Dingaan's Day" and
later the "Day of the Covenant," on which Afrikaner Nationalists
commemorated—as a holy day of thanksgiving to God—the

anniversary of their victory over the Zulu king, Dingane, in a historic battle in 1838. December 16 may have been holy for some Afrikaners, but for a gang of white motorcyclists from Lombardy East, a nearby white suburb, it was a day on which they liked to ride into Alex in force and roar around the township, just to remind us who was boss in South Africa. From a very young age, I remember that we weren't allowed to roam around the streets on "Dingaan's Day," instead having to hide away in our homes. According to the picture my mother painted, if I went back to Makgoba's Kloof, I would have to live perpetually in fear of that kind of person.

My first recollection of personally being unjustly treated by whites came at the hands of "Peri-Urban," the police employed by the Peri-Urban Areas Health Board, which governed Alex. I was about eight or nine at the time. Some of us Makgoba children had stopped going to ZCC services, having been baptized in Anglican or Catholic churches (and also because in those churches, you worshiped in the morning and then had the rest of the day free, while the ZCC service took most of the afternoon), but we were engaged in another activity close by. In an initiative started by my mother, we sat outside the ZCC services on Sunday afternoon selling to members of the congregation cakes my mother had made, as well as tea, groundnuts, and cooked mielies (corn) prepared by the granddaughter of Modjadji, the reigning Lobedu queen at the time. Near the place we sat there was a pothole in the road, which people slowed down to go through to avoid splashing us. One afternoon an "Afrikaans"—another name we used to describe a "Peri-Urban"—came by and sped through the pothole, sending water spraying over our food and ruining it. At first, we were inclined to forgive him, thinking he might be racing somewhere on duty, but then he came back and did the same thing. So we had no food to sell, and, thinking we would get into trouble, the girls began crying and I got really upset.

Other bad experiences at the hands of white South Africans occurred at the Alex Clinic. On one occasion a young intern spoke harshly to my father, and when he answered back we were banished to the end of the queue. On another a doctor told my mother that "you black women have too many children," making her cry. In later years a gang of white boys robbed me and my caddy friends of our earnings as we returned from a session at Royal Johannesburg.

Other experiences were more positive. I remember the caring doctor at Alex Clinic who treated my split upper lip as well as the people for whom my mother worked on two days of the week, especially the Keisers and the Bethlehems. Ma-Keiser supplemented my mother's pay with toasted loaves of bread and Jewish delicacies, but what I liked most when I was older was receiving her husband's hand-me-down clothes. In his shirts, pants, and shoes, I was top of the fashion parade, although he must have had big feet because I had to stuff newspaper in the shoes to make sure they didn't fall off. Ma-Bethlehem was Paulette Bethlehem, married to Ronnie, a renowned economist. She called my mother by her African name, Kedibone, and insisted on meeting us children. It was at the Bethlehems that I remember drinking for the first time a wonderful avocado soup, part of the Jewish Passover meal. Later when I went to the University of the Witwatersrand (Wits), my mother was too embarrassed to say so, because their son, Adam, was also there, and Mom was sensitive to it being known that the son of a "domestic" was studying with the son of the "missus." But after Paulette learned I was there and as I became politicized, we had long debates over whether Adam should serve in the military; under apartheid all white males were forced to become conscripts in the apartheid army. (Ronnie was tragically killed in a hijacking in his driveway at the height of Johannesburg's 1990s crime wave.)

My very limited wardrobe was what sent me off to caddy at the golf course. I may not have been able to verbalize what I saw at home in Alex, but I could see that it was tough for my parents. Each time I wanted a nice jersey, or other boys started wearing All Star shoes, my parents would say they didn't have the money. By caddying, I could earn enough regularly to take a little orange money-box to the post office, where my mother helped me open an account. In time I was able to buy canvas shoes and even a lumber jacket.

Once, however, caddying landed me in deep trouble. Usually I worked only at weekends, but on this occasion, I was asked to work during a professional tournament. I skipped school to do so but on the fourth day my father found out. He was furious with me for lying and escorted me back to school. Not only did I incur his wrath, but you didn't get paid until the end of the tournament, so I lost three days' worth of earnings—at 60 cents a day for 18 holes, that was R1.80 or just over two dollars at the time—a lot of money for a young boy in those days!

My father didn't make his living from being a ZCC pastor. He was what we would now call a "self-supporting" priest and had to fend for himself and his extended family. His way of doing so was to go every month to a factory shop in Johannesburg, Kitty Kit Hawkers' Factory Supplies, and buy clothing on credit. Then, starting around the fifteenth of every month, he and a friend, Dichabe, would drive west of Johannesburg through the gold mining areas of Carletonville, Fochville, Potchefstroom, Stilfontein, Orkney, and Klerksdorp, stopping at each mine, dropping off stock and collecting deposits, ending up at Lichtenburg, halfway to the Botswana border. Then they would turn around and travel back to Johannesburg. Every month, as they arrived at each mine and opened their trunk, the miners knew: "Makgoba and Dichabe are here." After payday my father and his partner would go back to their customers to collect their money.

Of course we weren't the only family my father had. His first wife had died by the time I was a child, but his second wife lived in Diepkloof in Soweto, so I assume that for some of the time he was away each month my father might have been there. For my shy, soft-spoken mother, this was just part of life—until the day he started a fourth family and hired a room in Alex in a yard opposite ours for his new wife and daughter. His new wife was the younger sister of the third wife of my dad's friend, who with no qualms had all three of his wives living in the same house. But for mother this was just too much. I was twelve or thirteen by then, and I remember the arguments as she remonstrated with my father. I think my father's friends regarded my mother as "matepe," or spoiled, but her case was that "you can do whatever you want to do, but not right here in front of my children and my friends." The young bride quickly read the situation and left with our new sister to return to the rural town from which she came. Calm returned to our household for another year or two.

From my account so far, the reader might think we were desperately unhappy in Alexandra, but there was a brighter side to the Dark City. Many plots were big enough for people to keep goats on, and as children we drank goat milk straight from the teat. We caught locusts and larks and ate them for lunch. We played with girls and swam in the Jukskei River. There was a big farm, named Molokoloko, across the main road and we "relieved" the farmer of his tomatoes, carrots, peaches, and plums. We crossed the river to Lombardy East, which we saw as a land of milk and honey, and there we relieved the white residents of what we saw as their bounty—the bottles of milk left outside their homes. We played "doll houses" and chose to be mothers, fathers, or children, holding mock weddings and observing gender stereotypes in our games: fathers smoked pipes and read newspapers while mothers cooked, cleaned, and watched over the children. Looking back, I realize that Guy Fawkes' Day, November 5, which commemorates a plot in Britain to blow up the Houses of Parliament, was an opportunity for those boys so oriented to acknowledge that they were gay. Some young men hugged and kissed openly; other young men could be comfortable in public wearing women's clothing. For some this would go on for weeks. Our math teacher, known for his strictness, high heels, and tight pants, loved Guy Fawkes, the only day on which he could relax and express his true sexuality.

For adults, says Madiba in his autobiography, life in Alex in the 1940s was precarious but also exhilarating: "Its atmosphere was alive, its spirit adventurous, its people resourceful."[54] Twenty-five years later, it was still the same. The streets were open-air theatres and at the weekends the township was vibrant with music. On Saturdays a ZCC brass band marched up and down the streets, hoping to attract worshipers, as did the "amaPostile," members of the Apostolic churches, in their green and blue uniforms. We heard jazz bands, we watched drum majorettes and our mothers warned us against dancing to the seductive music of the sangomas—indigenous healers—playing their drums and working themselves into frenzied trances. It was a multicultural world, in which Indian traders would be welcomed for the clothes they sold but treated with suspicion as "maslams" (slang for Muslims) because of their religion, and Chinese visitors in black cars came to fetch the takings from "fafi", our version of a numbers racket. Alex even had a little three-hole golf course.

Madiba's taste for smart clothes was an Alex trademark. When we dressed up, we would wash, cover ourselves with layer after layer of Vaseline, then walk up and down the street in our best clothes as a fashion statement. "Jy moet my mooi kyk," you might hear,

54 Mandela (1994), 71

"ek dra nie Wallabees nie, ek het 'n Florsheim en London Fog.
Ek is nie 'n barrie nie, ek is 'n clever van die township, jy moet
notcha!" (You must be careful around me, I don't wear cheap
shoes but Florsheim and London Fog. I am street-wise and a boss
around here.) The top shots, those who rode around the township
in stolen cars, would congregate at local shebeens, drinking
expensive liquor and playing music loudly from their cars. Alex
was an open university, a school for life where we learned tenacity
and resilience.

Then "the system" caught up with us. According to the history
I have previously cited, "Alexandra's place in the new apartheid
order had been largely settled ... in 1953." Five years after the
Afrikaner Nationalists took power, the government decided to
reduce Alex's population, sending away everyone other than those
who worked for whites in the northern suburbs. But it took until
1958 for the removals to begin. Then came the decision to turn
Alex into a township of huge single-sex hostels, a catchment area
for controlled slaves—although the first of the hostels wasn't
completed until the early 1970s.[55]

My father resisted the first removals by "vanishing" so that he
could not be served with eviction papers. In that way we dodged
being moved to Diepkloof in Soweto, then to Meadowlands, also
in Soweto, and then to Tembisa, east of Johannesburg. But the
pressure to move steadily intensified in our part of the township.
In August 1974, the government said 13,012 adult men living in
Alex were going to have to be rehoused in single-sex hostels and
4,800 families moved to Soweto or Tembisa.[56] Our family was
among them.

---

55 Bonner and Nieftagodien, Ch 8
56 *A Survey of Race Relations in South Africa, 1974.* (Johannesburg: SA Institute of Race Relations),
166

Alex was too filthy, too dangerous, too dark a city for the neighboring white suburbs. So our home was to be destroyed. Our bucket toilet system, our shared yards and taps had to go. Molokoloko farm was to be expropriated. The little golf course was to be closed. We had to go. In December 1974, after my father had delayed a move to Pimville in Soweto for a year, the threat of having his family—my mother, sixteen-year-old Mataps, two thirteen-year-olds (Tobi Tobi and me), eleven-year-old Esther, and our little brother, nine-year-old Thomas—thrown into the street forced his hand. He finally gave in to the power of "Peri-Urban." For the first time I saw him scared, lacking in concentration and angry. And I still recall the day on which he became violent.

I had just come home after playing marbles with my friends. My mother and father were arguing, and it became clear to me that she had lost patience with his "vanishing." Hearing the argument from another room, for the first time I understood the painful reality for my mother that each time my father disappeared and gave us a reprieve from having to move, he also started another relationship elsewhere. I learned that my sister, the child of his fourth wife, had been born out of wedlock. I was devastated. Cornered by "Peri-Urban" and embarrassed, my father responded to my mother's remonstrations by slapping her. Going into the room, I saw that she was red in the face. A beautiful woman, very light in complexion, she tried to hide her tears and gave me a smile. She tried to say something, pretending that things were okay. But things were not okay. "How dare you!" I said to my father. Fuming, he pushed me aside in rage and hit me. Then, in shock, he broke down crying and embraced me. "I'm sorry, son," he said. "I'm not coping with this poverty and all the demands on me." Those words are engraved in me; in our home my father was always right, and it made a big impression on me to see him cry and hear him say sorry.

Chapter 3

Soweto

I recall clearly the day the dreaded "GGs" arrived to take us to Soweto. These were the big white trucks with Government Garage number plates that people across South Africa feared during the era of forced removals. They came a few days before my fourteenth birthday, probably December 13 or 14, 1974. My parents didn't prepare for the move—I think as a continuation of my dad's attitude of passive resistance. We children didn't see the removal notice, which would have been stuck to the front door the night before. Sometimes the glue on the notices wasn't very sticky or perhaps our parents quietly removed it after dark. But there was no more dodging the move. The GGs came at around 10 or 12, and someone knocked on the door with a long spanner. If we didn't open up, we knew they would break the door down. My mother realized that the forced removal was actually happening; we had run out of options.

For what seemed like hours, a gang of laborers worked to clear the house and throw our stuff onto the back of the truck. My mother would rush to take plates and wedding gifts and wrap them up safely in the household linen or our clothing. Often during removals, a number of families and their possessions would be crammed onto a single truck. Sometimes workers would refuse to take big or heavy furniture, saying the houses to which the victims were going were too small, and neighbors staying behind would inherit these items. In our case, we were lucky and had our own truck. But that didn't save my boxes of carefully

collected, precious comics—*Chunky Charlie, She,* and the like. The
workers said they were too heavy and left them behind. Those
comics created a whole world as I was growing up; sometimes I
would sit daydreaming on the stoop with the boxes alongside me,
imagining Chunky Charlie to be real, or picturing the character
She as my mother or my older sister, a protector who could
overcome any challenge. For me, the greatest loss of the move
was that collection, and I was deeply upset. Also left behind was
a swing in the yard that had been given to my mother by one of
her "madams." When the house was empty, my father called us
together and said, "Let us pray." I can't remember what we prayed,
but it was as if we were in mourning, sitting there saying goodbye
to the house. An atmosphere of gloom settled on Alex during
these removals. Those who got to stay behind—at least for the
time being—would gather round, everyone holding hands, no
one saying anything, just expressing dismay and sadness as if at a
funeral.

Then we were off, my father, my mother, and five children, on the
back of the GG to Soweto, fifty kilometers away and on the other
side of Johannesburg. Past the city center we drove, past Crown
Mines, onto the Potchefstroom road, past Baragwanath Hospital,
finally to be dumped at house number 3458B, Zone 3, Pimville.
There were no street names or numbers.

The original township of Pimville was older than Alex,
having been founded in 1904. Its very establishment was the
consequence of a forced removal, in which people were taken
from an area of central Johannesburg called the "Coolie[57]
Location" during an outbreak of pneumonic plague and
transported to isolation camps on the farm Klipspruit, twenty
kilometers southwest of the city.[58] Later renamed Pimville after a

---

57 A derogatory word for people of Indian descent.
58 Howard Phillips (2014). *Locating the location of a South African location: the paradoxical pre-
history of Soweto.* Urban History, 41, pp 311-332

city councilor, it was the first township in what was to become Soweto. Its people resisted repeated attempts to move them again in the decades that followed but eventually succeeded in having the township rebuilt in the 1960s.[59] When we arrived, there was no question of people who had been living together in Alex being allowed to stay together in Soweto. We were categorized as "Basotho" so we went to Zone 3, which was dubbed "Maseru" after the capital of neighboring Lesotho. Similarly, Shangaan-speakers from the northeast of South Africa went to Zone 4, or "Giyani", and Zulus to Zone 1. Other language groups were sent to Tembisa, east of Johannesburg. Our old Alex community was lacerated.

Devastated by the move, we nevertheless tried to find something positive in it. Our new home in a newly built area was bigger and better than the one in Alex. The streets were relatively clean, and although the yard was sandy, I was able to start another vegetable patch. Here I grew spinach, carrots and cabbages. The house was what we in Soweto called a "matchbox." Made of unplastered red brick and attached to its neighbors in what looked like a row of train coaches, it was still a home of our own. There were two bedrooms, so my parents and my sisters each had one. Tom and I slept in a separate living room, and we had a kitchen. There was no bathroom but we had a flushing toilet outside, which fascinated us so much that we would flush down anything that was on hand.

Still we could not escape a sense of internal conflict and tension. With the houses so close together, we could hear what was being said and done in the toilet next door. The newspaper we used instead of unaffordable toilet paper sometimes clogged up the

---

59 JT Campbell (1987). T.D. Mweli Skota and the making and unmaking of a black elite. Paper presented at Wits History Workshop, pp 35-37; James Ball (2012). *"A Munich situation": pragmatic cooperation and the Johannesburg Non-European Affairs Department during the early stages of apartheid.* Master's thesis, Wits University, pp 105-110

pipes. The house turned out to be more cramped than I first
realized. Tom and I hated having visitors, especially if they arrived
after eight in the evening, because it meant we quickly had to
remove our bedding from the floor and toss it into our sisters'
room. To cover up for the delay in opening the front door, we
would pretend we had lost the keys.

I was in pain—sad, angry, broken down, and confused—feeling
a welter of the emotions that go hand in hand with relocation
and loss. I was losing my roots, my base, my space, the source of
my spirituality, and what made me who I was. And although my
father was just as unhappy, I held him responsible.

I had grown up regarding Dad, whom we called "Ouman"
(old man), as a hero, even though we didn't see him very often
because he spent a good deal of each month away. He also
often traveled to Moria to consult with the Lekganyanes, with
whom he had close ties. As an entrepreneur, he didn't depend
on anyone else for his income and his letters to Moria show that
he was a strong, independent-minded person. When it came to
politics, he demanded silence when the news broadcast came
on the radio, and if the news was bad, he would denounce
"maboer" (the Boers) and say the country needed a strong black
force. He encouraged me to be independent and to be wary of
unscrupulous traders. At the same time, he taught me not to
judge people on the basis of their race. Looking back on our
history, he would say that even if the Makgobas had weapons,
they couldn't fight the government. I should rely on the power of
education, he said. He was also progressive for his time when it
came to personal belief, insistent that we should be believers but
open to us choosing the religion we wanted to follow.

At the same time, I had a particularly close relationship with
my mother. My sisters felt that "Aus Kedibone" (older sister
Kedibone), as we called her, had too much of a special place in

her heart for me. As a child, I spent a lot of time with her. She was firm but extra tender toward me, so I guess I was spoiled. She urged upon me the virtue of modesty, telling me in Sesotho: "*Ngoana mosotho senne o ipolela ngoana motho o motle ha a bolela Ke ba bang*" (Mosotho child, don't praise your efforts, you are more beautiful when others praise you). After I had left home, she bought basics such as toiletries for me; after I married, she would buy an extra tin of canned tuna for the family; and even after I became a bishop, she continued to buy me socks, vests, and underwear.

After the move to Pimville, I was disgusted and disappointed with my father, my hero who had wronged me thrice: disgusted because he had lost his temper and hit my mother; disappointed because had failed his family by carrying on an extramarital affair; and disillusioned because he had failed to protect his family against a forced removal and its consequences. I was angry and became scared of the capacity of my anger to destroy both my father and me. Anxious and hopeless, tired because of lack of sleep and energy, I cried as my hero had cried, my feelings eventually turning to numbness.

I still had two years of senior primary school to complete when we moved. I was happy at Pholosho: I had good friends there and was regarded as a bright student, so I decided to travel back to Alex every day to attend my classes. My commute to school involved walking to the bus, which took me to the railway station at Nancefield, catching the 4:45 a.m. train to the city, walking to the Noord Street bus ranks, queuing for the bus to Alex, and then either walking from the Alex terminus to school or catching yet another bus—a good three and a half hours of traveling in all. Coming home, I would begin with a 4:30 p.m. bus and do the return trip, getting home around 7:15 p.m.

This daily trip not only taught me what hundreds of thousands of black South Africans had to endure to get to work, forced to live as they were outside the main cities, but it also exposed me to the gauntlet they ran every day under the pass laws. Transport hubs were a favored spot for police to raid when looking for people whose presence was deemed illegal.

At fourteen, I was tall for my age. One morning I alighted from the train at Park Station in the city center on my way to Noord Street to be confronted by a posse of police. Although I was in school uniform and carrying books, they wouldn't believe that I was too young to carry a dompas—a sort of internal passport—and arrested me. They shoved me into the back of a police van, where I waited until it was full of other alleged offenders. From there, we were taken to the dreaded "Number Four." This was a prison for black men, part of a complex known as The Fort on a hill just north of the city center. The original prison was built to hold white male prisoners by the Zuid-Afrikaansche Republiek in 1892, then converted into a military fort to defend Johannesburg during the Anglo-Boer War. Number Four and a women's prison were added later.[60] By the time I arrived for my brief sojourn, The Fort had accommodated rebels ranging from Boer military leaders to Indian passive resisters (including Mahatma Gandhi) to 1950s treason trialists, including Nelson Mandela.[61] My cellmates were black men who either didn't have permission to be in Johannesburg or who hadn't been carrying their passes. I could hear from their accents that many had just arrived from rural areas. Fortunately for me, I was taken before a magistrate late that afternoon. Seeing my uniform and books, he dismissed the case

---

60 The Fort is now part of "Constitution Hill", a heritage site comprising museums and a new building housing our Constitutional Court, designed to reflect the values of our constitutional democracy.

61 Constitution Hill heritage site website: https://www.constitutionhill.org.za/site/our-history/; Constitutional Court website: http://www.constitutionalcourt.org.za/site/thecourt/thebuilding.htm [Accessed 4 May 2016]

and told me to make sure in the future that my school gave me a letter to verify my age and that I was a scholar.

According to figures tabled in parliament later, I was one of 61,002 people arrested under the pass laws in Johannesburg that year and one of 268,985 people across the country as a whole.[62]

Despite that incident, I was not particularly politically conscious. I don't recall experiencing at school in Alexandra the levels of tension that built up in Soweto's senior primary and secondary schools ahead of the historic youth uprising of 1976. In Soweto the enforcement of a government directive that math and social studies be taught in Afrikaans at high schools, when most teachers weren't even fluent in the language, was the main flashpoint sparking a rebellion that began on June 16 of that year. In Alex, secondary education was being closed down ahead of the planned removals, so by 1976, many pupils were already going to high schools elsewhere.[63] In addition, we hadn't taken exception to the introduction of Afrikaans, perhaps because the tsotsi-taal (the hybrid language the tsotsis used) was prevalent in Alex and mainly comprised Afrikaans. However, we shared in common with Soweto the difficulties created by another controversial government decision: to reduce schooling from thirteen to twelve years. This intensified overcrowding in classrooms in Alex as in Soweto. Even before it came into effect, classrooms were overflowing; I recall classes of more than ninety students at Emfundisweni and more than seventy at Pholosho.[64] Not only that, the decision was also traumatic for parents as well as children because it abolished Standard Six, the final year of senior primary school. We placed a high premium on the Standard Six certificate; if for some reason you had to leave high school early,

---

62 *A Survey of Race Relations in South Africa, 1976.* (Johannesburg: SA Institute of Race Relations), 207-208
63 Bonner and Nieftagodien, 201
64 Op cit, 202

perhaps because of pregnancy, the certificate could get you into a primary teachers' training course or a job in the mines. I recall a brilliant classmate in tears because she was going to be forced to go to secondary school before her parents felt she was ready for it.

Unlike most of the children of Soweto, I actually went to school on June 16. I had heard that protests would begin that day but decided that since they were in Soweto and not Alex—and my principal at Pholosho was very strict—I had better attend classes. So I left Pimville in civvies, changed into uniform when I arrived in Alex and, as I recall, had a normal school day before returning home to Soweto. But my three sisters, who had transferred to Soweto schools when we were moved, were caught up in the tumult. They were all at different schools but all three joined marches. Mataps was writing a math paper when other pupils came in, shouted "Pens down!" and got the class to go out onto the streets. When the clashes with police began, she ran home with a friend, afraid of what our mother would think. My sister Nthabiseng joined another group of marchers, one of whom was shot and killed. She loved fun and was disappointed not to have been injured so that she could avoid her chores. Esther, who was twelve, joined yet another group, which reached its destination with her exhausted and hungry, yet excited. But then havoc broke loose, and she took refuge with a kind family nearby. Not knowing this, we panicked when she did not come home that evening. My mother spent the evening in silence, as if crying within. Esther came home the next day.

I have since learned that some children who lived in Alex but went to school in Soweto started organizing students in Alex that night.[65] The next day a few students put up a barricade on 6th Avenue. I traveled to Alex as usual and had another normal day at school.

65 Op cit, 205-207

Two days later, the uprising spread to Alex. I now know that while I was at home in Pimville, about a hundred older students had met the previous night in a dark spot behind the Alex stadium and planned a protest march.[66] When I stepped off the bus in that morning, it was unusually quiet. Unaware of what was about to happen, I went, as I had the previous two days, and changed into my uniform in the toilets at the bus rank. Beginning the walk to school, I met a group of about twenty children from different schools who were clearly not heading to class. I joined them because one of the leaders was a friend from a well-respected business family and the son of a former principal of Ezenzeleni. The leaders split us into smaller groups and told us to take off our school ties to make it difficult to identify us. I was in a group sent to a Chinese-run shop near the stadium. The shopkeepers must have decided to steer clear of Alex because the shop was closed. But they rented the premises from the respected business family, so we fetched the keys, opened the shop, and proceeded to loot it.

What I remember in particular is me and a tiny fellow dragging a five-kilogram bag of mielie-meal (corn meal) and wondering what I was going to do with it. I couldn't take it home on the train that night. When the police arrived, we scattered, regrouping as previously planned at the stadium, but the police followed us. They lined us up and said, "Now you, you, and you—you were involved in the looting." We vehemently denied this, but since we were covered in white mielie-meal, of course they didn't believe us. We were made to stand aside and told to wait to be picked up by "thisa-abantwana," the truant van. By then, however, Alex was burning, and the van was working overtime. They had to let us go. Police later told a commission of inquiry that looting occurred all over the township. They admitted shooting dead twenty-nine people, four of them youths between the ages of sixteen and twenty-five who were looting a bottle-store and one man who

---

66 Op cit

had attacked a fish-and-chip shop.[67] I can't recall how my parents learned I was all right, but it was decided that I would stay with relatives in Alex for a while to avoid the dangerous travel.

I don't recall feeling on that first day that we were engaged in an overtly political act. It was more as if, acting as a group, we felt we could go out, break the mold, and have some fun. We justified what we did by saying, *Well, after all, these Chinese sell us rotten bread, and they would never take it back.*

Historians say the first few days of the uprising were characterized by "the almost spontaneous involvement" of hundreds of students.[68] (They also describe our looting of Indian- and Chinese-owned shops as "a more sinister side of the youthful demonstrators.") A day or two later, one of our school's soccer stars addressed us and denounced the teaching of Afrikaans. Apart from the fact that we hadn't rejected its introduction earlier, our Afrikaans teacher was a much-loved person who had the ability to make the language come alive for his students— especially after taking a slug from the bottle he kept in his side pocket—so we were somewhat conflicted over the issue. Still, the rebellion left our strict principal suddenly unable to tell us what to think and do, and amidst the anarchy we could have fun. This was reinforced
by the views of student leaders from Soweto who told us that the issue went beyond Afrikaans. At its heart, they said, the revolt was about justice.

Despite joining those early protests, I still felt that my vocation was to continue my schooling and so I returned to class. In the weeks that followed Alex was occupied by a force of brown army "Hippos" and police "Mellow Yellows," armored personnel carriers

---

67 Op cit, 207-209
68 Op cit, 210

filled with white army conscripts as well as regular policemen. In both Soweto and Alex, police and soldiers roamed the townships, shooting at young people, often indiscriminately, whether they were arsonists, protesters, or teenagers throwing clenched fist salutes and shouting "Amandla!" ("Power").

One morning, after getting off the bus, I was walking to school when I heard the roar of an open-topped Hippo. Looking over my shoulder and seeing armed troops standing up in the Hippo, I fled. As the vehicle came alongside me, I dashed into the yard of a local mechanic, Mr. Shongwe, who was fixing a car. Terrified, I asked him to hide me. Leaving me under a car, he went out to the Hippo, which was now parked outside his gate.

"Where's the terrorist?" a soldier shouted.

By God's grace, Mr. Shongwe stood up to them. In what I saw then, and still see now, as an immense act of faith and courage, he told them off in language that I can't repeat here, accusing them of wanting to kill schoolchildren because they couldn't catch "terrorists." He must have pricked their consciences because they responded by leaving. I lay under the car weeping, feeling useless, scared, dirty with oil, not sure whether to go to school or back home. I slid out from under the car and asked Mr. Shongwe what he thought I should do.

"I think go to school," he said.

"I'm scared," I said.

"Then go home."

"I'm scared."

"Then I will take you to school," he said, "and explain to the teacher. And then you can go home and clean up because you are covered in oil."

As I write, recalling the incident, the panic and tears surge up inside me again. Looking back, it marked a point in my life in which I first understood the harsh reality of South Africa—and what it said about the spirituality of those in power. Through the prayers I offered while under the car, I think I subconsciously began to think about the man I wanted to be—and that the Hippo and soldiers epitomized the opposite of what I wanted to become in life.

I continued to stay with relatives in Alex whenever marches, boycotts, or other protests were planned, either in Soweto or Alex. When I had completed my time at Pholosho, I transferred to the only high school in Alex, Alexandra Secondary School, or "Seco." As political and student activism picked up in Alex, my parents decided that living there had lost its advantages for me and so, like many other urban parents in that era, they moved me to a rural boarding school in an attempt to have me escape the turmoil. I packed my trunk and traveled there, first by train and then on a bus service called Setsokotsane, which on the gravel roads lived up to its name (meaning "to shake up"). Within a few weeks at the school, however, there was a disruption (the nature of which I can't recall) and we urban boys were expelled. I returned to Jo'burg.

I was sent to join my sister Mataps at school in Orlando East, Soweto, first to Selelekela Secondary and then to Orlando High across the road until I matriculated, but to this day I see myself as an Alex boy. The circumstances of our move to Pimville and the wider world within which I began my final years at school and then university, meant that I never identified with Pimville in the way I did with Alex.

Sadly, my father's experience was similar to mine but with more dire consequences. The ZCC said if he did not live in Alex, he could not remain as the priest there. The congregations in Soweto had their own clergy. At first, he traveled to Alex to worship but slowly the joy and laughter went out of him. His ancestral roots were in the ZCC, and he had poured his energy into building the community in Alex. It had been everything for him. It gave him a sense of who he was and of his value in society. Finding himself in a different place, where he had no sense of belonging, stripped my father of his sense of identity. One Sunday he told my mother that he was "too lazy" to go to church. It was as if he had lost contact with his vocation in Alex and his resulting closeness to the church leadership in Moria. One evening late in 1978, as we were waiting for my end-of-year school results, I had a sense of unease—call it pending anxiety. The next morning, my father died peacefully in his sleep. He was drained, he was tired, and I think he felt that he had failed the family he loved. "Peri-Urban," the system, apartheid, finished him.

We had no phone, so I ran nonstop to the police station in Kliptown to report his death. They took five hours to come and fetch his body, during which time he "lay in state" for his family as my mother and I waited at his bedside. My sisters were paralyzed with pain. When the police finally arrived, we sang *"Hamba nhliziyo Yam, Uye eZulwini"* (Take flight my dear heart, Flee to heaven) with broken voices, full of tears and all that goes with uncontrolled weeping. As the yellow van took my father away to the morgue, I quietly offered this family praise song:

"Ke Ramaite wa ho loka, Bolepye wee: Tlou, Tloukgolo di tswa Bolepye!" (Hail, Father of Maite, a good and noble man from Bolepye; Elephant of the great/royal elephants of Bolepye!)

Chapter 4

Science, Politics, or Theology?

By the time I arrived in Orlando East to finish my schooling, I and my former classmates at Pholosho and Alexandra Secondary had been grounded in an independent, critical approach to learning that gave us the confidence to challenge our teachers, many of whom were not much older than we were. At Pholosho, the principal, Mr. Phahle, taught us never to take anything at face value. He would walk up and down the classroom, cane in hand, telling us that the best learning comes from asking relevant questions. The principal at Seco, Mr. Rikhotso was just as strict and strong an influence on us, underscoring what my father used to say: Work hard and don't pay attention to the poverty around you because that's not your destiny. He was also a follower of the Pan Africanist Congress (PAC)—a rival to the African National Congress (ANC) which Nelson Mandela was later to lead. He had served time as a political prisoner and liked to use Shakespearean characters in his English classes to allude to historic figures such as the PAC leader Robert Sobukwe and the black consciousness leader Steve Biko.

But math and science were the subjects that propelled my high school and then my university career. This began at Selelekela. On a visit to the school recently, I went to the classroom in which I'd studied the subjects and was encouraged to see a group of dedicated young students studying on their own long after school hours. However, anyone in Soweto who was serious about math and science aspired to attend Orlando High. TW "Wilkie" Kambule, a legendary teacher and brilliant mathematician, built this school into an institution that attracted the cream of Soweto students, and you had to compete to secure a place. Not to be outdone, the teachers who taught subjects other than math and science—Afrikaans, geography, history and the like—were committed to excellence in their fields too.

At Orlando High I took math, accountancy, geography, biology, and physical science. For languages, I studied Afrikaans, English, and Sesotho. The education was conventional, almost orthodox; there was no reinterpretation or adding of political nuance such as had been our experience in Alex. Orlando High taught what was in the syllabus. The only time the school allowed student activism was in the debating society, where we could discuss, for example, whether we wanted a Students' Representative Council (SRC) or whether to allow the Congress of South African Students (COSAS), established in the wake of the Soweto uprising, to organize at the school. Even when you weren't in uniform, you were representing Orlando High, so students were expected to wear a tie, trim and comb our hair, and polish our shoes. There was—and still is—a large rock in the school grounds, and "The Rock" became the nickname of the school and a metaphor for the solid, resilient education it provided. To supplement our schooling, we were encouraged to go on Saturday mornings to Wits University in town for extra classes run by Star Schools, associated with *The Star* newspaper.

Attending Selelekela and Orlando High cut my traveling time dramatically, down to half an hour if I went by train. As the train moved through the Klipspruit valley and up to Orlando East, I could look up to the left and see "Beverly Hills," the area of Orlando West near the homes of Nelson Mandela, Desmond Tutu, and professional and business people. If I squandered my train money on the movies in Fietas—the Fordsburg and Vrededorp communities on the edge of the city—then I either had to walk all the way to school or follow cleverer boys who knew train movements well enough to work out how to dodge paying the fare.

But even though school was now only two stops up the line, I still had to be careful. The station closest to home was near hostels that accommodated migrant workers from rural areas of KwaZulu/Natal. We called them the "Inkatha" hostels, because most if not all of the residents were assumed to belong to the Zulu cultural movement of that name. Since the 1976 uprising, when young people in Soweto had tried—and failed—to get hostel residents to join anti-apartheid boycotts and work stayaways, relations between us had been difficult.

Once, forgoing my usual caution, I took a shortcut across a field near the hostels. Seeing two men approaching, one carrying a stick, I wondered if I should run. I decided that running would be provocative and that I should be bold and walk on normally. But as they came closer, they adjusted their pace to mine, slowing when I slowed and speeding up when I did. So I decided to run. Accusing me of being a "comrade," they chased me and one beat me badly across the back of the head. I think I was slipping in and out of consciousness but the last words I remember them saying were: *"Ufile inja!"* (The dog is dead.) After I don't know how long, I gained enough strength to pick myself up and I walked, my head bleeding, to the nearby home of one of our teachers at Orlando High. The teacher was Angie Motshekga, who would later become the minister of basic education. Her family took me to Baragwanath Hospital, where I was x-rayed, and my head wounds were stitched up. But my main worry was not my injuries. It was the embarrassment of telling my mother that I had been foolish enough to have walked across that open field at night—and telling my friends that I hadn't fought back.

During my school years, I never really developed a close identification with Pimville. Even after I had moved schools, my social life revolved around my school friends from Orlando East. Pimville was where I went to sleep and perhaps on Sundays to slip into church, then to slip out before the end. I played tennis there only because I wasn't good enough to get onto a team in Orlando East. Otherwise I mixed with school friends, pursuing interests such as cars, fashion, following South African Premier League soccer, and, in time, politics.

Apartheid made sure that politics was always in your face. I grew up aware that my maternal grandparents had been forcibly removed twice before ending up in Sharpeville, a Pan-Africanist Congress stronghold. My mother was staying there with her parents when the police gunned down protesters during a PAC demonstration against the pass laws in 1960, the infamous Sharpeville massacre. Alex was the home of many African National Congress people, and community meetings at the stadium promoted the ANC. And of course I had experienced at firsthand the pass laws, the threat of the army, and our forced removal from Alex.

In Soweto, my first awareness of the political environment came through my sister, Mataps. She started attending "power" meetings in Pimville in the late 1970s, an era in which the black consciousness philosophy propagated by Steve Biko and others played a prominent role. Everything I heard was about "the system." Initially I thought "the system" was a person or a group of army personnel—it was not "Peri-Urban" that had moved us from Alex but a vicious system. I first heard about Madiba and Robert Sobukwe of the PAC soon after arriving in Pimville. My father was not the only one who struggled to adapt; everyone who had been forced to move there struggled as well. I recall people saying that the turf battles and other problems were so complex that we needed the wisdom of a Mandela, or a Sobukwe, or a

Zeph Mothopeng, the Soweto-based PAC leader, to solve them. Perhaps my first attendance at a big political event was when the community held a meeting at Orlando Stadium to discuss whether the American rhythm and blues group, the O'Jays, should tour South Africa. The group ending up cutting their tour short, condemning the "humiliating and dehumanizing effects" of apartheid and promising not to break the cultural boycott again.[69]

At university, I became more actively involved in political organization, experiencing for the first time the tensions between the different strands of our liberation movements. I also began to feel the competing attractions of science and the church.

After being baptized at St. Michael's Anglican Church in Alex, I played an active role there as a child and a teenager, especially when I joined the youth group when I was staying in Alex to avoid the commute to Pimville. My faith was strengthened by my brush with the army Hippo in Alex: in fact the incident marked something of a conversion, helping me realize that it was only by the grace of God, or gods, or some higher being, that I had survived the dangers inherent in living in gang-infested Alex and during a time of political conflict. Later in Soweto, I was profoundly moved by the worship that took place on train number 0713, the 6 a.m. train from Nancefield to school. I was repeatedly attracted to a carriage in which the same group of people gathered every day on their way to work. Amid beautiful African choruses sung to the clanging of a cowbell, the people listened to itinerant preachers whose exhortations and prayers spoke not only to the commuters' sense of desperation, pain, and fear but also to their hopes.

Inspired by the examples of Desmond Tutu and Dean Simeon Nkoane of Johannesburg, at age eighteen, I approached the

---

69 *Jet* magazine, 4 June 1981, 3 September 1982, 27 May 1985

bishop of Johannesburg, Timothy Bavin, to offer myself to be ordained as a priest. Accustomed to the ZCC, where priests were simply appointed, I didn't realize I would have to go through a course of study. Bishop Bavin said I was too young. He was also concerned that I was running away from the pressures of living in the black community. He told me that after finishing school, I should go and study anything other than theology. If I still felt called to ordination once I had completed a degree, I should come back to him.

So when I finished school, I applied to study science at the University of the Witwatersrand in Johannesburg, where I was accepted. In those days, however, black students needed permission from a cabinet minister to study at what apartheid had designated a white university. Permission might be granted if your course of study was not available at the university set aside for your ethnic group.

For two successive years I was accepted at Wits, but permission from the government to actually enroll arrived long after the academic year had begun. By then, in both years, I had already enrolled at the institution that apartheid had created to serve the Bantustans of Lebowa, Gazankulu, and Venda in the northernmost parts of South Africa. That was the University of the North, now the University of Limpopo, generally known as Turfloop, the name of the farm on which the campus was built. It was also close to my paternal family's ancestral home, about halfway between Makgoba's Kloof and the town of what was then still called Pietersburg (now Polokwane).

At Turfloop I found that people who knew my surname accorded me space and a respect I had not encountered before. I registered for a pre-med Bachelor of Science, a degree that prepared you either to go to medical school or to stay and qualify as a laboratory scientist. In the first year I passed physics and biological sciences

in both semesters but failed math in one semester and chemistry
in both. In my second year, I passed math and chemistry but fared
badly in anatomy. I had deep misgivings about anatomy classes,
the origins of which I did not fully understand but were at least
partly a result of my concern about the source of the cadavers we
dissected. They were of black men, and we understood they might
have been from Angola or Mozambique, two countries in conflict
with the apartheid government. We had to swear an oath not to
disclose anything about the dissections, and the white professor
teaching us was not happy with my questions about the origins
of the bodies. I nevertheless continued to go to practical classes.
One result of taking the course was that the unique scent of
embalming fluid made me lose my appetite for meat, which I have
never truly regained.

I wrestled with the dissections and the issues they raised for me,
including whether the bodies would be afforded a decent funeral
and whether cremation, which was not easily accepted in African
tradition, was appropriate. During this time, I consulted with
Father Hendrick Nkadimeng, the rector of the local Anglican
church in the adjoining town of Mankweng. Away from home
and living apart from family for the first time, I had become much
more active in the church than I had been at school. It was at St.
Michael's in Mankweng that I found God—or at least that God
found me. Two years after my father's death, Father Nkadimeng
filled his place in many ways. Not only did he counsel me and
lend me Bible commentaries to study, but he also introduced me
to people who could tell me more about my Makgoba ancestry.
When he fell ill and later died of leukemia, his replacement,
Father Nehemiah Mothiba, quickly filled the gap.

Both university and church life were inextricably bound
with politics. The architects of apartheid intended that their
network of ethnically exclusive universities, mostly situated in
rural areas, should train black students to become obedient

servants in their rural Bantustans. But many of us dismissively regarded them as "tribal" or "bush" colleges. Turfloop, which was situated in Lebowa, was a cauldron of student protest from early in its life. Notably, at a graduation ceremony in 1972, the president of the SRC, Onkgopotse Abram Tiro, made a stinging attack on Bantu education, the inferior education system the government introduced for black children, in the presence of the government officials and apartheid-aligned professors who ran the institution.[70] Infuriated, they expelled him, but their actions triggered sympathy strikes on black campuses across the nation.[71] Tiro was killed by a parcel bomb in Botswana on February 1, 1974.

In 1981, the year I arrived, students decided to launch a series of political activities, motivated partly by the desire to regain the spirit of Tiro but also by the ideals of Steve Biko and our rejection of the ethnic Bantustans. At mass meetings of students, the SRC resolved to stage a food boycott, not only to protest at the quality of the food the university provided but also to highlight demands that the Bantustans be abolished, that political prisoners be released, that Afrikaans not be introduced in the university, and that the institution be transformed.

I was part of the group that kicked off the boycott with a raid on the kitchens. In response, the university called in the vicious Lebowa police, who camped around the main kitchens to prevent us from repeating the raid. Students responded to the presence of the police by trashing the bottle-store and setting the student center alight. More police flooded onto campus, chasing us with dogs and beating some of us. I still shiver when I recall girls being whipped and bitten, breaking legs or stumbling away bleeding after they crashed through windows to escape. The university

---

70 http://www.sahistory.org.za/archive/graduation-speech-onkgopotse-tiro-university-north-29-april-1972 [Accessed 28 June 2016]
71 http://www.sahistory.org.za/people/abram-ramothibi-onkgopotse-tiro [Accessed 28 June 2016]

administration called on us to stop the protests; we refused, and they closed the campus and sent us home. About three months later, the campus re-opened, and we returned. We remained politically engaged, however. One of our strategies was to throw parties to keep up the interest of those reluctant to attend mass meetings!

Apart from joining the parish in Mankweng, I also joined the university's Anglican Students' Society (Ansoc). This was part of the Anglican Students' Federation (ASF), which organized students on campuses across southern Africa, and I was soon elected as a representative of the ASF's Transvaal region, covering what is now South Africa's four northern provinces. The ASF required its members to do community service, and encouraged by Father Mothiba, we took part fully in the activism on the Turfloop campus. My first intervention was to get our local Ansoc to write to the authorities to oppose the forced removal of the Bakwena people of Mogopa, an area in the western Transvaal.[72]

Soon after that, the campus chairperson of Ansoc and I went to a meeting of the local wing of the national student body, the Azanian Students' Organization (AZASO). The group decided we should organize a big protest march from the campus to the Mankweng police station, and they needed a safe place off campus to plan the event, so with Father Mothiba's agreement we volunteered St. Michael's. As the church was across the street from the police station, we were planning an illegal march on the Lebowa police almost literally under their noses.

On May 31, 1981, supporters of apartheid celebrated the twentieth anniversary of South Africa's break from the British Commonwealth and the declaration of a republic. For Afrikaner Nationalists, the reassertion of independence in 1961 after the

72 BKM Molokoe (1998). *A historical study of the Bakwena ba Mogopa as victims of forced removals, 1983-1994.* MA dissertation, University of the North-West, Ch 4

defeat of the Boer republics at the hands of the British six decades
earlier had been a significant day in their history, and they marked
the anniversary with a massive military parade in Durban. For
black South Africans, the declaration of a republic was a disaster
second only to the implementation of apartheid in the previous
decade, so we marked the anniversary with an "Anti-Republic
Day" campaign. In the weeks leading up to May 31, student,
church, and other groups across the country issued statements
and held demonstrations.[73] Ours was one of them.[74]

Hundreds of us marched that day. It was the biggest protest I
have ever been part of. We sang and danced our way from the
campus, some wearing T-shirts of banned organizations and we
Anglicans wearing ASF shirts, while the police kept their distance
in their vans. By the time we reached the police station, the crowd
overflowed across the street to the churchyard gate. There, we
were addressed by a student leader. Our intention was to hand
the police a petition and then tear down and burn the South
African flag that flew over the station. As the ASF, we identified
with this act as a nonviolent, Christ-like act of civil disobedience
to show the police that by serving masters in Pretoria, they were
poor servants of the public. To get to the flag, we chose Shakes
Makhado, the son of a Venda chief. Shakes was well-known
for partying in nice cars but as the slimmest and most athletic
of us, he was best able to climb the flagpole. We cheered as he
went up and grabbed a piece of the flag, but then the police
intervened. They told us we had one minute to disperse but
almost immediately fired shots into the air and lobbed teargas at
us. Pandemonium broke out. Shakes was left alone up the pole
while we scattered in all directions. While police were beating and
arresting other students, I ran into the rectory behind the church,
which I knew well, and hid under a bed. To my consternation,

73 http://www.sahistory.org.za/1900s/1980s [Accessed 5 July 2016]
74 Ineke van Kessel (1999). *Beyond Our Wildest Dreams: The United Democratic Front and the
Transformation of South Africa.* (Charlottesville and London: University of Virginia), 96

Father Mothiba's young daughter, who regarded me as an elder brother, cried out, saying I was there and calling for me to read her a story. As police roamed the yard, Father Mothiba sought unsuccessfully to hush her, telling her that I had run away across the fields. The police were in the yard, suspecting he had hidden some of us, but fortunately they respected the sanctity of the church and the privacy of his rectory. I had no desire to be in their hands.

Again the campus was closed, and we were sent home. Again it re-opened later, and we returned to classes.

The mass meetings and unrest bubbled on throughout my two years at Turfloop. During the second year, the police and army took over the campus. They controlled movement at the main gates, and the main administration block and student center were under their guard. They pitched a tent permanently on a hill that overlooked the campus so they could watch our actions. The watching was reciprocated. Father Mothiba still tells visitors how he allowed us to use the bell tower adjoining the church as a lookout post from which to spy on police movements across the street. He supported us in other ways too, such as allowing us to use the church duplicating machine to produce pamphlets. His identification with students seems to have been acknowledged by the police; the station commander warned him at one point to speak with caution among his fellow pastors in Mankweng, as some of them were informants.[75]

In 1983 I was finally able to attend Wits, my university of first choice, after the government decided to scrap the permit system for black students. Transferring universities meant that I had to start over again almost from the beginning, as Wits accepted only two of my Turfloop course credits, those for physics and

75 Interview with Father Nehemiah Mothiba, October 2015

biology. The standards at Wits were far higher than at Turfloop
so although attending the Star Schools and a summer bridging
school were helpful, I still struggled to adjust. I began by
taking classes in math, chemistry, psychology, and genetics but
floundered in genetics so I dropped it. By the end of four years
at Wits, I had also studied biochemistry, applied psychology, and
industrial psychology but still needed one course of chemistry
to graduate. I loved chemistry but as it later turned out,
psychology—with its natural affinity with the calling I eventually
followed—assumed a greater importance in my life.

As at Turfloop, study at Wits was intertwined with both politics
and church life. Although we could attend classes on the main
campus near the Johannesburg city center, black students could
not share residences with white students. We had to live in Glyn
Thomas House, a segregated residence (named after a Wits
academic and administrator) in the grounds of Baragwanath
Hospital in Soweto and travel into town each day by bus. Initially,
I found this new world depressing. I was rubbing shoulders with
students whose backgrounds and financial circumstances differed
completely from mine; they were the children of Bantustan
leaders, or engineering and accounting students with bursaries
who had cars, duvets, radios, TVs, bar fridges, and spare cash. I
felt alienated.

In contrast, my second year at Glyn Thomas House was
liberating. Coinciding with the abolition of the permit system,
we were joined by an influx of gifted third-year students from
black campuses across the country, among them people who later
became prominent in South African public life. These included
Saths Cooper, an internationally-renowned psychologist; Mojanku
Gumbi, the legal adviser to Nelson Mandela's successor, President
Thabo Mbeki; Bheki Mlangeni, a human rights lawyer who was
later assassinated by police; and Tiego Moseneke, later a leading
businessman. They came from a variety of political traditions, and

it was at Glyn Thomas House that I first saw how pronounced these political differences were.

In retrospect, I see my upbringing in Alexandra as having been in an environment in which underlying loyalties were to the African National Congress and its allies, specifically to the aspirations of the Freedom Charter, the declaration adopted in Kliptown, near Pimville, in 1955 which declared that "South Africa belongs to all who live in it, black and white." Turfloop, along with most black campuses, had in Tiro's time been heavily influenced by the black consciousness philosophy, and he remained an activist in that tradition until he was assassinated in exile in Botswana. During my time there, the SRC decided to adopt the Freedom Charter, and this led to tensions among the student body. I had golf-playing friends from Sharpeville supporting black consciousness and tennis-playing friends from Johannesburg supporting the charter. Anglican students were formally affiliated to the non-racial "charterist" groups but we had people of all persuasions in our ranks, and so we decided that political leanings should not dictate church life; rather, we should play a distinctive role as Christians in promoting levels of political engagement and enhancing the values that undergirded it.

When I moved into Glyn Thomas House, the charterist South African Students' Congress (SASCO) dominated student life and received most of the money allocated for student activities in the house committee's budget. The arrival of followers of the Azanian[76] Students' Movement (AZASM) came as a challenge to SASCO, and I quickly learned that there wasn't much tolerance for difference among some of my fellow students. I recall an occasion when a meeting ended in a free-for-all in which adherents of both sides pressed sand into little pebbles and proceeded to hurl them at one another. For my part, I had friends on both sides. I

---

76 Africanist supporters prefer Azania as the name for South Africa.

didn't want to be defined by my political loyalties, and I did not aspire to hold political office, so I joined the house entertainment committee. We tried to plan activities to bring students together, which led some to suggest that I was clearly destined to become a priest. I am not sure whether they continued to think that when, to keep students out of local bars and shebeens, we succeeded in petitioning the university to open a bar at Glyn Thomas.

Nevertheless, my fundamental allegiance was to ANC-aligned thought. By the early 1980s, the Anglican Students' Federation, in which I was to hold various leadership positions over the decade, had formally adopted the Freedom Charter. In my first year at Wits I joined fellow students in traveling by bus to the launch of the United Democratic Front (UDF) in Cape Town. There I saw clergy deploy the power of words to inspire and incite the 12,000 people who attended. I remember in particular the oratory of UDF founder Allan Boesak, a leader of one of the black Dutch Reformed churches, who said that "three little words" summed up our objectives in the struggle against apartheid: "We want ALL of our rights," he said, "and we want them HERE, and we want them NOW." [77] In other speeches, Helen Joseph, an Anglican and the leader of an anti-apartheid women's movement who had been living under restriction orders for many years, and Trevor Manuel, an activist who later became finance minister, conveyed the demand for respect and equality that epitomized the struggle. Back in Johannesburg, I joined protest marches organized by the Black Students' Society on the Wits campus. We were teargassed by police and often defended by staff, including the internationally renowned paleo-anthropologist Professor Phillip Tobias. I also witnessed a police raid at Glyn Thomas House during which Bheki Mlangeni and Tiego Moseneke were arrested.

---

77 http://www.sahistory.org.za/archive/speech-rev-dr-allan-boesak-launch-united-democratic-front-20-august-1983-rocklands-civic-cen [Accessed 19 July 2016]

At Wits I engaged in less public activism than I'd done at Turfloop. This was because I turned to underground work. I was recruited to the ANC in 1984 by Jabu Ngwenya, a UDF activist and founder of COSAS.[78] As an ASF office-bearer, I had a passport enabling me to visit Anglican students in other parts of southern Africa, including travel to Zimbabwe for ANC briefings during university vacations. I like to say that in contrast to operatives of the ANC's guerrilla army, uMkhonto weSizwe (MK), who skipped the country illegally for military training, I skipped the country legally and repeatedly between 1984 and 1986. I was schooled in the "M-Plan," the basis of the ANC's underground operations within the country, by Elias "Roller" Masinga, a successful ANC recruiter and organizer going back to the 1970s.[79] Military training was not for me, Roller said. MK had enough soldiers. Instead I should provide the ANC with intelligence on what was happening in my circles. Also, I should recruit young women to the ANC's cause at campus parties on my travels around South Africa! He wanted them to help smuggle weapons across the border from Zimbabwe. I nearly recruited one but after consulting with her twin sister in exile, she turned me down.

Also at the urging of Jabu Ngwenya, I joined the Release Mandela Campaign (RMC), which Roller described as a platform for implementing the M-Plan within an approved structure within the country. But the experience that cemented my developing political commitment was attending a rally at which I saw for the first time the depth of Nelson Mandela's faith and courage. It is important to explain the context. By late 1984, when Desmond Tutu was awarded the Nobel Peace Prize for his role as "a unifying leader figure" in the struggle against apartheid, Madiba (the clan name for Mandela) had been in prison for twenty-two years.[80]

78 http://www.sahistory.org.za/archive/biography-of-jabu-ngwenya [Accessed 6 July 2016]
79 South African Democracy Education Trust (2011). *The Road to Democracy In South Africa* (1970-1980), Volume 2. (Pretoria: Unisa), 381-398

Archbishop Buti Tlhagale of Johannesburg, then a radical young
Soweto priest, has said that in the late 1970s Tutu and the Soweto
community leader Dr. Nthato Motlana were better known to the
young activists of the June 16 generation than Nelson Mandela.
Since then, the RMC had helped to popularize the Mandela name
as the principal icon of the struggle. Nevertheless, no one in
South Africa had heard Madiba's words in the two decades since
the famous four-hour speech he delivered at his trial, ending
with the dramatic declaration that he was prepared to go to the
gallows for the ideal of a democratic and free South Africa. The
law banned the publication of his writings, prohibited the taking
of photographs, and even outlawed the publication of sketches or
photographs taken before he was jailed.[81]

Against this backdrop, in February 1985 the UDF hosted a
celebration of the then-Bishop Tutu's Nobel Prize at a rally at the
Jabulani Stadium in Soweto. Viewing archival video footage of
events, I recall the fear that the prospect of attending the rally
evoked: Jabulani was best known for the Inkatha gatherings, and
we were afraid of being attacked by Zulu warriors for intruding
on their space. Anxious to show that I was prepared to be
counted as a supporter of the struggle, I decided I would face the
risks. So in my yellow UDF T-shirt, I joined a group from Glyn
Thomas representing the Wits Black Students' Society and went
along. Seeing Bishop Tutu, shining out amidst the crowd in his
long purple cassock, I realized anew the relevance of the church
to angry young people in the midst of pain and struggle. The
appearance on the platform of Helen Joseph and the Rev. Frank
Chikane, later to become general secretary of the South African
Council of Churches, underlined the point. Led by a sloganeer
(in church we would have called him a cantor, elsewhere the

80 http://www.nobelprize.org/nobel_prizes/peace/laureates/1984/presentation-speech.html
[Accessed 12 July 2016]
81 Prisons Act. No 8 of 1959, Sections 44(1)(e) and (g)

leader of a war-cry), we did the revolutionary dance known as the "toyi-toyi," singing our hearts out with liberation songs celebrating UDF and ANC leaders.

Cantor:	*Ma-guerilla ubaba wethu*	*Us: Hayi-Hayi! Hayi-Hayi!*
	Ma sothsha ubaba wethu	*Hayi-Hayi! Hayi-Hayi!*

While UDF co-president Albertina Sisulu, the wife of Mandela's mentor and fellow prisoner Walter Sisulu, and a leader in her own right, was escorted to the stage:

Sisulu lona umama wethu	*Hayi-Hayi! Hayi-Hayi!*
Nelson Mandela ubaba wethu	*Hayi-Hayi! Hayi-Hayi!*
Oliver Tambo ubaba wethu	*Hayi-Hayi! Hayi-Hayi!*[82]

The most dramatic moment came when Madiba "spoke" to the crowd. Winnie Madikizela-Mandela and the couple's youngest daughter, Zindzi, had been to see him in Pollsmoor Prison in Cape Town a few days earlier. Winnie had been banished by the government to the small town of Brandfort in the Free State, four hours' drive from Johannesburg but had been given permission to visit Madiba. At the prison, they discussed how he should respond to an offer from the president, P.W. Botha, to release him if he renounced the armed struggle. Madiba decided to use the Tutu rally to give his reply. Winnie was unable to attend; she was required to return to Brandfort after the visit. So Zindzi came instead. I remember wanting to join the young people who lifted her high on their shoulders when she arrived.

Defying the ban on quoting her father, and to cheers and whistles from the crowd, she read his message verbatim:

---

82 "Guerrillas (MK), our protectors! Soldiers, our protectors! Ma Sisulu is our mother! Nelson Mandela is our father! Oliver Tambo is our father!" (Tambo was the ANC leader in exile.)

I cherish my own freedom dearly, but I care even more for your freedom. Too many have died since I went to prison. Too many have suffered for the love of freedom. I owe it to their widows, to their orphans, to their mothers and to their fathers who have grieved and wept for them. Not only I have suffered during these long, lonely, wasted years. I am not less life-loving than you are. But I cannot sell my birthright, nor am I prepared to sell the birthright of the people to be free. I am in prison as the representative of the people and of your organization, the African National Congress, which was banned. What freedom am I being offered while the organization of the people remains banned?

Mandela also touched on issues close to me: the laws that forced us to carry the hated dompas that denied us freedom of movement and those that empowered the government to banish people from their homes. He turned the tables on Botha: "Let him renounce violence. Let him say that he will dismantle apartheid... Let him free all who have been imprisoned, banished or exiled for their opposition to apartheid. Let him guarantee free political activity so that people may decide who will govern them." He unequivocally rejected Botha's conditions: "Only free men can negotiate. Prisoners cannot enter into contracts...I cannot and will not give any undertaking at a time when I and you, the people, are not free." Then the final, ringing words: "Your freedom and mine cannot be separated. I will return!"[83]

Nelson Mandela's words that day, the strength of his commitment, and his willingness to sacrifice himself for the sake of the nation, gave me the clarity I needed about the heart of the struggle, and I knew I wanted to be supportive at a deeper level. I intensified my activities in the Release Mandela Campaign and was subsequently fetched from Glyn Thomas House from time to time to meet UDF

83 http://www.mandela.gov.za/mandela_speeches/before/850210_udf.htm [Accessed 12 July 2016]

and ANC stalwarts in Orlando West such as Mrs. Sisulu and the RMC leader Aubrey Mokoena. We discussed how Madiba would be welcomed if he was to be released. I also distributed RMC pamphlets and T-shirts. On one memorable occasion I was asked to drive some activists in Aubrey Mokoena's long and ugly red Nissan Skyline to deliver tracksuits and clothing to Winnie Madikizela-Mandela in Brandfort. The prospect both of driving this big car and of making what I feared was an illegal visit was daunting. But I had a license and the only other person who could have taken control was a bad driver, so I agreed to go. First, we ran short of gasoline, forcing me to stop at a church on the way and borrow money. When we got to Brandfort, my companions also handed a little parcel to Winnie. I didn't know what the contents were, but the episode impressed upon me the seriousness of the task. Then on the way back we nearly had a bad accident while I was passing a truck and another car came toward us. By God's mercy we averted it and blamed one another for the near miss. We didn't tell "Bra Aubs" about this when we returned his car.

At the same time as I was pursuing political activism, my commitment to the church was growing. As far back as my time at Turfloop, the ASF encouraged members to be active in their home parishes. I became involved at St. Andrew's Church, Pimville, so much so that I intervened in defense of our rector, Father Mashikane Montjane, when he, as someone with black consciousness leanings, was facing pressure from charterist youth to leave the parish. During my years at Turfloop and Wits, the African Bursary Fund of the South African Council of Churches provided me with financial support and caring mentors, in exchange for which I worked in the photocopy room during vacations or when classes were disrupted. This gave me insight into another aspect of the church's work. Desmond Tutu was general secretary of the SACC at the time, and I learned something of the politically sensitive nature of its anti-apartheid work from the contents of the documents I was asked to shred. I was also attracted to the rhythm of regular Morning Prayer and Communion, which he insisted on as part of the life of the council.

When defending Father Montjane's presence at Pimville, I had told Timothy Bavin, the bishop, that the youth would nevertheless continue to engage the rector vigorously, even to the point of forcing him out or being forced out ourselves. Amused, the bishop asked when I was becoming a priest, prompting me to remind him that it was he who had urged me to go and study. Later, he encouraged me to broaden my church experience by joining St. Francis of Assisi church in Moroka, Soweto. This was a congregation largely comprised of people who had been forcibly removed from Sophiatown in the western suburbs of Johannesburg twenty years earlier. It had a fine music tradition and an active youth ministry. I taught in the Sunday school and was mentored by Father Abel Molefe, a deeply spiritual man who earned his living as a chemistry lab assistant at Wits and supported us Anglican students at the university. He pressed me to complete the path Father Nkadimeng had set me upon at Mankweng, and after a short while, he asked Desmond Tutu, by now bishop of Johannesburg, to license me as a lay minister. He then sponsored my attendance at the diocese's Fellowship of Vocation, the group that helped aspirant priests decide whether they had a vocation.

At the same time, I was steadily taking on more responsibilities in the leadership of the Anglican Students' Federation. This not only enabled me to travel around South Africa and neighboring countries but it also opened up other new experiences: getting to know the leaders of the church and learning how its structures operated and how decisions were made. I remember with some pride the day I met with the church's secretary-treasurer, Sid Colam, to complain that the ASF's budget was too small, to see him erase a figure in his black book and write in another. I later learned he had increased our allocation by two-thirds.

I was less successful the first time I took on the leadership in a high-profile debate. Now entitled to attend and speak at the synods through which senior lay people, clergy, and bishops made policy for the church, at one synod I unsuccessfully argued in favor of the ordination of women as priests and against the deployment of Anglicans as chaplains to the apartheid-era South African Defense Force. When I saw that we were losing the debates, I angrily accused Bishop Tutu of being a conservative and a coward. One of the lay representatives, Sir Rupert Bromley, told me afterward I was putting up a convincing argument until I blew my case by losing my cool. To this day, Archbishop Emeritus Tutu still teases me about calling him a conservative, especially since, unlike him, most of our church's bishops, who are decades younger than he is, still oppose church recognition of gay marriage.

Helping to lead Anglican students also transformed my understanding of white South Africans. The transformation began when I was first admitted to Wits. Black students were still a small minority then, and I went there thinking that all whites would act as if they were superior. A warm and welcoming classmate in the chemistry laboratory disabused me of that idea. We found common ground in that neither of us was much good at the subject, so we worked together, earning borderline marks. He genuinely didn't seem to think about race or color. I came to realize that it was I, not he, who was internally struggling. Early in 1986, I was moved when white students joined us in attending a mass funeral in Alexandra for people who were killed in what was dubbed the "Six Day War" by the media.

The "war" had its roots in an incident in which police fired teargas at mourners returning from a funeral. According to one researcher, "communal outrage" turned into "overt rebellion," and over the six days, forty-six people were killed and scores more injured. At Wits, we hired ten buses to take about 600 of us to the first mass funeral. On the way into Alex, white police stopped us, and whether we were black or white, videotaped us, subjected us to individual body searches, and confiscated cameras, posters, and banners. It opened my eyes: apartheid fathers were scared of their own children and of non-racialism! We joined 30,000 mourners in the stadium, where we chanted freedom songs, raised clouds of dust, and watched as seventeen coffins draped in banned ANC flags were carried to the cemetery. Young militants booed Bishop Tutu, who had ten days earlier flown to Cape Town in an attempt to negotiate an end to the conflict with the government and had been rebuffed. Behind the scenes, they tried to persuade Allan Boesak to help them leave the country for military training.[84] On another occasion I recall the Wits SRC president, Claire Wright, addressing a campus rally opposing the compulsory conscription of white men into the army. I loved her speech and her courage: Here was a white woman who knew what her brothers were doing and rejected it, and her words helped to ameliorate the pain of my experience with the Hippo a decade earlier.

In the ASF, I had closer, more personal experiences in the company of white students. Once a fellow student drove me from Johannesburg to a meeting of the ASF executive in Durban. I had never been in such close company with a white person for so long. He spoke freely and at length. I, feeling inferior, answered but as briefly as I could. On our return he went through a breakup with his girlfriend who, wanting none of it, cried and remonstrated with him. It was a revelation to me that white people cared to the point of fighting and crying over relationships; I assumed that they thought you were just meant to move on. In

---

84 Bonner and Nieftagodien, 286-291; Wits Student, Vol 38, No 2, March 1986, 9

Durban, we were hosted by local families, and lo and behold I was assigned to a white family. Because of the fear of white people that I had grown up with, this was a traumatic experience.

At another ASF meeting at a rural retreat center run by the Diocese of Zululand, students of different races stayed together for a week, eating together, debating one another, and worshiping together, even hugging one another during the passing of the peace. At one stage there was a rumor that police would raid us because they suspected that students of different races were sleeping together, in contravention of what apartheid called the "Immorality Act." I carefully brushed my jersey every day to ensure that if there was a raid, no white person's hair would be found on it. Words don't capture the fear I felt; just writing about it now is a healing experience. Interracial relationships on campus were fraught for other reasons too. I recall angst and criticism among black men when a black woman fell in love with a tall, good-looking white student leader: He had taken away from us the cream of the crop! I supported her on the grounds that if we wanted to live non-racially then nothing stopped us from loving non-racially. When I discussed the issue with my mother, she pointed out that disagreements about relationships across barriers went further than race; moreover that they might affect me in the future: "Love is love, my son. It's a pity that you are a Makgoba. Partners who are amaXhosa[85] or of other races will be problematic for Makgoba royalty."

As my time at Wits came to an end, I finally had to make up my mind about my future. Should it be science and chemistry? Or politics? Or theology and the church?

My teachers had been urging me in the direction of the sciences, but I was still short of a credit for chemistry. My mother, my

---

85 People originally from the Eastern Cape region who speak isiXhosa.

friends, and people at Wits thought I should complete chemistry
and explore medicine or dentistry or perhaps teaching. This was
tempting. Even now I enjoy chemistry and science, to the extent
that when I played a role in a joint religious community-civil
society campaign at the Paris climate talks in 2015, I related to
the debate on the science as much as to the social justice issues
at stake. But Wits would not finance another year of study for a
single course, and my mother could not afford the fees. I could
go out to work and study part time, but I was worried that then
I wouldn't complete the course. I was set to become my family's
first university graduate. A lot of people in Pimville were looking
to me to succeed, and I feared becoming a dropout.

As for politics, my ANC recruiters had already steered me
away from going for military training. So had Desmond Tutu.
Some time earlier, I was among a group of young people who
had sought his opinion on the matter. His response had been
that there were other ways of expressing how we felt, among
them organizing young people in the church and educating
the community about our struggle. As an Alex boy, I wondered
whether joining MK was what the people of Alex wanted of me.
Apart from the fact that I would have been reluctant to leave my
twin sister behind, I had other reservations. If I got killed, yes,
I would be a hero but who would help educate people in the
church in the discipline and courage that were needed to enable
them to stand up selflessly to the fierceness of the system? By the
time I left Wits, I was questioning how military training would
help bring about the kind of healing that my exposure to the
struggle for justice convinced me South Africa needed.

In the end I did two things: I applied for a job as a researcher
with the Lowveld Council of Churches, and I also agreed to my
name going forward to the Diocese of Johannesburg's selection
conference— the group that decides whether to accept one as an

ordinand, that is, as a student to be trained for ordination to the priesthood.

When the Lowveld council offered me the job, I decided to take it. Then a letter arrived from Bishop Tutu. I still have it. It told me: "Those who interviewed you are unanimous in their view that you have a definite vocation to the ordained ministry. I am happy to tell you therefore that I am accepting you as an ordinand to start training at St. Paul's College in 1987. Acceptance for training is no guarantee that you will be ordained as the period of training is still part of the process of testing your vocation."

I had been very uncertain about going to selection conference. During my time in the Fellowship of Vocation, everyone else seemed to think they had a vocation for sure: They had met the Lord in some specific way, and they were definitely called to preaching, pastoral visiting, or whatever. In contrast, I had to be open about the fact that I wasn't sure. I enjoyed church music, processions, and the liturgy through which we worshiped, but what particularly attracted me to the church was its teachings on peacemaking. Seeing Tutu, Chikane, Helen Joseph, and the Afrikaner church dissident Beyers Naudé in action, teaching the eternal ideals, the values of the Bible, in a stadium filled with angry young people was what inspired me. Challenged by my interviewers on whether I wanted to preach or to teach, I kept on saying the teaching ministry of the church was what interested me. I left the conference thinking they were either going to throw me out of the fellowship or at least say they were not certain I had a vocation. So when the letter came, I wrestled over what to do: Go to work in the Lowveld or study at St. Paul's, the Anglican theological college in the Eastern Cape city of Makhanda, for another three years?

I consulted with my mother and Father Molefe. My mother wasn't sure that I was cut out to be a priest, but she also worried for my

safety. I had been told that at the Lowveld council, many of the
refugees I would serve were actually MK guerrillas, and she was
worried that I would end up getting raided, detained, or even
killed. Part of me wanted to chicken out of the Lowveld job for
that reason. With Father Molefe, who was also a lab assistant at
Wits, I discussed my continuing love for science. He pointed out
that I could still pursue this. One of my options, he said, was to
become a self-supporting priest like he was, ministering part-time
and with a full-time job in another field. Anyway, he added: "It's
not your science; it's God's science." He also said the teachers at
St. Paul's included priests who already had B.Sc. degrees and he
thought they would allow me to complete mine.

I decided, and my mother reluctantly agreed, that I should go
to St. Paul's. I now realized that what I thought then were my
choices paled in insignificance to the decision made by the
Diocese of Johannesburg's selection conference. It wasn't a matter
of me finding or choosing the church. Nor was it a case of me
offering the church my talents and skills—I had none that were
immediately relevant. No, the church found me. It called me and
molded me. And although in the decade to come I was exposed to
the possibilities of pursuing an academic or professional career as
a psychologist, it was as a priest, then as a bishop, and finally as
an archbishop, that I found myself. There is nothing bigger than
that which I have been formed to be in service to God through
being who I am, warts and all.

Chapter 5

Into a Boiling Pot

The city of Makhanda is a small city with a big reputation. Its main business is education; the city's handbook records more than a hundred educational institutions, including Rhodes University and a number of nationally known private schools.[86] It is the center of South Africa's biggest arts festival. Despite being much smaller than other cities in the region such as Port Elizabeth and East London, it is the judicial capital of the Eastern Cape. Its plethora of steeples, most prominently that of the Anglican Cathedral of St. Michael and St. George, which looms over High Street, has given it the nickname "City of Saints." The local diocese was the first Anglican diocese to be created in southern Africa after Cape Town, and it has a proud history of its bishops going on to be elected as archbishops of Cape Town.

However, when I arrived in Makhanda, I just found it depressing. I had been there before for an Anglican Students' Federation meeting, where our host, who was looking after the bishop's home while he was abroad, entertained us by raiding the bishop's whiskey cabinet. But living near the heart of town you could see and feel poverty in a way I had not experienced. Blacks and whites lived in closer proximity to one another than in Makgoba's Kloof or Johannesburg, and people who were obviously hungry roamed the streets, selling four bananas, or three boxes of

---

86 http://www.grahamstownhandbook.co.za/grahamstown5.asp [Accessed 17 August 2016]

matches, or two oranges. And the city's history was as steeped in brutality as that of Makgoba's Kloof. When I went there, the city was still named Grahamstown, after its Scots founder, Lieutenant-Colonel John Graham. The territory around the city had initially been seized in one of the earliest of the 19th-century frontier wars in which the British crushed the Xhosa-speaking kingdoms of the Eastern Cape, long before the Boers killed my ancestor, Kgoši Makgoba. Both men and women had been killed and crops destroyed in Graham's campaign to subdue the region, of which the British governor who ordered it said "there has not been shed more Kaffir blood than would seem necessary to impress on the minds of these savages a proper degree of terror and respect." The epic history of the wars describes the outcome of Graham's offensive as "the first great 'removal' in South African history."[87]

The annual arts festival is based in the monumental building memorializing the original English settlers. It looks down on the town from an adjoining hill. So the City of Saints, we used to say, was also a colonial town of great inequality and pain, living under a mountain of sin.

My gloom at the nature of the city was compounded by my first experience of St. Paul's College. I became very ill with the flu for the first time in my life. Further, the hierarchical and rigidly disciplined regimen of the college came as a shock to those of us who were part of the post-1976 Soweto generation who questioned our teachers and were accustomed to negotiating our relationship with them. Coming from a university environment, where you didn't attend lectures if you didn't want to, I now had to adjust to a tightly ordered daily schedule imposed from above. On weekdays, this was how it looked:

---

87 Noël Mostert (1992). *Frontiers: The epic of South Africa's creation and the tragedy of the Xhosa people.* (New York: Alfred A. Knopf), 377-389; Ben Maclennan (1986). *A Proper Degree of Terror: John Graham and the Cape's Eastern Frontier.* (Johannesburg: Ravan Press), 128

6 a.m.	A bell rings to get you up.
6:15 a.m.	You must be in the chapel, in your long black cassock, ready for meditation.
6:20 a.m.	Meditation begins, in compulsory silence.
6:55 a.m.	Bell rings. Prepare for morning service. Altar party processes into the chapel.
7:15 a.m.	On the dot, the introit hymn begins. Formal Morning Prayer or Eucharist. Second- and third-year students take turns to deliver the homily, to be critiqued by the lecturers.
7:55 a.m.	Service ends.
8:15 a.m.	Breakfast.
8:45 a.m.	Morning lectures begin.
12 noon	Bell rings. Students stop and pray the Angelus.
1 p.m.	Lunch, followed by a break.
2 to 4 p.m.	Chores in teams. (There was a window-washing team, a gardening team, a maintenance team, a chapel team, and a library team. Because I had been at Wits, I had the privilege of being in the library team in the first year, until I was kicked off it because I would retreat to the back of the library to read. I was transferred to washing windows.)
4 p.m.	Bell rings. Tea.
4:30-5:30 p.m.	Free time. (You could dash to town if you needed, but if you were a single student you had to wear your cassock—until we single students rebelled at the favoritism toward married students and the rule was abolished.)

5:45 p.m.	Bell rings for chapel.
6-6:30 p.m.	Evening Prayer.
7 p.m.	Dinner.
7:30-9:30 p.m.	On Thursdays, we had a weekly meeting of all the students and staff in the Common Room.
11 p.m.	Curfew, enforced even for students working in the Rhodes University library.

In time I came to value the way in which the regimen broke down our preconceived ideas and habits and molded us as priests, but at the beginning it was a struggle. In the classroom I had to adapt from the language of science to that of theology, the Old Testament, New Testament, and church history. It seemed as if everything was about words, words, words—words in chapel, words in hymn-singing, words in prayers. It was as if the part of my brain that enjoyed science had to shut down for my first year. Some of the words were disturbing. I assumed we would be taught literal interpretations of the Bible, but we were challenged to think through our faith to its roots, having to answer questions such as: Who is God? and What if God is dead? Also, what we did out of the classroom was under as much scrutiny as our studies in the classroom. What went into your mouth was of concern to others. If you weren't eating, or weren't eating enough, you would be asked why. For me, the answer to my eating habits was often because the food, prepared on a tight budget, was not as good as that at Glyn Thomas House.

St. Paul's was founded in 1902, and for most of its life trained only white priests, with black priests trained at other colleges. But by the time I came, the college was admitting substantial numbers of black students. There were also a few woman students, although they couldn't be ordained as priests until 1992. One of my fellow ordinands, Henry Mbaya, has written extensively of the disputes over integrating the institution, from issues about what sport we took part in to how we commemorated anniversaries of national political events.[88] By my second year, half the students were black, but many of those tensions continued and others emerged. Henry's narrative quotes students describing college as a melting pot, but I think of it more as of a boiling pot, a cauldron in which your skin was peeled off and you had to re-form yourself. There were only fifty-four of us, black, colored, Indian, and white, so you couldn't retreat into a crowd as you had been able to among the tens of thousands at Wits. You had to face your fellow students, and the process of forming you as a priest— especially the meditation— forced you to face yourself.

There were also tensions over more issues than that of race. Class, ethnic and national origin, and marital status all played a role in how we interacted, as did theological differences over attitudes about ordaining women, gays and lesbians, and around "churchmanship"—whether you were a "high church" Anglo-Catholic or an "evangelical." Students from the big cities wanted to relax watching soapies, while those from the Transkei and KwaZulu preferred other television programs. Cultural differences, sometimes over small issues such as approaches to personal hygiene or how loudly one's fellow students spoke, could lead to tensions too. Henry Mbaya records the uproar when a white student told someone from the Diocese of Zululand, "You Zulus make a lot of noise!" He also reports how black students found it strange—and selfish—when white students put "Do not disturb" notices on their doors. Zululand students thought it was sinful to go out for an evening dance at St. Clement's, the church serving the local "colored" township. The college warden, Chich Hewitt, discouraged me when I was invited to play golf because in previous years, those who believed there could be "no normal

---

88 Henry Mbaya (2016). *Resistance and Acquiescence to Apartheid: St. Paul's College, 1965-92.* Publication pending at the time of writing.

sport in an abnormal society" had persuaded students to boycott any sport that excluded blacks. So amid some uncertainty, I went to play squash at Rhodes.

Politically, we were a hodgepodge: radicals from the Western Cape, PAC supporters from Sharpeville, Inkatha supporters from Zululand, ANC supporters from Johannesburg, who bitterly opposed Inkatha, and white liberals who had been brought up to think of ANC and PAC followers as terrorists. The tensions these differences generated could erupt at the weekly house committee meetings on Thursday evenings as we we discussed how and where we would commemorate the Sharpeville massacre every March 21 or the Soweto uprising on June 16. We liked to observe such memorials by attending a community event in a local black church, but some of the white students feared—unnecessarily—for their safety. Unlike at a university, St. Paul's had no student representative body; students were represented by one person: the head student. If he was perceived as being too close to the lecturers, fellow students would pull him apart during those Thursday evening meetings.

Off campus, Makhanda lived up to its brutal past. Coming from Makgoba's Kloof, Alex, and Soweto, where people respected graves, I was shocked when I learned that a shack settlement had been built on a graveyard and that the authorities seemed to have allowed it. It was called KwaNdancama, or "the place of giving up." I experienced more fear in Makhanda than I ever had during my activism at Wits or in Soweto. I took part in launching branches of SASCO and the Release Mandela Campaign at St. Paul's, and on one occasion we hid Mcebisi Jonas, later South Africa's deputy minister of finance, when he was on the run as a student. The Special Branch—the dreaded security police—enforced a modern-day "proper degree of terror," and a particular black security policeman, known as Diliza, was as feared as the white officers, so much so that if you were abused in detention, you said that you were "diliza-ed." Police in the nearby Ciskei, nominally an independent Bantustan, had an even worse reputation; if you were seen as an awkward customer, you might be dropped off in their territory to be dealt with. Even a visit to the beach at Kenton-on-Sea, about sixty kilometers away, on a Saturday could be a tense affair unless we were in a mixed group of students, the presence of white students making police harassment less likely.

Immersed in the cauldron of the college and the surrounding town and subjected to college discipline, I was stretched in every way, emotionally, academically, and physically, making my three years at St. Paul's a time of enormous personal growth. When I was assigned to a prison ministry, I was upset at the number of able young black boys I found locked up awaiting trial for offenses such as stealing milk at the local supermarket. Some begged me to contact their parents who didn't know they were there. I could not write details down for fear of being accused of smuggling out information, so I would memorize the home addresses of two or three at a time and quietly visit their families afterward. Before I went into the prisons, I had not thought through what I could expect to find, so I arrived thinking most inmates would be political prisoners or would deny guilt. When prisoners acknowledged they had killed others and asked only for my prayers, my initial instinct was to wonder what I was meant to pray for. For them to be released? But what about the families of those they had killed? As I gained more experience, I realized that teaching the word of God should not be limited to those who came to church or to the crowds I had seen at Jabulani Stadium. We needed to pray for prisoners and also for the warders who asked for our prayers as we left at the end of every session.

In our second year, we were sent out to local parishes to practice preaching. I was sent to the cathedral and was confronted by nineteenth-century reminders of our past and the church's complicity in colonial conquest: the old colors of British regiments laid up there and plaques afffixed to the walls memorializing soldiers who had died fighting in what the plaques called the "Kafir Wars." I promptly decided to do something about them and recruited some students from the Diocese of Zululand onto my side. Two members of the St. Paul's staff, Chich Hewitt, and a lecturer, Torquil Paterson, didn't discourage us but warned us that making such changes would be divisive. When we asked whether we were risking expulsion from the college, we were told it depended on how we conducted ourselves; we might get into trouble over how we fought the issue but not for raising it. Members of the cathedral congregation asked us what we proposed should be done with the offensive language; we said it should be chipped out. They replied that to do so would require a "faculty," a legal document authorizing the alteration of the fabric of a church, and they sent us to David Russell, the bishop.

David was, and after his death still is, renowned and deeply respected across the church and the nation for the radicalism of his fight against apartheid and misrule. But, he explained, he could not act unilaterally. Church law stipulated that the parish had to push the case for a faculty. In the meantime, Dorothea Russell, David's wife and my spiritual director, was egging me on. She said she would come with us without a faculty and help us chop out the words. Eventually, the dean at the time, Roy Barker, proposed an extensive process of consultation. But by the time the consultation was completed, I had long left Makhanda. Present-day visitors will find that a memorial to Colonel Graham has been turned to face a pillar so that much of it is obscured, and the offensive wording on the plaques and on part of the memorial has been covered over with marble.

At a personal level, I was finally healed of my childhood fear of and feelings of inferiority around white people, mainly as a result of my continued role as a leader in the ASF. I had already been mentored by a legendary Anglican couple in Johannesburg, Deane and Dot Yates, who took me under their wing when I was living in Alex and they were running welfare projects and worshiping at St. Michael's church. Deane had been headmaster of St. John's College, the elite Anglican school for boys in Johannesburg, before going to Botswana to start the pioneering multi-cultural and non-racial school, Maru-a-Pula (meaning "clouds of rain" or, more idiomatically, "promises of blessings"). The couple had then returned to Johannesburg, where Deane helped found the non-racial New Era Schools Trust (NEST) network. He became almost like a father to me, one who had hopes that I might become the first black science teacher at St. John's. Later, when I came home from Makhanda for holidays, Deane and Dot gave me refuge in their home when the security police were arresting young men in Pimville.

In my first year at St. Paul's, their influence on me was reinforced when I was elected deputy president of the ASF and became close to the president at the time, Richard Shorten from the Diocese of Natal. He was a conscientious objector who refused to be conscripted into the apartheid army, but he was also able to help me understand the fears of white South Africans. We shared deeply, becoming like brothers. The following year I became ASF president and worked closely with my deputy, Jane Saunders, a medical student at the University of Cape Town who shared a passion for activism and justice. These experiences were reinforced by David Russell, who was the liaison bishop between the ASF and the rest of the church and impressed us not only with his commitment to our struggle but also with his extraordinarily fluent grasp of isiXhosa and its idiomatic expressions.

As ASF president, I was sent on my first overseas trip as part of a delegation to an international Anglican youth conference in Northern Ireland. There I learned about kinds of segregation

other than that based on race. When I challenged an archbishop
in the robust style we used in South Africa on why the Irish
church was confining itself to "ambulance ministry" and not
intervening more directly in trying to end the conflict, an elderly
lady in the room responded with warm amusement and support.
Aleen Herdman went on to become like a second mother to me,
visiting her "South African son" a number of times before her
death. During that first visit, she also helped relieve my anxieties
over the prospect of returning home; with other South Africans
on the trip I had visited the writer Mongane Wally Serote at
the ANC offices in London, and I had once again discussed the
possibility of going into exile for military training, this time en
bloc with other students. Wisely, and like Desmond Tutu, Wally
told us to return home and prepare the way for negotiations.

In my second year at St. Paul's, I decided that I could not just
abandon my B.Sc. so I simultaneously continued my theological
studies and enrolled at Rhodes to earn my remaining chemistry
credits. My teachers were concerned that the course load would
be too heavy, but I followed my father's philosophy—which I
still do—encompassed in the Sepedi phrase "ha ho na kgomo ya
boroko", idiomatically translated as "you don't herd your cows by
sleeping," meaning that you don't achieve anything without hard
work. Lectures and a weekly tutorial indeed piled extra pressure
on me, so halfway through the year I declined to stand for another
term as ASF president, but not before the post exposed me to my
first encounter with the security police.

A group of us, traveling in a couple of cars, were on our way to
help resuscitate an ASF branch in the neighboring country of
Lesotho when I was pulled aside by a South African immigration
officer at the border post. After writing the symbol (K) in my
passport, which was not explained but which I later assumed
meant "Kyk" (Watch), I was called into the back of the offices.
The immigration officers ordered my fellow students to continue

into Lesotho and refused to tell them what would happen to me.
In the back, my face was compared to a series of photographs.
Late in the afternoon, a yellow police van arrived. I was put in
the back of the van, taken to the police station in the nearby
town of Ladybrand, and then left in a holding cell without any
explanation. After some time, three white plainclothes security
policemen fetched me for the first interrogation. They were hostile
but not aggressive, asking why I was going to Lesotho. On church
business, I said. What church, they asked. "Die Engelse kerk"
(the English church), I replied. What church was that? I decided
not to beat around the bush, for fear that it would lead to trouble
later. Desmond Tutu's church, I said. Did I know him personally?
Yes, he was a good preacher. What about his politics? He never
brought politics into the pulpit, I answered. Really? Then they
returned me to the cell.

My main fear was that they would see in my passport that I had
been to Zimbabwe. Did they perhaps know I had been in contact
with the ANC there? While I sat back in the cell, not knowing
what awaited me, I learned the power of prayer as a tool to sustain
me. I also concocted a story that I had gone to Zimbabwe to visit
a girlfriend. When the police summoned me again, they were
more aggressive but they didn't want to know about Zimbabwe.
Instead they searched my bag and interrogated me about Lesotho.
Did the Anglicans really have a church there? Yes, I said. Would
my meetings include ANC members in exile? We all shared the
fear of identifying people and subjecting them to harassment.
So I responded by asking whether ANC members still lived in
Lesotho (having been the targets of cross-border military raids
a few years earlier). Drilling down, my interrogators questioned
me intensively about a convent at Masite in Lesotho, situated
in a rural area and run by mostly English nuns of the Anglican
religious order, the Society of the Precious Blood. The sisters
at the convent hid ANC thugs, I was told. (I later learned they
had once given refuge to Chris Hani, the chief of staff of MK,

and his wife, Limpho.) I insisted that I was going to meetings
to reconstitute an Anglican students' society. After 9 p.m. they
let me go, in time to hitch a ride in a minibus taxi back to the
border post and to cross into Lesotho before it closed at 10. My
companions, who had been holding a prayer vigil, welcomed me
like a hero.

In my third year at St. Paul's, I was chosen as head student of the
college. This gave me invaluable experience of management and
leadership of a non-racial institution going through tumultuous
change. But the most important decision I made that year had
little to do with my studies or the college.

When I first went to university, my mother warned me against
the pitfalls of getting a girl into trouble. She told me I was going
there to get a degree. If I impregnated a girlfriend, I would have
to drop out, go and live in a shack, get a job and look after the
mother and child. In my early years at university, I had a fear of
intimacy. The more serious a relationship seemed to be getting,
the more I backed off. I had one long-term girlfriend at Wits, but
she struggled with my decision to train for the priesthood, and
we parted amicably. At St. Paul's, the pressure to be careful grew.
Don't fall in love with a choir member or any other member of
your congregation, we were told. Fortunately, in my last year, at
the age of twenty-eight, I was about to return to the Diocese of
Johannesburg to be ordained a deacon, then a priest a year later,
when I met Lungi Manona.

The Manona twins, Linda and Lindiwe, and their little sister
Lungelwa (Lungi) were Makhanda royalty. Fashionable but
inaccessible to boys (they were always with friends when out
in the town), they were the daughters of the anthropologist Dr.
Cecil Wele Manona, and his wife Nobantu. Dr. Manona was a
pioneering black academic at Rhodes, one of the Eastern Cape's
most respected social researchers. Mrs. Manona was a descendant

of the royal family of Pondoland in the far Eastern Cape. I first came across Lungi when she was head of the student council at the Diocesan School for Girls (DSG), a private Anglican school, and I was sent to practice my preaching there. DSG was a tough assignment: Services could last for no longer than forty-five minutes, and your sermon had to be between seven and nine minutes. Preach longer than nine minutes, and you would be silenced by the impatient shuffling of young women's feet on the chapel floor! Lungi had an aura around her: When I greeted the girls as they left after services, most would thank me for my sermon but not Lungi. She might say, "I was absent-minded, I didn't hear what you were saying." On one occasion, she came past the chapel in her tennis shorts as I was finishing a service. Our interchange was typical of our early contact.

"You missed a great sermon," I said.

"It must have been a lousy sermon," she replied. "No preacher says his sermon is good."

"I am Thabo Makgoba."

"I am Lungelwa Manona, and I study at DSG." Then: "Is that it?"

"Well, I just wanted to introduce myself."

"Oh, we know of you. Everyone knows of you."

After Lungi left school, I came across her in Makhanda every now and then, in the streets or while she was playing tennis, and I asked her out a number of times, either to play squash or to a movie, then to Gino's, a local pizza parlor. I had no success. Once I waited in vain for a call back on the students' public phone at St. Paul's after I had left a message for her when she said I could call on her mother's number. Eventually, she agreed to come out and join a group of us for a meal. The next day, I asked her to come with me and another couple to the beach at Kenton. We bought wine, someone gave us Southern Comfort and Coca-Cola, and my friend got a little tipsy and lost his glasses in the sea. Oh dear, I thought, I've blown this opportunity.

But Lungi agreed to come out with me again, and our relationship developed from there, although not without hiccups on the way. I joined her and her parents for dinner—being who he was, Dr. Manona knew all about the Makgobas of Makgoba's Kloof—and Lungi agreed to come to Friday night formal dinners with me at St. Paul's. But her first response when I wanted to become serious was, "You are mad! I am only nineteen." And when she agreed to come up to Johannesburg to attend my B.Sc. graduation at Wits, and I introduced her as my girlfriend, she said, "Thabo, you lied to your family." That didn't stop her from eventually agreeing, over a meal at a steakhouse in Makhanda, to marry me, and we sealed the engagement with her grandmother's ring.

Then the negotiations between our families began. Bikitsha Njumbuxa, one of our lecturers at St. Paul's, agreed to begin preliminary discussions in the absence of my family. Later, two of my uncles and my mother flew from Johannesburg, then drove to the village of Peddie, Dr. Manona's hometown an hour from Makhanda, to negotiate how much "lobola"—traditionally a payment in cattle but nowadays usually cash—the Makgobas would pay the Manonas for my bride. Dr. Manona said he was an anthropologist, and he wasn't going to sell his daughter, but he respected the rationale behind the tradition of *ukulobola* as a guarantee that the bride's living would be secure. So he said that if the marriage didn't work out, Lungi could return to live with them, and he took my family's willingness to pay for three people to fly from Johannesburg—a substantial sum of money for us—as evidence of our seriousness. The negotiations were sealed with a bottle of whiskey.

So it came about that we had a traditional wedding in Peddie, which included the slaughtering of a sheep, and later returned to the village for a big Anglican marriage service in the Methodist church. David Russell refused to hold a state marriage license because it obliged him to obey the law prohibiting marriage across the color line, so he did not marry us but celebrated the eucharist. Canon JPM Ncaca, a veteran priest in the diocese, held a Ciskei marriage license so he handled the civil law formalities. Father

Lungi and I at our church wedding in 1991 in Peddie in the Eastern Cape, hometown of Lungi's father, the anthropologist Dr. Cecil Wele Manona.

Njumbuxa presided over the Christian marriage service, and Godfrey Henwood, the dean of Johannesburg (by then my boss at St. Mary's Cathedral in that city) preached. We attracted a big crowd of guests from all over South Africa, and Aleen came from Northern Ireland. So many whites came that the people of Peddie, unaccustomed to such an influx, thought Lungi must be marrying a white man.

Chapter 6

Hard Graft and Gunfire

When I graduated from St. Paul's, I was not destined initially to go to St. Mary's Cathedral. I was supposed to have been sent to a big Soweto parish to serve under one of the diocese's most senior priests, but I learned later that I had developed a reputation as a political agitator and he was not keen to have me. So after first being sent home to Pimville until the diocese decided what to do, the bishop, Duncan Buchanan, placed me under Godfrey Henwood's supervision at St. Mary's. I served as a deacon for only six weeks, instead of the customary one year, then was both ordained and licensed as an assistant priest for St. Mary's on the same day. I was allocated accommodation in Darragh House, the adjoining block of flats owned by the cathedral near the city's main transport hub at Park Station. Thus began a ten-year stint at the cathedral, an unusually long posting in one parish for a new priest. During this time, apart from my pastoral duties, I qualified and worked as a psychologist, acted as a university lecturer and chaplain, and ran a teachers' college residence. A number of these I did simultaneously, making for a busy and complex life.

Godfrey Henwood and Duncan Buchanan both influenced me greatly. Godfrey is an unsung hero of our church. He formed me as a priest in every way, including in my spiritual life, and I owe who I am to his teaching, his criticism, his affirmation, and his patience with my stupid questions. He was a hard worker, a structured person, and he gave me the tools of the trade. We argued a lot: He used to accuse me of being a humanist and not a Christian, telling me that caring was always the content of my message but that "I don't hear Christ there." I would reply that I did not want to be a biblical literalist and ask why I couldn't talk

about what Christ meant to me and to others and how we encountered him without using the words "Jesus Christ" in every second sentence. He wasn't a political person, but he understood the suffering of ordinary South Africans and was good at mediating conflict.

Duncan Buchanan was a great teacher and pastoral counselor who operated with intelligence and order and practiced a style of leadership that empowered those who worked under him. He,

Offering a blessing after my ordination as a priest at St. Mary's Cathedral in downtown Johannesburg in 1990.

too, became a mentor. I had an easy relationship with Duncan, in which we laughed a lot but also argued freely. I used to tell him that although I could argue fluently with anyone in Sepedi, he was the only person I could get mad at in English without getting tongue-tied. He also opened many doors for me, pressing me to keep growing, exposing me to many ministries within and beyond the church. The variety of assignments he entrusted me with and the range of initiatives he allowed me to pursue made for a challenging and enriching experience.

After Lungi and I married, we were moved into an old two-story house on the western edge of the Jo'burg city center, near the Selby Hostel for migrant workers and the West Street taxi rank, the terminal for many Soweto routes. The house was in the grounds of St. Alban's church, which had been built in one of Johannesburg's first mining camps, an area known as Ferreirasdorp, that had long served a vibrant, racially mixed community.[89] The community had been torn apart by forced removals in the 1960s, however, and the congregation had dwindled on Sundays to a small but lively congregation of about 90 Xhosa-speaking domestic servants and hostel residents. Since it was now a chapelry of the cathedral, I was made responsible for the congregation. Before we moved into the house, it had served as the bishop's offices, and Lungi and I slept in what had been Desmond Tutu's office when he was bishop of Johannesburg.

The hooting of taxis from the early hours on weekdays and the meetings of church guilds at weekends made for an interesting, if at times impossibly noisy, sojourn at St. Alban's. It was a rundown part of town beset with problems, and Lungi made it her project to open our home up to street children who had no prospect of going to school, in time recruiting two teachers and volunteer student teachers. We called our little school Nothemba Crèche. As the violence of the transition from apartheid intensified in the early 1990s, life also became dangerous. Taxi bosses employed violence as they battled over routes, and hostel residents launched murderous raids on one another in their quest for political advantage in the negotiations for democracy. There were times when we locked ourselves in our isolated house with only hostel dwellers and street children for neighbors, listening to the gunfire and keeping watch on the street outside the hostel, praying for protection against stray bullets. Once I arrived home at 8 p.m. to

---

89 https://en.wikipedia.org/wiki/Ferreirasdorp; http://www.newtown.co.za/heritage/history

find the area cordoned off by police. I was barred from entering until I persuaded them that my wife was trapped and alone in what they had declared was a war zone, after which they allowed me through at my own risk. Passing through their roadblock, I roared up to our locked gate, opened it, drove through, re-locked it, and parked the car, expecting bullets to fly at any moment. Speechless and scared, Lungi opened the door for me, and we spent an uneasy night.

Contrasting with this experience was the exhilaration of election day, April 27, 1994, when St. Alban's became a polling station in South Africa's first democratic elections, with Lungi as the presiding officer. Helped by parishioners, representatives from Selby Hostel and Wits students, she stored all the election materials in our home overnight before opening the station to long queues of voters at 6 a.m. I put my cross on the ballot paper and jubilantly helped vote a government into power: Ai, Ai, Ai! If you've not been disenfranchised all your adult life, you will never comprehend the excitement. At the end of each of the two days of voting, Lungi had to accompany the ballot boxes to the Jeppe police station for safekeeping, traveling with the police who in my mind were no different from those who had arrested me as a boy in the same city center, people still not to be fully trusted. That, together with the stress we were living under at the time as a result of her losing a number of pregnancies, developed and intensified my prayer life, teaching me to look at prayer not as a passive tool but rather as a powerful contemplative action that forced me to examine where I was, where I was going, and what tools I ought to be using to effect a particular outcome.

At the same time as ministering in the cathedral parish, I was studying. Ever since my mother had worked for the Bethlehems and seen the red gown Ronnie was entitled to wear as a Ph.D. graduate, she had aspired to see me in one. I took until 2009 to earn mine, sadly graduating from the University of Cape Town three months after she died, but I took the first step the year I arrived at the cathedral. I won a place in an honors course in applied psychology, which I hoped would open the way to a master's degree in clinical psychology. I earned an upper second pass for my honors degree but that, combined with my lack of practical experience, was not good enough to get me onto the right course. I was accepted instead for a master's in educational psychology. Here, I found my academic vocation, earned good marks and gained in confidence, qualifying for an internship in the area of substance abuse and psycho-addictive work at the South African National Council on Alcoholism and Drug Dependence (SANCA).

Combining study and later the internship with my pastoral work made for, as they say, hard graft. I typically started my day by taking a 7 a.m. service at the cathedral (once embarrassing myself by oversleeping and, with my cassock covering my pajamas, arriving late for the service to find Desmond Tutu, by this time Archbishop of Cape Town and known as a stickler for punctuality, among those waiting for me. I was very relieved when he gently forgave me.). Then I would attend lectures or report to SANCA for my clinical work. Later I returned to the cathedral for evening prayer. After that, I would do hospital or home visits or night-time street ministry jointly with the local Methodists. On Saturdays I took youth groups, and on Sundays I preached and took confirmation classes. Three times a week I also took an afternoon Mass and every Sunday I returned to the cathedral for formal Evensong. On Monday the cycle started again.

Unless you are lazy or thick-skinned, there is never a dull moment in the life of a priest, and this was certainly so in a cathedral serving parishioners both in the Johannesburg city center and beyond. One writer has referred to the queues of people seeking pastoral intervention as being a priest's "stoop traffic"—referring to the days when you could expect to find a queue of people waiting to see you on the veranda, or stoop, outside your rectory, much like people awaiting attention in a police station charge office.[90]

From my stoop traffic, I learned a lot about human nature and God's love for me and all people. Once, I had to take a neat and respectable but poor young man to hospital after he came for help. He broke down and started crying as he explained how, returning from a gardening job, he had been accosted by three men, stabbed, sodomized, and robbed of his wages. On another occasion, a woman carrying an ax and a can of paraffin woke me up at 3 a.m. She asked me to take her to the Hillbrow police station before she "damages someone." I did so but the police could not act because no crime had been committed. In the year I began my M.Ed., a number of gay men who attended services at the cathedral were found murdered in their flats, traumatizing the community. Then there were the funerals of tuberculosis sufferers (TB was often the final cause of death for AIDS patients). One of the prayers I used at such funerals was from a text in Luke's Gospel, also known as the Song of Simeon. In burying the beautiful young sons and daughters of Africa, it was difficult to keep one's composure while praying: "Now, Lord, you let your servant go in peace; your word has been fulfilled. My own eyes have seen the salvation which you have prepared in the sight of every people..." After bursting into tears at one funeral, sparking off almost everyone else at the graveside, I delegated the task to lay ministers.

The demands of my stoop traffic were unending:

"Father Thabo, our son has hanged himself."

"Father, I have a court case...You won't understand but I acted in self-defense. I shot and hurt somebody. Please pray for me."

---

90 Alan Wilkinson (1992). *The Community of the Resurrection: A Centenary History* (London: SCM Press)

"Father, thank goodness we have found the body of our son. [But] the family is fighting. They do not want his body in the house for the vigil." "Why not?" "He is rotten, Father. He was found in Thokoza hostel (meaning he was a victim of political conflict), he had (bullet) holes all over. They identified him by the birthmark on his shoulder." (Viewing the body was a dreadful experience and, during the funeral, the odor was unique, to put it mildly.)

"Father, our sister, one of the street ladies, has died and she is at the Hillbrow government morgue. They will only allow a priest to identify her." I went with them. The morgue attendant opened drawer after drawer of corpses before we found the body and called in the family to confirm the identification. They asked me to say a prayer, but in my fear, all that came out was "Good morning, Amen," causing a police assistant no end of hilarity.

During my decade at the cathedral, I also served for some years as a chaplain to Anglican students at Wits, where I again ran into the controversies around race that I had experienced as a student. Added to that were tensions over gender relations and disagreements over the church's response to those who identified themselves as gay and lesbian. I was also challenged for the first time on how to handle religious difference. Wits had strong Jewish and Muslim constituencies, and I had to decide how to defend and promote my Anglican strand of Christian belief in a way that did not seek to trample on other people's identities. On one issue, we could unite: When the practice of Satanism appeared on the campus, the chaplains and the dean of students united to close it down in the face of criticism that we were not respecting other people's religious faith. In these years, I was again stretched by Duncan Buchanan when he appointed me as a church representative to the council of St. John's College, where in my thirties, I helped guide the school's direction with leading Johannesburg lawyers and businessmen—all men until, near the end of my time, a woman joined us.

My appointment to the cathedral also brought with it the privilege of being introduced to ministry to some of South Africa's leaders. Although the Anglican Church in South Africa has never been an established church like the Church of England or the Scandinavian Protestant churches, with a formal place in official protocol, it was nevertheless often seen in the colonial era as the church of the English-speaking white establishment. This role declined over the twentieth century, but we entered the democratic era of our history, counting many prominent South Africans among our members. Albertina Sisulu, one of the presidents of the United Democratic Front, was an Anglican, and Winnie Madikizela-Mandela was ministered to at her time of greatest suffering by Father Leo Rakale, a South African monk of the Community of the Resurrection (and the person on whom the writer Alan Paton based one of the key characters in his book *Cry the Beloved Country*). Paton was also an Anglican who had represented the church abroad on occasion. So, too, were his friend, Prince Mangosuthu Buthelezi, leader of the Inkatha Freedom Party, and many members of the Zulu royal house. Up to the present day Prince Buthelezi speaks warmly of Bishop John Colenso, the nineteenth-century Anglican heretic who defended the rights of the Zulu monarchy and nation against British colonial oppression. Oliver ("O.R.") Tambo, leader of the ANC in exile, was a lifelong Anglican who had been accepted as an ordinand in the Diocese of Johannesburg in the 1950s before politics took over his life. When Buthelezi and Tambo met in London in 1979 to try to settle the political differences between the ANC and Inkatha, the talks were chaired by Bishop Alphaeus Zulu, South Africa's first black Anglican bishop.

So it came about that when exiles began to return home and emerge from prison and banishment after Nelson Mandela's release from prison, St. Mary's in Johannesburg became a place of remembrance, mourning, and celebration. In January 1993, Nelson Mandela and OR Tambo came to join Archbishop Tutu for the funeral of Helen Joseph, who had left those of us in the ASF with a powerful impression on the need for gender equity. A few months later, Archbishop Desmond sent me and a fellow priest to minister to the family of Chris Hani, by then general secretary of the South African Communist Party, after he had been assassinated by white right-wingers. Finding the family's home filled with party leaders, I was hesitant about saying prayers. "No, no, Father," they reassured me. "Please pray. We may be communists, but at least we know the Lord's Prayer." We ended by singing the well-known nineteenth-century Xhosa hymn, *Lizalis' idinga lako, Thixo nKosi yenyanyiso* (Fulfill your promise, Oh faithful God), the words of which most of us, whether Christian or communist, knew by heart.

Two weeks after that, we were back in the cathedral for a Requiem Mass for O.R. Tambo, who had died on April 24 after a long illness. The congregation still included conservative white Anglicans, and there was some debate over hosting the event. Godfrey Henwood decided to welcome it and to allow the body to lie in state. I was tasked with leading the prayers and incensing and blessing the remains before the final viewing. Accustomed to photos of O.R. looking like a venerable grandfather in suit and whiskered face, I was startled when I opened the lid of the coffin to find a body in full military uniform. For a moment I thought it was a trick of the forces of apartheid, but on recognizing the familiar markings of the amaMpondo people on his face, I realized it was indeed O.R., in the uniform of an MK soldier. Later, another priest and I, solemnly reading sentences from scripture as we slowly accompanied his coffin up the stairs of his home for it to lie there overnight according to African custom, were interrupted by Tokyo Sexwale, the premier of Gauteng province at the time: "Hey, fathers! Move up quickly. This coffin is heavy!"

Later, after Madiba became president of the country, his assertiveness in driving the process of reconciliation and development led to clashes with the church—one of them in St. Mary's. But more of that in a later chapter.

My study and practice of psychology opened new horizons for me, giving me experience and skills that have served me well in my ministry since. My clinical work during the SANCA internship introduced me to cross-cultural therapy in which I was counseling people from many different backgrounds. The most memorable client was a man who insisted on bringing his firearm to therapy because he "did not trust the black people at reception." After three months of working on his trust issues, the truth came out: He had never been in a closed room with a black man who was in charge of the encounter, and I was the one he did not trust. The confrontation that elicited this admission broke open the way for healing.

SANCA also exposed me early on to a societal crisis, the seriousness of which was only beginning to be recognized in the church: the abuse of women and children. Of course, I had my own experience of this in my own home, and I am by no means alone. Desmond Tutu, for example, has written of his rage as a young boy when his father hit out at his mother after having too much to drink. I once wondered if my mother had hidden the extent to which she had been abused, and, since I was a shrink after all, I once summoned up the courage to ask her. "Hey, wena (you)," she responded, "Who do you think you are?" I quickly backed off.

I saw at SANCA that much of gender-based violence was a consequence of substance abuse. So when I was asked to become the inaugural chairperson of a new initiative, the Tshwaranang Legal Advocacy Centre to End Violence Against Women, I readily agreed. But that wasn't enough for Mali Fakir, the dynamic head of a project called Women Against Woman Abuse (WAWA), which ran a shelter for women in Eldorado Park, south of Johannesburg.

We who were priests and psychologists talked too much at meetings, she said. We should come and see the problems firsthand. I did, and I was shocked. As a result, I became a weekly volunteer at the shelter. I listened to stories of men inflicting burns on women, kicking pregnant women, inserting objects into their orifices, stabbing them in their vaginas, or cutting off their labia. I couldn't believe that human beings could be so evil toward others. I wept with the women and children as I heard of obscene phone calls, incest, a boy allowing a friend to rape his girlfriend, and children being raped in front of their parents. The work was depressing, and it gave me a different attitude to life; I realized that man, if left to his own devices, could wipe out the whole of humanity. Adding to the trauma was the frustration and anger of reporting a case to the police, then finding the docket was lost. That was where Tshwaranang came in.

As chairperson of Tshwaranang, I was first exposed to the power of the media to expose society's evils when the case of an abused seven-year-old girl came to court. In 1996, a thirty-one-year-old self-proclaimed Christian man raped the girl. Two years later, while out on bail pending his trial, the man abducted the girl, throttled her to death, and buried her in a shallow grave, all in order to destroy the evidence of his crime. For the kidnapping and the murder, the man was given multiple jail terms, including one of life imprisonment. I had a phobia then about appearing in the media, but the trial was big news and I agreed to go on a popular morning radio news show. I welcomed the sentences not as a victory for the justice system, which had been too slow in reacting, but as a victory for the community, which through its lobbying had given the court little choice but to impose the sentences it did. I urged communities, NGOs, and individuals to unite and to report and publicize such cases for investigation and prosecution. The reaction was immediate: a stream of calls, of praise and thanks, but also some threats.

About a week later, I went through a low patch. Recalling one of David's psalms, I asked myself, *Why are you so full of heaviness, my soul, why so unquiet within me? What was the meaning of this abuse by one person of another? Was poverty to blame or the system of apartheid—or just plain evil?* I cast my mind back to the deaths of members of my family, from those in the wider circle made up of my parents' siblings' families, my father's "other" families, and within our own nuclear family. I thought of my father. I thought of a step-brother who had died, then a nephew, then another step-brother, this one of AIDS. I thought of my "little" brother, Thomas, whom we had lost much more recently. Thomas lived long enough to vote in the 1994 elections but collapsed in the street and died soon after, apparently having suffered an epileptic seizure. His death opened a floodgate of grief for my mother, and she never came to terms with his loss before her own death more than ten years later. As with my father, we waited for hours for the government morgue van to collect his body. Thomas lay out in the cold street in Pimville where he had died, his body covered in a blanket with the township people, as usual, watching. I thought of the times I had had to make the sad trip to a morgue to identify my father, my nephew, and now Thomas. That image of the corpse stays in your mind for months and the distinct odor of the morgue for days.

After three years at WAWA, the work was wearing me down, and I felt I had to move on. I try to keep in touch with those brave community counselors from time to time. Theirs is a thankless vocation but a vitally needed one.

As a priest and a psychologist, I saw the depths of depravity to which people could sink. But as a psychologist, I was required to debrief regularly with my own therapist, which helped me to cope. More importantly, Lungi and I experienced unalloyed joy when, after years of trying to have a child, we celebrated the birth of our son, Nyakallo ("Nyaki"), in 1996, and then rejoiced again

My mother, Elizabeth Kedibone Makgoba, holding our son and first child, Nyakallo.

when our daughter, Paballo ("Pabi"), was born on All Saints Day in 1999.

After graduation, I registered formally as a psychologist, and new opportunities emerged. As a professional who had identified with the liberation struggle, I began to receive referrals of returned exiles with deep psychological problems. This work carried a lot of baggage for me, so much so that I was relieved when my growing church responsibilities forced me to close my practice and pass my patients on to a colleague.

Perhaps the most challenging work pastorally for me was counseling miners who had suffered spinal injuries. Over a period of about five years, I saw about 400 patients at the Rand Mutual Hospital in Johannesburg, an institution with roots in the gold mining industry of the Witwatersrand. These young men, most between the ages of 22 and 29 and none older than 35, had traveled from their homes across Lesotho, Mozambique, and South Africa, to go down into the belly of the earth to earn enough money for lobola so they could get married. Then, while each of them was perhaps a kilometer or two underground (today some mines are nearly four kilometers deep) in temperatures as hot as a pizza oven, they had gone through the trauma of a rock fall. They had survived, but the lights had gone out and in the pitch dark they couldn't move their legs. They had suffered low-velocity, high-intensity injuries, which meant that there was usually no blood, just a bulge protruding from their backs indicating that their spinal cords had been crushed.

One day a young man would be fit, energetic, and looking forward to marrying and having children. The next he was lying in traction in a hospital, physically and emotionally devastated, the doctors praying that the injuries were low down enough on his back that he would only be a paraplegic, without the use of his legs, and not a quadriplegic, without the use of his arms and hands also. In an instant, this young man could be condemned to life in a wheelchair, unable to control his bladder or his bowels, fitted with a catheter and wearing a diaper, struggling to move about in the rocky areas from which some came. Unable to feel anything below the injury, he would have no sex life, no more children. After being discharged, many would return to hospital to have pressure sores treated, an indication not only of physical illness but of deep emotional stress. Counseling men in such great pain meant trying to bring life out of chaos, trying to instill faith in a place where your patient couldn't see the point of living: "Father, if God can't make we walk again, what's your issue?" "Father, doctor, I just want one child! "Father, I want my wife to stay with me." Or, "Father, I am a young woman; this is not the man I married." I ended up doing mainly psycho-sexual counseling, encouraging couples to think of in vitro fertilization if the young man was still producing sperm. (Later I was to use my case notes as the basis of my Ph.D. thesis on "Spirituality in the South African Mining Workplace.")

The stories of these young men were stories of despair, anger, and sadness, but there were also stories of resilience, faith, and courage. I remember "Masivango" from Xai-Xai in Mozambique, a tall, huge man with whom an interdisciplinary team tried all sorts of interventions. Finally, he said what we were doing would not bring back his manhood, so he was going to start a new manhood. He went back to Xai-Xai, opened a little shop, and taught other people business skills. We never saw him come back with pressure sores.

Apart from continuing my cathedral ministry and counseling patients, once I earned my M.Ed. I was recruited by the then-Johannesburg College of Education (now part of the Wits School of Education) to become first a tutor and then a senior lecturer, earning along the way a higher diploma in educational science. With the money Lungi earned as an electoral officer, we had enough to buy our first house, but that came to an end after two years when I was asked to become dean of Knockando, the college's historic residence for men. The job came with a two-story house with the best view in Johannesburg, looking out from the Parktown ridge, where it was situated, over the leafy northern suburbs. (At night, you could hear the lions roaring in the zoo in one of the suburbs below). In recent years the residence had been plagued by protests. When I took over as the first black dean, I was charged with the responsibility for the welfare of 250 students of all races—at a time when they were still learning to live with one another. In addition, the college was entering the process of being merged into Wits. Helped by another mentor, Graham Hall, a former dean and by now the rector of the college, I had no choice but to plunge into the everyday tasks of running a multi-million rand (dollar) operation employing thirty staff. I woke early to do my planning for the day, being visible in the dining room by 7 a.m., then returning after teaching to work with assistant deans and the cleaning and gardening staff, and putting my own stamp on the way in which we managed the operation. I valued Graham's insights and friendship greatly, and he and his wife, Prudence, remain great friends. At Knockando I learned that students were relatively easy to lead as long as I was present—and as long as I put my foot down when the testosterone hit the fan. It also perhaps helped that I stopped being a card-carrying member

of the ANC; I had been attending meetings of the Killarney
branch, which included a mixture of domestic workers and
Jewish ladies but decided that since the students had a range of
political affiliations, I should distance myself from any one party.

While I was at Knockando, Duncan Buchanan came to me with
another of his challenges: to become priest-in-charge of the
Church of Christ the King, Sophiatown. This was no ordinary
parish. Although the church was more than sixty years old, the
congregation had been torn apart, the community crushed,
and its people scattered by a forced removal thirty years earlier.
For those who don't know about Sophiatown, the name of this
suburb on the western edge of Johannesburg is synonymous with
the vibrant urban black culture of jazz, nightclubs, interracial
mixing and political, business, artistic, and literary achievement
that flourished there in the first half of the twentieth century.
The church, its bell tower standing proudly against the sky at the
suburb's highest point, was at the center of community life. Then
Sophiatown fell victim to an early display of the new apartheid
government's determination, which I experienced in Alexandra
later, to separate black from white by dispatching black residents
at gunpoint to live in areas in and around Soweto, far from work
and town. To mark apartheid's victory, the suburb was renamed
Triomf.

Some years after the removals, the diocese, sitting with a church
stranded on its own among the derelict ruins of destroyed black
homes and new homes being built in their place for whites,
controversially sold the building. For three decades the building
hosted in turn a congregation of the most right-wing Afrikaans
Reformed church (the only one formally to have a whites-only
constitution), a boxing club, and, finally, a congregation of one of
the Pentecostal churches that became popular among working-
class Afrikaners as the Dutch Reformed establishment became
more affluent.

But with apartheid now gone and the suburb's name changed back to Sophiatown, Duncan Buchanan had bought the church back with help from wealthy white Anglicans and sought to re-establish the congregation there.

I had to start from scratch. With only twelve members at the beginning, I built it up to thirty, then to forty-five, and, by 1998, to around seventy, when I was made rector of the parish. Our congregation continued to grow, to about 150 to 180, but the parish was beset by troubles on all sides. On the one hand, some of our white neighbors did not welcome the arrival of black parishioners. They threw firecrackers into the yard at Christmas, cut water and power off during our events, and confronted a Palm Sunday procession through the suburb, saying we were making too much noise. The Easter Vigil was a particular source of contention. One resident reportedly told the Johannesburg Sunday Times: "I don't care if they are black, white, or purple, people shouldn't start singing at 3 a.m. Is that the way Christian folk behave?" On the other hand, worshipers who had returned to Christ the King after living for many years in a kind of religious exile were still hurting from the forced removals, traumatized not least by the way the diocese had treated them. The diocese had colluded with apartheid, they said, when it sold the building, and why had it paid so much to get it back? The poor church probably felt like a prostitute, changing hands so many times. Was the diocese now acknowledging that it had been wrong in selling, or was it just bending to people's pressure? Adding to the challenge, many features of the church had been demolished or altered and beautiful murals painted over, so that we had to raise money to restore it to its former glory. Fortunately for me, a number of retired clergy were interested in helping me with service and pastoral work, so that even after I was made archdeacon and responsible for a number of churches in the area, I was able to cope.

The interment of Trevor Huddleston's ashes in a memorial garden at Christ the King after his death in 1998. The plaque is dedicated to "Those who bore Christian witness in a time of persecution."

We cannot recreate the past or relive it, but we can keep its memory alive lest we forget the errors of our predecessors. As part of a process to heal those who were scarred by the apartheid church, we took a number of steps toward reviving Christ the King and its traditions as well as memorializing its history. Trevor Huddleston, O.R. Tambo's close friend who became a bishop in Tanzania and one of the world's leading anti-apartheid campaigners, had begun his South African ministry in Sophiatown as a monk of the Community of the Resurrection, and after he died President Thabo Mbeki came to hand over his ashes to us. Later we interred them in a memorial garden, unveiled his tombstone and dedicated a plaque to "Those who bore Christian witness in a time of persecution." We also established the Trevor Huddleston CR Memorial Centre, which is now home to initiatives in arts, culture, sustainable business, and training, especially for young people. The legacy of Sophiatown is at last being acknowledged and built upon for the good of all our people.

In September of 2001, a priest from the Diocese of Grahamstown (at the time of writing, the diocese retains the name Grahamstown) asked me to allow my name to go forward for election as a suffragan bishop, responsible for the northern region based further inland in the town of Komani, then called Queenstown. I had just turned forty, I had young children and had been the rector of a parish for only three years. I was enjoying my lecturing, and there was a possibility I might be a candidate for a top job at the Wits School of Education. On top of all that, we had recently moved into our own home again. With our daughter Paballo growing older, Lungi and I had moved out of the all-men's world of Knockando and had found a house nearby in Parktown, around the corner from the novelist Nadine Gordimer. The house was a gift from God. We had never thought we would be able to afford to live in such an area but the house had been owned by an old man who had died, it needed a lot of work, and we got it at a steal of a price. So I refused nomination, saying I did not want to be a bishop, certainly not then.

When I next saw David Russell, who was still the bishop of Grahamstown, he challenged me in a growl: "Dear Thabo, dear Thabo," he said, "don't you think the Lord is saying something?" I answered, "Yes, the Lord is saying you guys must look elsewhere!" I talked it over with Lungi, who was very clear: It was out of the question. She had no wish to return to the Eastern Cape, at least not at that stage.

The elective assembly duly met, but it deadlocked, unable to agree on a candidate after eleven rounds of voting. When that happens in our church, the choice is delegated to the Synod of Bishops, which meets twice a year and includes the leaders of dioceses across southern Africa. Ahead of their meeting, I came

under renewed pressure from a number of bishops, so I called
Duncan Buchanan, the person in the church with whom I had
argued the most but also trusted the most. Now retired, he told
me to "be obedient for once, Thabo." His admonition should be
viewed against our belief that in a prayerful elective assembly,
the outcome should reflect the presence of the Holy Spirit.
Archbishop Tutu used to tell candidates that they should not
obstruct the spirit by refusing nomination; if it was God's will that
they be chosen, it would happen, and if not, it wouldn't. Very
reluctantly, I sent in my curriculum vitae.

During the next meeting of the synod, I was painting our newly
purchased home one day when David called. The bishops, who
were meeting at a church conference center in Kempton Park,
east of Johannesburg, wanted to see me. "When?" I asked him.
"As soon as you're ready." "But David, I'm in dirty jeans and full
of paint." "It's not about the paint, it's you we want to see." So I
grabbed a bottle of turpentine, tried to clean myself with it, and
dashed into the shower. But turps and water don't really mix,
so when I headed out in our little red and white VW Citi Golf,
still in jeans, I looked a bit like a scruffy white fellow. Arriving, I
was told I had been elected by the Synod of Bishops. Faced with
the combined authority of Archbishop Njongonkulu Ndungane,
Desmond Tutu's formidable successor, and his bench of bishops,
I felt I had no option but to accept. By accident, someone phoned
Lungi with the news before I got home, so after rushing home I
took her out to a nearby restaurant, where over endless cups of tea
I told her the deed was done and that we had no choice but to go.
She was devastated, so it was not a good start to my ministry as a
bishop.

It was also a tragic time in our family life, on account of the
sudden death of my dearly loved twin sister, Nthabiseng. She was
a delightful person, loved too by Lungi, who had invited her to
visit both of our children on the day after their births. Her life had

deteriorated after her husband had been rendered quadriplegic by a gunshot wound and become abusive; her marriage broke down, she lost weight and began to drink, not taking medication for hypertension when she did so. She died of a stroke, but she still lives in my heart.

We arrived in Komani early in 2002, with me anxious, even scared, but having surrendered to what I accepted was God's will for me. Lungi was unhappy, albeit quietly so. She loved me but had agreed to marry a Jo'burg boy, not an Eastern Cape one, and definitely not expecting we would be sent to Komani. Smaller than any place either of us had lived in as adults, the town was not seen by people elsewhere in the Eastern Cape as a

Lungi, our daughter, Paballo, and I at my consecration as bishop of Grahamstown.

desirable place to live. "Queenstown!" they would say if you were transferred there. "What have you done wrong?"

We spent six years in the Diocese of Grahamstown, two based in Komani, and then four in Makhanda after I was elected to succeed David Russell as bishop of the diocese as a whole. Komani in particular stretched my spiritual resources to the limit. I spent most of my time there caught up in bitter conflict within a parish, one which went way beyond what I had imagined the church could do to its own. Briefly stated, members of a parish who were unhappy with their priest staged a fake robbery during a service. Tipped off that it would happen—but not that it was staged—the priest fell into the trap they had set and responded by reaching into his cassock, producing a firearm and brandishing it in front of the whole congregation, which included children. He was charged in court, and I had to suspend him. Then, after he was acquitted, I tried to broker his return on the basis that he would apologize and that our churches would all be declared gun-free zones in future. Part of the congregation resisted, but I insisted on exerting my authority. Subsequently, they disrupted the service at which the priest was meant to be reinstated, blowing whistles to drown out proceedings. Some congregants were armed, and the police were called. Young, foolish, and faced with a challenge to my authority, I took one of the dissenters into a room and told him, "Don't think because I'm dressed as a bishop that I can't 'klap' (whack) you." "Ah, the bishop is threatening me with violence!" "Yes, I'm threatening you with violence," I responded, and I took off my cassock. Then I panicked and backed down. "No, I'm not fighting. Let's talk." After clearing the room, I broke down privately and wept, unable to believe that after successfully re-establishing the historic parish of Sophiatown and leaving it flourishing, I had walked into this chaos in Komani.

I completed the service without reinstating the priest, and as I processed out, I heard a drunk, who had been sleeping earlier in the service, asking loudly, "Who is this Thabo we were told to come and stab?"

With the congregation split into two factions, I closed the church. For seven months, there were no services, although people would toyi-toyi outside in protest, and my family was harassed with dead cats thrown into our swimming pool and at our front door. Eventually—after I had moved to Makhanda—I sent a team to effect a reconciliation, and we appointed a new priest. Although I can laugh about the episode now, it was a real baptism of fire for one newly elected to leadership. It was also valuable training in how to—and how not to—make peace in a community. I am all the better as a leader for the experience.

More productively, both in Komani and Makhanda we were able to launch a number of initiatives close to my heart: a community center with a library and computers; training in computer skills and farming methods; a legal advice center; a farm school; a retreat house; and theological training for teachers who became part-time priests in outlying parishes, supporting themselves on their teachers' salaries. We also tried to be leaders in land restitution by donating to the government a piece of the land originally granted to the church by local chiefs. With David Russell, I visited King Sandile of the Rharhabe branch of the Xhosa nation to apologize for the church's role in the colonial era suppression of his people in the nineteenth century and to offer restitution.

The Eastern Cape provided plenty of cause for the church to speak out on matters of public policy, and our history gave us the platform from which to do so. Grahamstown wasn't the only Anglican diocese in the Eastern Cape—there were three others at the time—but as the oldest it enjoyed a profile out of proportion to the size of the cathedral town. In addition, David had drawn on the credibility he had built as a campaigner against apartheid: At times he laid down in front of bulldozers to stop forced removals, as a result, lived for years under banning orders. He campaigned against the failures of democratic government in the Eastern Cape, notably in the provision of education and health services. When I became bishop, the first black South African to lead the diocese in its 150-year history, I found that columns of the most influential newspaper in the diocese, the *Daily Dispatch*, were wide open to me.

Over the years I was in Makhanda, the *Dispatch* carried regular comment from me and from other religious leaders on issues of public concern ranging from the HIV and AIDS crisis and the behavior of the supporters of South Africa's deputy president, Jacob Zuma, during his trial on rape charges, to corruption, land reform, poverty, inequality, and the high number of deaths of babies in one of the province's hospitals. Further, in an area which a senior journalist once described as the "Bible belt" of South Africa, the newspaper was willing to run a regular column dealing with issues of faith in the public space, which allowed me to write at length for its opinion pages on ethical issues in explicitly religious terms.

Although those who suffered most in society, and thus deserved most of our attention, were overwhelmingly black, I tried to reach out to the whole community. Thus when the wife of an Afrikaner farmer was murdered, I reached out both to her widower and the local black community and went to pray with them. When the government wanted to move the main seat of the High Court in the Eastern Cape to Bisho, an old Bantustan capital which had become the post-apartheid provincial capital, I became the public face of a campaign that included both white and black Makhanda as we argued—eventually successfully—against the proposal on the grounds that it would devastate the local economy.

After the dilemma over whether to accept my election as a bishop for Komani, Lungi and I found the decision to accept nomination for Makhanda came relatively easily. Lungi's parents were there as were good church schools for our children. Plus, I turned out to be the only candidate in the election. We moved into Bishopsbourne, the historic bishop's residence (where we had raided the liquor cabinet as students), and we were quickly surrounded by a loving and supportive church community who made us feel completely at home. I loved traveling out of town, appreciating the beauty of the Eastern Cape and the rhythms of rural life: lambs and calves being born, pythons along the road catching the sun, snow lying on high ground, and the blackened veld after fires. I was also deeply moved by the generosity of the poor who would share their last eggs, or bread, or milk with me because I was their bishop, coming hopefully to give them spiritual nourishment.

As I settled into the diocese, we managed to turn around the finances and to attract young people and potential ordinands to the church. We also began the process of carving out a new diocese based on Komani, where past enemies became firm friends, excited that despite our past history I saw fit to delegate real power to them. I thought I had come to the job in which I would happily serve until my retirement—until I was approached by a group of people from St. George's Cathedral in Cape Town. Would I stand in the forthcoming election of a new Archbishop of Cape Town, to replace Archbishop Njongo, who was retiring?

Chapter 7

Bishopscourt

The implications of asking a forty-seven-year-old priest to allow his name to go forward to the assembly that chooses the Anglican Archbishop of Cape Town can best be explained by describing the historic nature of the office.

Since the Diocese of Cape Town was the first to be established in southern Africa, in 1848, it is regarded as the mother diocese of the church. By tradition and church law, the bishop is automatically the "Metropolitan," or head, of what is now called the Anglican Church of Southern Africa (ACSA), and carries the title of archbishop. The first two bishops of the diocese were sons of the British establishment sent to serve the colonial church while still in their thirties, but they presided over only a handful of congregations and dioceses. Not since the office of archbishop was created in 1897 had anyone as young as I was held it, and ACSA now comprises twenty-eight dioceses in six nations, from Angola, Namibia, and the island of St. Helena in the west to Mozambique in the east, and includes Lesotho, Swaziland and, of course, South Africa. We are not subordinate to the Church of England or to the Archbishop of Canterbury; our synods and the archbishop are the church's final authority. In this respect we are like all the other churches in the Anglican Communion, each member church is an autonomous partner in a community of interdependent churches, and the Archbishop of Canterbury chairs our meetings as a "first among equals."

Although the church in South Africa has never had any official status in the eyes of the state, St. George's Cathedral has a prominent location in Cape Town, situated across the street from Parliament and a block away from the mother church of the Dutch Reformed Church, initially the church of the Dutch establishment. As leaders in the English-speaking community, archbishops enjoyed a high profile in colonial times, reinforced by their often lengthy terms of office. Once elected, an Anglican bishop usually remains in office until retirement. Since 1848, the archbishops have lived in the most exclusive suburb of Cape Town, Bishopscourt, named after the archbishop's official residence, an 18th-century mansion built on an estate owned by the country's first Dutch settler, Jan van Riebeeck, in the seventeenth century. Two Cape Town schools were originally established in the outbuildings of Bishopscourt: Diocesan College, known as Bishops, and Zonnebloem College, which the first bishop, Robert Gray, founded in collaboration with the British governor of the Cape in the 1850s to teach British ways to the children of defeated African kings. Among those schooled at Zonnebloem were the

Bishopscourt, the residence of the archbishop of Cape Town, was bought by the Anglican Church in 1851. Built on the farm of the first Dutch settler to arrive in South Africa, it was also where Nelson Mandela spent his first night of freedom in 1990 as a guest of Archbishop Desmond Tutu and his wife, Leah.

sons and daughters of Maqoma and Sandile of amaRharhabe in the Eastern Cape, of Moshoeshoe I of the Basotho, and later of Lobengula Khumalo of amaNdebele in Zimbabwe and Lewanika from Barotseland in present-day Zambia.[91]

When Afrikaner Nationalists took power in 1948 and the Dutch Reformed Church became the unofficial church of the establishment, the profile of the archbishop of Cape Town remained high, partly because the incumbents spoke out against the new policy of apartheid. In the 1950s, Geoffrey Clayton dramatically dropped dead in his study after signing a letter to the prime minister of the time, saying the church would defy a law that sought to impose racial segregation in church services. His successor, Joost de Blank, who was born in the Netherlands, was a harsh critic of apartheid who famously told the prime minister, H.F. Verwoerd, also Dutch born, that he would resign as archbishop and return to his country of birth if Verwoerd did so too. Clayton and de Blank's successors continued the tradition in one form or another, with Desmond Tutu the prominent voice of opposition against apartheid. Then Archbishop Njongonkulu Ndungane carried the tradition into the democratic era, campaigning on issues including the eradication of poverty, the cancellation of international debt, converting the arms industry into a civilian peacetime industry, and famously getting under the new government's skin by courageously denouncing its slow response to the AIDS pandemic as a crime against humanity.

When first approached to stand for election, I was conflicted and ambivalent. I felt too young, and I had a young family. I was about to start my Ph.D. and had been offered a sabbatical at the Episcopal Divinity School in Boston. Moreover the idea of stepping into my predecessors' shoes was intimidating.

---

91 Janet Hodgson and Theresa Edlmann (2018). *Zonnebloem College 1857-1933: The development of an African intelligentisa.* (Johannesburg: African Lives)

The responsibility to the church and its role in public life in southern Africa was too big. The other potential candidates being spoken of were established leaders in church or public life: David Beetge, the powerful bishop of the Highveld and Archbishop Njongo's "number two"; the experienced Bishop Bethlehem Nopece of Port Elizabeth; Barney Pityana, a leader of the black consciousness movement alongside Steve Biko and a vice-chancellor of the University of South Africa who had served in other high profile positions, including chairperson of the Human Rights Commission and head of the anti-racism program of the World Council of Churches; and Jo Seoka, the Bishop of Pretoria, a pioneer of industrial mission who had secretly helped channel large amounts of foreign funding into the country to fight apartheid.

The introvert in me, the boy from Alex and Pimville, felt inadequate to such a high calling alongside leaders of that ilk. But on the other hand, I was a Makgoba, a descendant of a king who had fought against the odds for our people's freedom. I asked for time to consider the request from those who had approached me, including Professor Njabulo Ndebele, a former vice-chancellor of the University of Cape Town, Erica Murray, a Cape Town priest, and Di Oliver, a member of the cathedral congregation who was a social activist and had been an anti-apartheid politician. There wasn't much time, I was told. I consulted people in Makhanda and was told that this was what they had been expecting: like other former bishops of the diocese, I might go on from there to Cape Town. Di Oliver, obviously prepared by David Russell for my "no," went straight to the heart of my dilemma by telling me I didn't have to enter on my own the process of prayer and discernment through which we believe God's will is tested; others would be helping me pray and discern whether this was right.

The assurance that I would not be alone put me in my place, so to speak. In trepidation and fear, and after writing and tearing up five drafts, I sent the sixth version of an acceptance letter and told David Beetge, who was to chair the elective assembly, of my decision. Shortly afterward, I had a call from Njongo, who was disappointed that I had allowed my name to go forward and concerned that it would upset David. My impression was that he thought that, being as young as I was, I would have another chance to stand for election in future. I arranged to see David, who told me that after hearing of my nomination he did not want to run against me and was withdrawing his name. I felt humbled but also sore for David and hoped he was not angry. I began to hear stories of others saying complimentary things about me, but that "he's too young." Grahamstonians assumed I would be elected and began to talk of holding farewells and "last meetings." Lungi loved Makhanda but said she had married me knowing we would move elsewhere. She also liked Cape Town.

I was beset by a jumble of different emotions, fearful and anxious but not wanting a repeat of what had happened when I'd rejected the call to Komani. Bottling up my anxiety, two months after submitting my acceptance letter, I was diagnosed with hypertension. Uncertain of myself, I withdrew to spend more time in prayer and self-examination.

Despite all the feelings of uncertainty and confusion—and I still have feelings of confusion about the process—I left my name in contention. The elective assembly was held at an Anglican school, Diocesan College, in Cape Town, where Jo Seoka, the other candidate for election, and I sat alone together in a staff room while the elective assembly deliberated. Sitting reading or contemplating, sometimes with our eyes closed, it felt like the quietest day in my life, almost as if I were dead. David Beetge and Professor Ndebele visited us at one stage to clarify an item on my curriculum vitae. When David appeared a second time with Rubin Phillip, the bishop of Natal, I thought there were more questions. But no, it was to tell me I had been elected on the third

ballot, which was surprisingly quick. In shock and disbelief,
I hugged Jo and assured him of my love and prayers and said
I hoped we could continue to work together. As one who had
seen myself as a relatively quiet person who worked behind the
scenes, I walked down the aisle of the bishops' chapel to accept
election, feeling that this was the longest walk, either to freedom
or incarceration, of my life.

I was installed as archbishop in St. George's Cathedral in March
2008, in the words of Jim Rosenthal, the Anglican Communion's
communications director, "amidst clouds of incense, [the]

The new archbishop blesses the city of Cape Town.

sprinkling of baptismal
water, anointing [with
oil], seven processions,
and a colorful array of
copes and miters." The
service was "rich in
symbolism," he noted,
held in six of southern
Africa's languages,
with music ranging
from an indigenous
setting of the Mass to
Schubert, and instruments from trumpets and the cathedral's
organ to "the haunting sounds of a kudu horn."[92] Although my
mother didn't live to see me capped with my Ph.D., she did live
to see me become archbishop. (She died at the age of eighty some
eighteen months later.) Archbishops and bishops from churches
in the Congo, the Indian Ocean, Tanzania, the United Kingdom,
and the United States came, and President Thabo Mbeki brought
greetings from the government. In accordance with tradition,

---

92 James Rosenthal, Anglican Communion News Service, 1 April 2008 http://www.anglicannews.
org/news/2008/04/festive-beginning-for-new-archbishop-of-cape-town.aspx [Accessed 15 February
2017]

With my predecessors, Archbishops Emeritus Njongonkulu Ndungane and Desmond Tutu at the awarding of my doctorate at the University of Cape Town in 2009.

he also announced that he was giving me a goat to mark my installation—a gift for which I am still waiting! When I raise the issue with him, he reminds me that Cape Town city bylaws won't allow me to slaughter it at Bishopscourt.

Almost immediately, I was pitched into crisis ministry. In my first months I led a march through Alexandra to protest against xenophobic violence, visited displaced migrants from other parts of Africa in safety camps, and heard a despairing woman say she possessed nothing except the power to take her own life. I also visited Zimbabwe at the invitation of the local church, negotiating police roadblocks and accompanying the then-archbishop of Canterbury, Rowan Williams, to tell President Robert Mugabe about the persecution of the church by a deposed bishop who supported his ruling party. Later I joined Archbishop Williams in a phone call to the United Nations secretary-general, Ban Ki-moon, over the escalation of violence in Zimbabwe. I was critical of President Mbeki's quiet, behind-the-scenes diplomacy on Zimbabwe, and after making a public appeal for an arms embargo on Harare, I was summoned by the president for a robust, two-hour session on what he was doing to try to resolve the impasse. Later, after he was deposed by his own party, I felt compelled to speak out against the tone of the rhetoric being used against him in the intra-party squabbling, condemning those who described him as a "dead snake" and their opponents as "dangerous snakes."

Against this backdrop, it came as a bolt out of the blue when, in June 2009, a request came that I would never have thought in my wildest imaginings I would receive.

Chapter 8

"Religion is in our Blood"

The call I took that day was from Zelda la Grange, Nelson Mandela's long-time assistant. She was calling to say that Madiba and his wife, Graça Machel, were in Cape Town, and he was ill. Mrs. Machel was asking: Would Lungi and I pay them a pastoral visit and pray with them?

For some of my readers, it might come as a surprise that I should be called to pray with Madiba. After all, he was not generally perceived in the country, let alone in the world, as a person of faith. For those who believe he was a communist, this call might be seen as an even bigger surprise. So before I tell of my spiritual journey with him, let me sketch the background of his faith and of his relationship to other people of faith.

In many rural areas in South Africa, Christian religious affiliation is strongly influenced by which European missionaries arrived first or came to be dominant. Nelson Mandela was born, brought up in, and educated in a world in which the Christian faith was represented primarily by the Methodist Church. His mother was a Christian, and he was baptized in a Methodist church, attended Methodist "class meetings" as a child, studied at Methodist schools, stayed in the Methodist hostel at the University of Fort Hare, and became a Sunday school teacher there. Researchers have found little evidence of a church life after he went to Johannesburg to work, then to study and practice law and to become involved in politics. But he married his second wife,

146 Faith & Courage

Nomzamo Winnie Madikizela, in a Methodist church, and when he was jailed Methodist chaplains were among those who visited him in prison.[93]

Despite these strong Methodist roots, when Madiba emerged from prison in 1990, little was known about the nature of his faith. In his prison correspondence, his subsequent writings, and in speeches and discussions with church leaders and pastors, he emphasized the importance of the role of churches and their ministers as educators, community leaders, opponents of apartheid, and boosters of prisoners' morale, but he refrained from speaking about his personal beliefs. At the same time, politicians, writers, and polemicists from right-wing, liberal, and anti-Soviet left-wing backgrounds debated among themselves whether he was or ever had been a communist.

In his autobiography, published in 1994, Madiba described himself in the 1940s as being "quite religious" and put off by the Communist Party's "antipathy to religion." When he and others founded the ANC Youth League, he said he shared the view that communism was "a 'foreign' ideology unsuited to the African situation."[94] But he told the American ghostwriter of his autobiography, the *Time* magazine journalist Richard Stengel, that although he was "not a Party man" when he was young, he was "impressed to see whites (communists) who were *totally* divested of color consciousness."[95] And when, in 1961, he launched the armed struggle against apartheid as commander-in-chief of uMkhonto weSizwe, it was in close alliance with the Communist Party. Upon his death in 2013, the party claimed him as one of their own, saying that when he was arrested in 1962, he was not only a party member but also a member of their central

---

93   Dion Forster (2014). "Mandela and the Methodists: Faith, fallacy and fact." *Studia Historiae Ecclesiasticae*, 40, Supplement, 91-94
94   *Nelson Mandela* (1994), 69, 94
95   *Nelson Mandela* (2010), 43-44

committee.[96] The nature of his relationship to the party remains disputed among academic researchers: The main proponent of his allegiance has said that although Madiba always denied being a party member, "he certainly attended top party meetings from 1960 to 1962. Not only the SACP but also the ANC has stated that he was a member of the Communist Party. Many senior communists thought that he was a member or that he had been 'recruited'..."[97] The principal skeptic on the issue argues that "it is possible that Mandela attended one or two meetings of the central committee in 1961-62 in his capacity as commander of MK. He may have been briefly co-opted to the central committee, but that does not mean that he was a member of the party. There is no compelling reason to doubt the word of one of the world's most respected people."[98]

Madiba's relationship to the Communist Party is not a subject of much interest to Christians in South Africa today, nor was it a matter of controversy to my generation. To us, capitalism was associated with apartheid. We saw no contradiction between our Christian faith and our admiration of the Communists' commitment to our shared ideals and to the common good. As students at Glyn Thomas House, we sang slogans advocating socialism, and Mac Maharaj, who later became a cabinet minister, taught us about Marxism. My communist idols were Che Guevara and Trotsky. My favorite Che mantra was "the revolution is not an apple that falls when it is ripe, you have to make it fall," and we used to rehash Trotsky's saying that "the end may justify the means as long as there is something that justifies the end." While we did not see socialism as a political ideology hostile to the church, my appreciation for this ideology could never replace my love for the Anglican students' movement.

---

96   Umsebenzi Online, Vol 12, No 43, 6 December 2013
97   Stephen Ellis (2015). Author's response. AFRICA, Vol 85, Cambridge University Press, 158
98   Hugh MacMillan (2015). *Debating the ANC's External Links During the Struggle Against Apartheid*, AFRICA, Vol 85, Cambridge University Press, 156

Perhaps the best early inquiry into Nelson Mandela's faith after he
came out of prison was conducted by Charles Villa-Vicencio, who
was for many years a professor in the religious studies department
at the University of Cape Town and formerly a Methodist minister.
In an interview for a book published in 1996, Madiba implicitly
explained why he did not discuss his faith in public. He told Villa-
Vicencio:

> The relationship between a person and his or her God is a
> deeply intimate and private matter. It is not a matter I usually
> regard as open for public discussion...There is a sense in which,
> for me, it is a matter beyond articulation. It is an experience I do
> not fully comprehend.

Asked whether he thought it important to try to comprehend
religious experience, Madiba added:

> I think it is more important to live in accordance with one's
> deepest values and convictions, whether religious or otherwise,
> rather than to fully understand them. But yes, I suppose all of us
> try to some extent to make sense of what drives us.

Would Madiba regard himself as a religious person, Villa-Vicencio
asked.

> No, I am not particularly religious or spiritual. Let's say I am
> interested in all attempts to discover the meaning and purpose of
> life. Religion is an important part of this exercise.

Did he believe in a God?

> As I have said, the relationship between a person and God
> is personal. The question concerning the existence of God is
> something I reflect on in solitude.

Villa-Vicencio reports that he was about to change the subject
when Madiba quoted a verse from Tennyson:

Strong Son of God, immortal love,

Who we, who have not seen thy face

By faith, and faith alone, embrace,

Believing where we cannot prove.

Told that his comrade, Govan Mbeki, a former fellow prisoner and father of Thabo Mbeki, had also quoted those words but insisted that he was an atheist, Mandela responded: "Oh, no! I am not an atheist. Definitely not."[99]

The role that the clergy of Madiba's primary spiritual home, the Methodist Church, and leaders such as bishops Don Dabula, Stanley Mogoba, Peter Storey, Mvume Dandala, and Ziphozihle Siwa played in his life has been well-documented in a recent book by the journalist Dennis Cruywagen, entitled *The Spiritual Mandela*.[100] I will introduce my ministry to Madiba with a brief account of his prior exposure to the Anglican Church.

We have already seen that he rented a room from St. Michael's church in Alexandra when he first arrived in Johannesburg. He went on later to work with Anglicans in the early years of the fight against apartheid, including Trevor Huddleston and Ambrose Reeves, bishop of Johannesburg in the 1950s. In letters from prison to Desmond Tutu and Archbishop Tutu's predecessor, Philip Russell, Madiba voiced his admiration for the church's "noble record of resistance against all forms of racialism" and for clergy who had been "uncompromising in their demand for political change."[101] He also spoke warmly of Alan Hughes,

99 Villa-Vicencio, Charles (1996). *The Spirit of Freedom: South African Leaders on Religion and Politics.* (Berkeley: University of California Press), 146-149
100 Dennis Cruywagen (2016). *The Spiritual Mandela: Faith and Religion in the Life of South Africa's Great Statesman.* (Cape Town: Zebra Press)
101 Nelson Mandela to Desmond Tutu, File C3.11.1-C3.11.2, O. R. Tambo Papers, Liberation Archives, Fort Hare University; Nelson Mandela to Desmond Tutu, 21.8.89, AB2668 Arc, Anglican Archives, Historical Papers, William Cullen Library, Wits University

Anglican chaplain in the 1960s to political prisoners jailed on
Robben Island, off Cape Town, whose preaching "left one full of
hope" and so attracted "atheists, agnostics, Christians who last
attended service on the day they were baptized, and Muslims and
Hindus who have never set foot inside a temple." One of Hughes'
successors was Harry Wiggett, a Cape Town priest who first met
Madiba and his fellow prisoners while accompanying Hughes to
Robben Island. Later, in the 1980s, Wiggett ministered to Madiba
and other leaders who had been transferred to Pollsmoor Prison
on the mainland, and he was once temporarily suspended for
writing a letter to a newspaper defending Madiba.[102] He tells this
story of celebrating a service in Pollsmoor:

> On this particular occasion, when I reached the Peace, Nelson
> gently stopped me and went over to the young warder on watch.
> "Brand," he asked, "are you a Christian?" "Yes," the warder,
> Christo Brand, responded. "Well then, you must take off your
> cap and join us round this table. You cannot sit apart. This is
> holy communion, and we must share and receive it together."
> To my utter astonishment, Brand meekly removed his cap and,
> joining the circle, received holy communion.[103]

After Mandela's release, Archbishop Desmond Tutu became
one of his informal political and personal counselors—one
who supported, admonished, or otherwise expressed strong
opinions on matters both national and domestic, both great
and small. These included issues such as when to suspend the
armed struggle and sanctions against apartheid; the government's
decision not to close down the apartheid armaments industry;
high salaries for cabinet ministers; and even what to wear at
funerals. The archbishop also ministered to both Madiba and
Winnie over the breakup of their marriage. Madiba was "a broken

---

102 Harry Wiggett (2007). *A Time to Speak.* (Cape Town: Pretext), 63-70
103 Harry Wiggett, *Church Times,* London, 13 December 2013

man" and "a lonely figure" after their divorce, Tutu later said.[104]
He was thrilled when Madiba found happiness with Graça Machel
and publicly put pressure on them to marry. When they did so,
on Madiba's birthday, "the Arch" was one of a handful of witnesses
to their wedding, which was conducted by Mvume Dandala, the
Methodist Church's presiding bishop at the time.[105]

Some of Tutu's disagreements with Madiba were amusing rather
than serious: When the archbishop said the president ought to
wear a jacket and tie at funerals instead of the loose, colorful
Italian-made shirts he loved, Madiba reportedly retorted that the
remarks were rich, coming from a man who wore dresses. But
they clashed more fiercely, and memorably, over the arms trade
and the high salaries awarded to ministers in the first Mandela
cabinet, with Tutu criticizing the government publicly and the
president giving as good as he got, accusing the archbishop of
being a populist playing to the gallery.[106]

My own experience of Madiba at odds with the Anglican Church
came during a stormy two weeks early in 1998. I was still in
Sophiatown when Duncan Buchanan asked me to join Bishop
David Nkwe of the Diocese of Matlosane, in North West Province,
and about nine other clergy for lunch at the presidential residence
in Pretoria. A few weeks earlier, on the eve of the president's
annual address to the opening of parliament, Archbishop Njongo
had criticized the government for a number of failings, including
neglect of the poor. Referring to the president's reputation for
bringing about change, he had told a Cape Town newspaper:
"Madiba magic won't be solving our problems." We prayed with
Madiba, had a lovely meal, and then he tore into our archbishop.
My impression was that because Njongo had been imprisoned on

104 Desmond Tutu's obituary for Nelson Mandela, 5 December 2013, at http://allafrica.com/
stories/201312051793.html [accessed 1 March 2
105 Zelda la Grange (2014). *Good Morning, Mr Mandela*. (London: Allen Lane), 103
106 Desmond Tutu (2011). *God is Not a Christian*. (San Francisco: HarperCollins), 177

Robben Island as a young man in the 1960s, not for the ANC but for its rival, the Pan-Africanist Congress, Madiba suspected him of party political motives.

What shocked us most was that the president went behind Njongo's back. It was as if he wanted to set the record straight about this archbishop of ours, and now that he was in power he was behaving like P.W. Botha, the notorious apartheid president of the 1980s, metaphorically wagging his finger at us and telling us: "Ostracize your Archbishop." Bishop Duncan was furious and wrote to Madiba afterward that "we all came away with a clear sense that you were trying to isolate us from our Archbishop, and equally that in spite of what you said to the contrary, you and your government are in fact extremely sensitive to criticism."[107] Madiba had said he would be having further meetings with religious leaders, so Duncan, in another letter, wrote warning them that the president would "attack Njongo very forcibly without any chance for discussion or reply...What came through from the President was that: you are bigger than the Archbishop—keep him in order."[108]

Archbishop Njongo followed up by asking for a meeting with the president to clear the air. I did not attend but for an insight into Madiba's thinking, the notes he made for the meeting in his diary, which is now in the archives of the Nelson Mandela Centre of Memory, are instructive. Defending the government's record, he cited its achievements, praised the role of past bishops, accused Archbishop Njongo of identifying with the opposition in parliament, and underlined his own allegiance to institutions of faith: "My generation are the products of religious institutions," Madiba wrote: "Religion is in our blood."[109]

---

107 Letter of Duncan Buchanan to President Mandela, 26 February 1998, AB3347/J2.8, Ndungane papers, Anglican Archives, Historical Papers, William Cullen Library, Wits University

108 *Sunday Times*, Johannesburg, 1 March 1998

109 Notes for a meeting with Archbishop Ndungane, 5 March 1998, 1998 diary, ZA COM NMPP-2009/8-2-10, Nelson Mandela Centre of Memory

Two months later, along with Archbishop Njongonkulu and
about 3,000 others, I again experienced the feisty side of
Madiba's nature. We were holding a memorial service for Trevor
Huddleston in St. Mary's Cathedral in May 1998, shortly after
he had died in Britain. Speaking as head of state, the president
delivered a eulogy in which he said that in Huddleston "we
see exemplified in the most concrete way the contribution that
religion has made to our liberation."[110] Then, at the end of the
service, the congregation sang our national anthem, *Nkosi Sikelel'
iAfrika*. But we didn't use the words of the official anthem, which
included an Afrikaans verse from white South Africa's previous
anthem and a new concluding verse in English. Instead we
sang the hymn in isiXhosa, Sesotho, and isiZulu, as originally
composed and developed in the early twentieth century as the
national anthem of black South Africans. Madiba, in his drive for
reconciliation between black and white, wasn't having any of it.
Dismayed, he reprimanded us and made us sing it again, this time
using the new, official anthem.

Despite these experiences, there was no question about how I
would respond to Mrs. Machel's request to pray with them in
Cape Town. Apart from my involvement in the Release Mandela
Campaign, I remember my father fondly speaking of Madiba in
the late 1960s and early 1970s, seeing him as a younger brother.
Dad had prayed, in vain during his lifetime, for Madiba to be
released from prison. I remember as a student yearning to get to
know Madiba. I read Fatima Meer's biography of him, *Higher Than
Hope*, and found it useful, but it didn't quench my thirst to know
more. So of course I agreed to visit him.

Thus began a deeply enriching experience in our lives, which
lasted until Madiba's death, in which either I—or both Lungi

---

110 Address by President Nelson Mandela at a memorial service for Father Trevor Huddleston, 5
May 1998 http://www.mandela.gov.za/mandela_speeches/1998/980505_huddleston.htm [Accessed
on 1 March 2017]

and I—would visit Madiba, or Me Graça, as I called her, or both of them together, to pray and talk.[111] Between the visits, which most often happened when Madiba went through health crises, we exchanged a steady stream of text messages in which I tried to keep ministering to them even if I was traveling—a sort of "ministry by SMS." There are pastoral confidences around some of the visits, especially the text messages, which I cannot disclose, but I will share a number of the interactions that inspired me.

---

111 "Me" denotes respect, similar to "Ma'am."

Chapter 9

The Quietening Years

When the summons came to minister to Madiba, he was living a quiet life. He had retired from public life five years earlier and was a few weeks from his ninety-first birthday. Me Graça, or Me Machel as I also called her, was a bubbly, beautiful woman, a leader in her own right as a former Mozambican cabinet minister and the head of a major United Nations project studying the effects of armed conflict on children. She was also the widow of the founding president of Mozambique, Samora Machel, who had been killed in an aircraft accident, probably caused by the apartheid regime. She had her roots in a part of Mozambique served by Dinis Sengulane, our bishop in the southern part of the country, and he spoke warmly of how she helped him establish a new communal irrigation scheme in her home district. As Archbishop Desmond has observed, Madiba doted on her, and in my five years of ministry to them, I witnessed the depth of her love for him, expressed through an unwavering, selfless dedication to him and his best interests in very difficult circumstances.

Madiba had suffered various health problems through the years: eye problems as a consequence of the blinding white limestone quarry in which he and other prisoners had to work on Robben Island; tuberculosis in Pollsmoor Prison; and, most recently, prostate cancer. So Zelda's suggestion that he was ill was worrying. Whenever rumors of illness circulated, the newspapers and

social commentators would ask: Will South Africa survive when
Mandela dies? What will happen to the ANC? Is there a suitable
heir? Such worries were misplaced, as later proved to be the case,
but the questions were nevertheless there.

We didn't have to travel far for our first visit to Madiba; he and Me
Graça were staying around the corner from us in Bishopscourt,
in a house owned by one of the foundations that bears his name.
As it happened, Me Graça couldn't be there on the day I was
available. As chancellor of the University of Cape Town, she
was presiding at graduations, so Zelda la Grange took care of
the arrangements. Preparing for the visit, I knew Madiba didn't
take words lightly: They had significance for him, so I wanted to
locate a prayer that would come naturally to me and also speak
to him. I looked in our Anglican Prayer Book for inspiration but
could not find anything so I turned to the readings of the day. In
our church calendar, on the day of the visit, we celebrated the
feast of Saint Barnabas, a Cypriot apostle of Christ from the first
century, who was known to his fellow apostles by the nickname
"Son of Encouragement." The theme of encouragement seemed
an appropriate one to sustain both Madiba in his frailty and Me
Graça against the pressures on her, so I scribbled down what I
wanted to say, then asked my research and ecumenical adviser,
Sarah Rowland-Jones, to edit it for me.

When Zelda first contacted us, I had tried to find out what was
wrong with Madiba. No, she said, we can't talk over the phone.
We set a time on a Thursday morning. Just before we were due
to leave, Zelda called. If my diary allowed it, she asked, could
we delay coming? Madiba wasn't awake yet. I was a little put out
because I didn't want to cancel appointments that had long been
scheduled, but we had to recognize his frailty, and besides, it was
an enormous privilege to minister to him. We cleared the diary
for the day, except for one special call that I had to make—to
my mother on her birthday. After a couple more calls and texts

Photo by: Trevor Slade

My son Nyaki, then three years old, and I stand with Nelson Mandela at a memorial service for anti-apartheid activist Trevor Huddleston in 1998 in Johannesburg.

delaying our arrival yet further, it was nearly lunchtime when we eventually arrived. Madiba had just woken up, and at first he seemed disorientated. But he asked Lungi and me to join him and Zelda for breakfast. As he began to engage with us, he livened up. Taking me by surprise, he began to joke: "Ah," he said, "Zelda and my family don't want me to go to Saint Peter, so they've asked you to come and pray with me. But I'm ready to go to Saint Peter, so please, please, please, Archbishop, don't pray for something else! I'm ready for Saint Peter anytime, so you can book me."

He also said something to me that I will never forget. I am an introvert, someone who enjoys sitting on my own and reflecting, going on a silent retreat before venturing into the public arena. Hearing from Zelda that other visitors were waiting, I asked him if he tired of the many people coming in and out while he wasn't well. Instantly, his mood switched, and he rebuked me: "Archbishop, I don't understand you. Would you rather have me quiet and dead and not relating to people or engaging people and talking with them? How can you get tired of people? People give me energy. That's why I am up now. You can't get tired of them."

He spoke with a degree of lightness, but there was no mistaking that he was deadly serious. He couldn't understand someone being tired out by another human being. Coming from a politician to an archbishop with a duty to pastor to people, it was a profound learning experience for me. Ever since, I have tried to enjoy being with groups of people, using the opportunity to energize myself to give back to the community.

It was also an eye-opener to see Madiba interact with Zelda, whose book *Good Morning, Mr. Mandela* tells the remarkable story of her life as a young Afrikaner girl raised during apartheid and her decades-long dedication to Madiba.[112] She called him Tata (Father) or Khulu (Granddad). He, in turn, often called her Zeldina. Over breakfast with us, he said, "Zelda, Archbishop and Mrs. Archbishop are saying I don't like these raisins in my muesli." It was obviously not the first time the issue was in contention. "You always allow these ladies (the cooks) to give me raisins," he told her. "I don't like raisins in my muesli." "No, no, Tata," she replied firmly. "I know you don't like them but you mustn't bring the Archbishop into this debate. It's our debate." He conceded defeat: "If you insist, I will eat them." It was so wonderful to see how she had become his trusted soulmate.

After he had finished his breakfast and Lungi and I had finished our coffee—it was too late for breakfast for us—Zelda and other staff helped him into another room. After a brief *ex tempore* prayer, I asked him whether I could read my written prayer to him. "Oh

112 Zelda la Grange (2014), op. cit.

sure, sure, sure. Let me adjust my hearing aid. And Archbishop, read it loudly. You're speaking too softly." Despite having to raise my voice more than I would have liked, it was a precious spiritual moment as I began:

Bountiful God, giver of all gifts,
Who poured your Spirit upon your servant Barnabas,
[nicknamed "Son of Encouragement"]
And gave him grace to spend his life in encouraging others;
We thank you for those whom you have led to follow his example
Through generous and selfless service.

In the season of his birthday,
We thank you for the inspiration and strength
That you have given to Madiba,
Enabling him, over so many years, to draw out the best in others,
Rousing us always, by word and example,
To seek the highest good for every child of this nation.

We pray that you will prosper the labors of his life
So that all we have received from him
May continue to grow and flourish and bear fruit.

Give us that same courageous spirit of generosity and selflessness
so we may persevere in bringing true freedom to all our brothers
*   and sisters,*

And we ask that now, in the quietening years,
He may find around him those who may be as Barnabas to him,
Warm friends to delight his heart, and cheer his days,
And, dear Father God, we pray that you will hold him close
In your ever-loving, ever-lasting arms,
Today, tomorrow, and always.

In Jesus' name, Amen.[113]

---

113 Drawn in part from a Collect for Saint Barnabas published in *Exciting Holiness*, edited by Brother Tristam SSF (Norwich: Canterbury Press), 1997

On occasion, after praying with him, Madiba would ask me to
expand on the meaning of a word or phrase, although I cannot
recall if he did so on this first visit. Generously, he said that it was
an interesting prayer. "Thank you so much for that. Will you give
Zelda or Mama (Graça) a copy?" "Well, I have a copy I can give to
you." "No, no, I will lose it. Give it to Zelda."

Our time with him was over, but Zelda asked us to stay with
Madiba as he saw the next group in the stream of visitors. They
were the family of an Afrikaner farmer who had lost two children
in tragic circumstances: The children had fallen out of a car
and their father had accidentally run over them. As Madiba
prepared to see them, we discussed what he planned to say. I
can't remember his exact words, but they were along the lines of:
You just have to love them and help them love themselves. The farmer
and his wife were traumatized, almost inconsolable. As a priest,
I would have fumbled and struggled to find words to use and
would probably have turned to the formulations in our prayer
book. But Madiba gently reassured the farmer that he shouldn't
blame himself for the deaths. For him, life and death seemed just
to be different places on a continuum of loving oneself and loving
the God who had created you. The spirituality and the healing
gift of forgiveness and reconciliation that emanated from him
overwhelmed us. Recalling my own pain at being expelled from
Alex, remembering the challenges I had faced since, I admired
the faith and courage of Madiba, who cut across the boundaries
of race and culture to reach out to another human being in pain
who was searching for something tangible that could help him
forgive himself. Again the politician was teaching the pastor about
ministry.

Soon after I saw him, Madiba traveled to London for his last visit
to Britain, where he rallied support for his charities, spoke out
against the misrule of Robert Mugabe in Zimbabwe, and visited
the Queen (whom he addressed as "Elizabeth," Zelda records).

In the months that followed, I developed a ministry of intimate
text messages and phone calls, often six or seven times a month.
In public life, after I made a call on the church for donations for
Haiti in the wake of their devastating earthquake in 2010, Me
Machel asked me to join an "Africa for Haiti" initiative to campaign
more widely for support for the country's people. Privately, Lungi
sometimes visited her separately. At times when Graça or Zelda
felt Madiba was in need of prayer or they needed to share news
about his health, they would send me a text message and I would
respond by text or a phone call. As Me Graça put it, and I am
paraphrasing her:

> Quietly, I'm offering Madiba to you to journey with him in his
> spiritual life. Madiba is a believer but he struggles between
> ideology and really living the life of a believer, but he agrees that
> you should come and pray for him.

However it was some time before I saw him again. In the
intervening period were developments that would lead to a
disagreement between us later: Jacob Zuma succeeded Thabo
Mbeki as South Africa's president early in 2009. Madiba had
stood firmly in support of his party through all the controversy,
going back nearly a decade, surrounding then Deputy President
Zuma: the allegations of corruption against him, President
Mbeki's decision to fire him, Zuma's rape trial, and his subsequent
comeback to lead the ANC. Madiba liked to joke that if Zuma
got to heaven, he would join or start an ANC branch there. In an
apparent attempt to help the deputy president out of his financial
entanglements, Madiba donated a million rand to him a few days
after he was fired.[114] Zelda la Grange reports in her book that
some government leaders felt Madiba backed Zuma over Mbeki,
leading to diplomatic slights aimed at Madiba, although she is

---

114 Report prepared for the National Prosecuting Authority, carried in the *Mail & Guardian*, 7
December 2012. R1 million was worth about U.S. $150,000 at the time.

careful not to attribute them to Mbeki himself. After the party
forced Mbeki to step down as president, precipitating a split in
the ANC, Madiba made a rare public appearance alongside Zuma
at an ANC rally two months ahead of the election that brought
him to power—at a time when Mbeki had refrained from backing
Zuma as president.

When President Zuma took office, I expressed disquiet over what
I called the "unanswered questions" hanging over him, referring
in particular to more than 700 counts of fraud and corruption
over which, at this time of writing, he is due to go on trial.
Soon after Zuma took office, just after I had visited Madiba in
Bishopscourt, Mr. Zuma told a church congregation that the ANC
would stay in power for ever. There were believers, he said, who
were saying "the time is coming when the Son of Man will come
back to earth. The ANC will rule this country until then."[115]

It would have been unthinkable for Nelson Mandela to claim
religious sanction for ANC rule, and it wasn't the first time Zuma
had done so. I had been invited to return to Christ the King in
Sophiatown to receive their "Naught for your Comfort" award,
named for the book Trevor Huddleston wrote after the forced
removals of the 1950s, and I decided to use the opportunity to
reply to the head of state.

"President Zuma," I said, "does have the perfect right to express
the hope that South African voters will choose his party as the
country's government until Jesus returns. But it is a different
matter to predict the party will rule until the end of time
as we know it." I criticized him on three grounds: that one-
party rule, which his statement implicitly backed, had done
enormous damage to many of Africa's people; that his views
were anachronistic, reflecting a 1960s or 1970s view of Africa

115 *The Sowetan*, 22 June 2009

out of step with modern governance standards established
by the African Union, the body which collectively represents
African governments on the world stage; and that his views
were dangerous, in that they might encourage those who had
economic motives for prolonging ANC rule indefinitely to take
unconstitutional action to preserve it. This did not dissuade him
from continuing to make the claim in the following years.

By the second meeting of our synod of bishops following
the inauguration of the new presidential administration, my
criticism was expanded to the whole government and included
wider issues. In our statement afterward, we identified worrying
"common threads" running through how governments were
conducting themselves in southern Africa. First we laid out the
biblical basis of our critique:

> We believe that those in power are called by God to wise
> leadership and exemplary lifestyle, exercised on behalf of all
> God's people and for their upliftment and betterment—as Saint
> Paul wrote in his letter to the Romans. Of particular importance
> within
> God's economy are the poor and those who live on the margins
> of society.

Then we applied this to what we saw happening across the region:

> It is our observation that though lip service is widely paid to
> the notion of social upliftment, the reality is that most of the
> leaders of our respective nations seem more committed to
> self-enrichment than poverty eradication. We have listened to
> accounts of unbridled greed, a greed that is not simply limited
> to those in political power. Nevertheless, we are especially
> concerned at the levels of greed of those in power and at the
> manner in which political processes are manipulated and co-
> opted in the pursuit of self-enrichment. This has resulted in a
> serious undermining of democratic values to the point where, in
> some places, such values are non-existent.

The bishops went on to cite the situations in Angola and
Swaziland, then turned to South Africa. We added to the issues
we cited the admission by President Zuma during his trial on
a charge of rape (of which he was acquitted) that he had had
unprotected sex with a woman who was not his wife and who was
young enough to be his daughter:

> The almost unprecedented levels of alleged corruption among
> those in power within...South Africa, the seeming inability or
> unwillingness of the state to hold anyone accountable, and the
> recent revelations of the sexual misconduct of the president of
> that country do not bode well for the future and are cause for
> serious concern.

This and other expressions of our distress at the erosion of the
values by which Nelson Mandela lived and ran his government
were to set the pattern of the church's public ministry for my
time as archbishop: endorsing and helping to launch an anti-
corruption campaign, backing initiatives to improve standards of
governance, speaking out against the abuse of human rights, and
joining "Walks of Witness." These marches, mostly in poverty-
stricken areas, protested against corruption, inadequate services
in communities, failures in the education system, and xenophobic
attacks on refugees and foreign migrants living in South Africa.

The most challenging campaign I supported in the early part of
my ministry in Cape Town led some in the church to dub me
"the toilet archbishop." The campaign's objective was to improve
sanitation in the poorest areas of Cape Town, especially in the
settlements of Makhaza and Khayelitsha. At the time, 10 million
people across South Africa did not have access to basic sanitation,
half a million of them in the Cape Town area. In Makhaza, a flash
point was created when toilets were installed without any walls
or doors, giving users no privacy. The city council said they had
been unable to afford to build toilets and had erected them only

after discussion with the community and that the community had said they would enclose the toilets themselves. But on one of my visits, I saw elderly and disabled residents forced to use toilets that had been enclosed by hastily constructed planks of wood, and I also saw toilets that were exposed because the temporary structures around them had been demolished by the ANC Youth League. The dispute had become a political football in a struggle between the Youth League and the council, which was governed at the time by the opposition Democratic Alliance. On a Walk of Witness in Khayelitsha with other religious leaders—ahead of which I received a text message from Zelda la Grange to say the Mandelas were praying for my mission—we saw toilets that served an average of up to sixty people. Some were clogged; others were filthy or surrounded by waste of all kinds, and yet others were a long way from people's homes. At the request of the civil society group, the Social Justice Coalition, I offered to mediate between the parties, but my offer was not accepted; it appeared I was not very popular among any of the politicians for trying to intervene. I was told later by colleagues who met the Western Cape premier at the time, Helen Zille, that she was upset with us for interfering in the issue. As I write, local disputes over toilets still erupt within communities, and the struggle for adequate sanitation continues.

Madiba continued to live quietly out of the public eye. Much of his time was spent either at his home in Houghton in Johannesburg or at Qunu, his boyhood home in the rural Eastern Cape, where he had built a modest house patterned on the warder's house where he had stayed during his final months in prison. The public no longer saw him, except when he briefly attended the closing ceremony of the 2010 football World Cup, his last formal public appearance.

Then, early in 2011, the first major health scare of his final years occurred.

He had spent Christmas with his family in Qunu, then traveled
to Cape Town for the new year. I was away on my annual holiday
after our Christmas services. Zelda la Grange tells the story in
her book of how, when she arrived to join them, Madiba had
lost weight in the two weeks since she had last seen him, and he
had difficulty walking. His condition deteriorated steadily after
her arrival. He was admitted to 2 Military Hospital, the local
military hospital in Cape Town, for tests, generating rumors that
he had died. A statement was issued denying his death but did
not mention his hospitalization. He was discharged after a day
or two and appeared to be recovering at home when he began to
deteriorate again. Airlifted to Johannesburg, he was admitted to
the private Milpark Hospital, and another statement was put out,
saying he was undergoing "routine tests."

By this time, I had returned to work and was in London at a
meeting of archbishops from around the world. The Nelson
Mandela Foundation, the presidency, and the ANC all released
reassuring statements, but it quickly emerged that these were
misleading. Hardly had they been issued when the Reuters
news agency reported, apparently quoting a family source, that
Madiba had suffered a collapsed lung. He was released after two
days and returned to Houghton to recover, but the credibility of
public statements about his health was never completely restored,
with the public not quite sure whether to believe statements that
seemed designed to put their fears at rest.

For my part, in one of my regular public letters directed at
Anglicans, I appealed for prayers for Madiba but also sought to
prepare them for the inevitable. "He is an old man of 92," I wrote,
"and we cannot hope for him to stay with us forever. We thank
God for all he has done...but we must also commit him into God's
hands, asking, as the ancient prayers say, that when his time
comes, he may have a 'good end' and not be afraid to make that

final journey to his eternal home..." Soon afterward, I thought what I was gently warning about might come to pass.

I was in Cape Town when I received an urgent appeal from Me Graça and Zelda to fly to Johannesburg. They didn't spell out what was wrong but urged me: *Please, you have to be here.* It was obviously a pastoral emergency, so I took the earliest flight I could find. When I landed, a message from Graça told me to wait, that President Zuma was there. When I called, Zelda explained that television crews were outside the gates of the home in Houghton. Diplomatically, Me Graça asked what I was wearing: If I was in cassock and clerical collar, it might signal the crisis to the world. I explained that I was in a pullover that covered my collar. Then I went to an old family haunt, a restaurant nearby, to wait until the president had left. When the coast was clear, I drove to Houghton, where the security detail was expecting me. Me Graça was at the front door. Her first concern was not for herself or Madiba but for my welfare. She insisted that I have something to eat and told me that Madiba had not spoken for a week, even when Albertina Sisulu had visited. Despite having known her for more than sixty years, Madiba had not recognized her.

When Graça took me upstairs to Madiba, he was in a hospital bed, attached to pieces of medical equipment and apparently unconscious. He was surrounded by the specialist medical team who cared for him around the clock. I asked whether I could anoint him with chrism oil, and they agreed. One of them gave me disinfectant, and I wiped down my hands and my Anglican Prayer Book. The team quietly withdrew. "May I pray?" I asked Graça. "Of course," she responded. This was why she had asked me to come. I took out the prayer book and the chrism oil. I opened the book to the section entitled "Prayers for the Dying," which I probably hadn't used for three or four years. I began with "The Song of Simeon," a prayer excerpted from Luke's Gospel:

Lord, now you let your servant go in peace
your word has been fulfilled.

My own eyes have seen the salvation:
which you have prepared in the sight of every people.

A light to reveal you to the nations:
and the glory of your people Israel.

Then:

Lord, to you we commend Madiba. In your loving mercy forgive his sins,
that dying in this world he may be raised to life in the world to come;
through Jesus Christ our Lord.

I held the prayer book up so Graça could recite the responses to
the litany that followed. Her responses are in bold typeface:

Lord, remember not our offenses   **Spare us, good Lord**

From all evil and sin   **Good Lord, deliver us**

From the assaults of the devil   **Good Lord, deliver us**

As I read, I took the oil and anointed, I think, Madiba's leg. My
recollection of the words that triggered what happened next is
not clear, but either at the phrase "In the hour of death" or at
the words "Go forth, Christian soul" in the prayer that followed,
Madiba opened his eyes. Seeing me, in a strong voice he asked
sharply: "Graça! Who is this man? Who is this man, Graça?" "Oh
Tata, you remember the archbishop from Cape Town," she tried
to reassure him. "You know him." But he didn't want reassuring.
"Who is this man? Get out! He must get out! Bring me my sticks!
Bring me my sticks!"

I hurriedly left. Excited, one of the doctors asked me how I had
gotten him to respond. I learned that the medical staff thought
he was dying and were grateful for his outburst. Poor Graça,

however, was deeply embarrassed and apologized profusely. Over a cup of tea, I assured her that as a priest I was accustomed to such episodes. I had seen people who, when facing death, initially went through phases of anger and denial before arriving at a stage of acceptance. I interpreted Madiba's response as very human. After all, he had spent twenty-seven years in prison. He now had a beautiful wife whom he loved deeply, and he had comfortable homes, time to reflect, and a world to influence. His anger at the prospect of losing these things was legitimate. As someone who had grown up a rural Xhosa boy, learning the art of stick-fighting, Madiba's response was both natural and understandable. I was simply the accidental target of the anger, and I was profoundly privileged to have been so.

As I returned to Cape Town, I reflected on whether I had done the right thing in using prayers for the dying: As a pastor it is always difficult to know when one should do so. I never did learn whether he did in fact have sticks in the house!

After this incident, I held back for a time, communicating with Me Graça by text every now and then to ask how things were going but otherwise giving her space to digest what had happened. During this time Albertina Sisulu died, and I was honored to be asked to preside and preach at her funeral service at Orlando Stadium in Soweto.

It was a notable moment in South African public life. The story of Albertina and Walter, her husband (who died in 2003), may not be as well-known as that of Nelson and Winnie Mandela, but it is a powerful story of love and sacrifice. The Sisulus, who married in 1944, had known Madiba since his earliest days in Johannesburg. In many ways, Walter was Madiba's political mentor, an activist who identified in the young Nelson Mandela the qualities of a leader. Madiba stayed with the Sisulus in Soweto at one time and met his first wife, Evelyn, there. The Sisulu family became a powerful political force: Apart from Albertina's role in the United Democratic Front, to which I have already referred, Walter was one of those sentenced to life imprisonment with Madiba and was released only four months before Madiba. The story of their family is, in the words of the journalist Pippa Green, "a story of imprisonment, persecution, exile and suffering...There can be few families in the history of South Africa that have been torn apart as relentlessly by the political struggle, and few that have survived it so intact."[116]

The Sisulus had five children of their own and adopted another three children of relatives. For a thirty-year period, at least one member of the family was always in prison. At one time in the 1980s, six were in prison. One son, Max, was in exile for the whole time his father was jailed. A daughter, Lindiwe, was detained, held in solitary confinement, and tortured, both physically and psychologically. Security police told her that her mother had died, and it was three months before she learned they were lying. Albertina spent most of the twenty-four years during which Walter was in prison either restricted, under house arrest, or detained—once in solitary confinement for almost a year.[117] At the time Albertina died, Max was the speaker of parliament, and Lindiwe was minister of defense. (At the time of writing, she is South Africa's foreign minister.)

Madiba wasn't well enough to attend Albertina's funeral, but Graça came and delivered his tribute.

In my sermon, I recalled how forthright Albertina had been in her criticisms when we had gone to consult her as students in the 1980s. "Sadly today," I added, "too often criticism is labeled anti-revolutionary, and we are discouraged from speaking out. But we should follow Mama Sisulu's lead and say what needs to be said—

116 Pippa Green, "Reunion," *Leadership magazine*, May 1990
117 Pippa Green, op cit

for the good of our leaders and for the good of our country. Mama
Sisulu knew the power of Jesus' words, that 'the truth will set you
free,'" Citing her and Walter's selfless service to the country, I said
they pursued it for its own sake, "not because they knew they
would get something out of it. Not for them, the pursuit of power
for personal gain."

The next time I saw Madiba, he and Graça were in Qunu. It was
just after Christmas 2011, and I was in the Eastern Cape on my
way to preach at the funeral of Fikile Bam. He had been president
of the Land Claims Court and was also an old Sophiatown
resident who was, with his wife Xoliswa, a parishioner at Christ
the King. His sister, Hlophe, had a long history in the church,
working in the World Council of Churches and the South
African Council of Churches, and eventually chairing South
Africa's Independent Electoral Commission. Fikile, too, had
been imprisoned on Robben Island, not for the ANC but for
participation in a small group called the National Liberation
Front. He was in the same section of the prison as Madiba.
Despite coming from a different political tradition, they became
close, and he used to tell an extraordinary story of Madiba's
generosity and self-discipline. After he and Madiba discovered
that they shared a birthday, for the remainder of Fikile's ten-year
sentence, Madiba would set aside some of his Christmas gifts of
candy and cookies. Seven months later, on July 18, he would
bring them out and present them to Fikile on their joint birthday.

I called Zelda and Graça to say I was coming to the Eastern Cape,
traveling with Lungi and the children. Graça was enthusiastic.
Yes, she said, come, and Madiba would like you to come to
lunch. It was the day after Christmas, St. Stephen's Day, on which
we commemorate the first Christian martyr. We flew to East
London and drove up to Qunu with a police escort that had been
sent to accompany us. We were welcomed at Madiba's home in
Qunu by Graça, a local chief who was related to Madiba, and

members of Madiba's medical team. That group of young doctors and specialists who took care of him has not been accorded enough recognition. I always call them the unsung heroes and heroines of Madiba's last years. They did the medical profession proud, and we owe them a debt of gratitude for looking after the nation's icon. In time Madiba came in, propelling himself with what looked like a combination of an upright stretcher and a wheelchair, crutches under his arms so that he could walk slowly along, watchfully guided by the doctors.

Compared to the condition I had seen him in in Houghton, he was a man transformed.

"My wife tells me," he said in a jocular mood, "that I wanted to beat you about the head with sticks when you came to say the last rites without my permission. But don't worry, now you are my friend!"

Nyaki, Lungi, and Paballo pose with Madiba at his home in Qunu in the Eastern Cape just after Christmas 2011.

Being in the area in which he was brought up, we talked about
our antecedents. Lineage was key for Madiba. I was surprised that
he remembered I had served in Sophiatown. He was impressed
that I, an urban boy and a priest, knew my ancestry. He also took
a close interest in Lungi's descent through her mother from the
royal family of the amaMpondo people. He remained in high
spirits through the meal. When we were offered wine, a rosé, he
teased us: "Archbishop, you say you are a Christian, and my wife is
a Christian, so why are you denying me what she is having. Look,
she doesn't want me to have that red stuff she is drinking—she
gives me water!" Telling us that Madiba's doctors had advised
against wine, Graça offered to forgo hers. I joked that I should
bless it for Holy Communion, transforming it so he could have a
sip. "Oh well," he said to laughter around the table, "in that case,
I will have a big gulp!" After the meal, I took photos of him with
my family. The teasing continued: "Archbishop, everybody who
comes here wants to take a picture with me. You archbishops
are like chiefs or kings! You are a proud man, so important you
don't want a picture with me. Everyone who comes here wants a
picture with me—they come for the picture, not for me!" So I also
put myself into the picture. His wisecracks continued: "I'm not
sure if I should smile or not, now that you are next to me!" and
"Don't get too close—you may pray that I go to heaven!"

There was serious conversation too. We talked about the Libyan
leader Muammar Gaddafi, who had been killed about two months
before my visit. First as leader of the ANC and then as president,
Madiba had many dealings with Gaddafi, who was a supporter
of our liberation struggle. Toward the end of his presidency, he
had helped persuade Gaddafi to hand over for trial two Libyans
suspected of being responsible for the bombing of the Pan Am
airliner that crashed into Lockerbie in Scotland in 1988. As the
uprising and foreign intervention that had begun in Libya earlier
in the year was coming to an end, Gaddafi had been captured
by opposition militia members. They brutally assaulted and

slaughtered him, in public and on camera. Madiba was very distressed over the way he had been killed.

My views on President Zuma created a bit of a challenge between Madiba and me. My criticisms of the Zuma government had grown since the president's inauguration, focusing earlier in 2011 on the militarization of the police. In April, I had visited Ficksburg in the Free State, where residents protesting against the failure of local authorities to provide water and sanitation had clashed with public order police. In full view of television cameras, the police had beaten and kicked a local math teacher and political activist, thirty-three-year-old Andries Tatane, and he had died soon afterward. There was a national outcry, and back in Cape Town I took the opportunity in a sermon to condemn the police aggression: The police "seem to maim and kill rather than offer safety and security," I said. Although my discussion with Madiba did not concern the death of Andries Tatane, that event certainly reinforced my reservations about the new administration.

Madiba, however, defended his party and its leader. While he may not have said it explicitly, his attitude was that Zuma was a disciplined member of the ANC and a simple and accessible leader. President Zuma clearly had a special place in Madiba's heart. Everyone erred, everyone made mistakes, Madiba said, and I needed to give him some credit. At the same time, Madiba recognized where I was coming from: that as a priest I held people to high standards, and he did not expect me to deviate from that. While I cannot say that I changed Madiba's mind about President Zuma, he did not attempt to persuade me to change mine. I found particularly striking his acknowledgment of my right to hold the position I did and his respect for my independence and the autonomy of the church.

I believe that during this visit, I told Madiba my story of how, after Chris Hani had been assassinated, I had sought permission to say prayers in his home. Madiba loved that punchline I have already referred to: "We may be communists, Father, but at least we know the Lord's Prayer."

Turning to prayer, I recited one that we had written for this occasion:

> *The angel host that appeared to the shepherds*
> *sang "Glory to God in the Highest."*
> *Lord God, heavenly king, yet born a tiny baby*
> *We too sing your glory as we celebrate your coming as Emmanuel,*
> *God with us, our Friend and Savior and Prince of Peace,*
> > *in all that life brings our way.*
>
> *As we give thanks at Christmas for all the rich gifts you shower*
> > *on our lives,*
> *we thank you for the gift of Madiba himself,*
> *and all that you have helped him be and do in his years on earth,*
> *and for the health and strength he continues to enjoy.*
>
> *As we remember how, in Jesus, God was born into a human home*
> *we thank you for the gift of this home,*
> *for the loving marriage shared with Graça,*
> *for the joys of children, grandchildren and great-grandchildren,*
> > *of friends and family*
> *with whom we enjoy the love you pour upon us.*
>
> *As, today, we remember Saint Stephen, the first martyr,*
> *we thank you that you also inspired Madiba to devote his life*
> *to striving for all that is good and true, for all that is right and just,*
> *and to be a living sacrifice and a bright shining example for others*
> > *to follow.*
>
> *As we look to the year ahead, we remember the words of Gabriel to*
> *Mary, and the angels to the shepherds: "Do not be afraid!"*

And so we trust ourselves to you for all that is ahead,
committing ourselves to keep on walking your ways,
with our hand in yours, until that day you lead us safely home.

So today we ask your blessing on Madiba, and those he loves, and those
who love him:

May the joy of the angels
The eagerness of the shepherds
The perseverance of the wise men
The obedience of Mary and Joseph
And the peace of the Christ child
Be theirs, this Christmas;

And the blessing of God almighty, the Father, the Son, and the Holy
Spirit, be upon you, and remain with you always. Amen.

I was never again to see Madiba as lively as he was during that
Saint Stephen's Day visit. Subsequent visits often took place in
hospitals, and the medical staff often ascribed his more muted
response to us to the fact that he had just taken medication.
But you could see his condition was tough for him. Me Graça
urged me to continue visiting them, once saying, and I am
paraphrasing her:

> He connects with you. When people come, he sometimes
> pretends he's not conscious and tells me after they have left that
> he didn't want to talk to them. But when you're with him he
> wants to talk, so please keep coming.

I knew that other clergy also ministered to him, among them
Bishop Don Dabula of the Methodist Church when he was in
Qunu, and Bishop Malusi Mpumlwana of the Ethiopian Episcopal
Church (and now-general secretary of the South African Council
of Churches). Nevertheless, the responsibility Graça's words
imposed on me was awesome—and humbling.

Chapter 10

Facing the Setting Sun

Soon after that Christmas visit, Madiba returned to Johannesburg and fell ill again. By now, as Zelda la Grange has written, "Every time Madiba was admitted to hospital, we held our breath." His admission generated international headlines and fevered speculation, especially when it was disclosed that he was suffering abdominal pain. This time President Zuma took a hand in informing the public. He announced that doctors had performed a planned diagnostic procedure and pronounced Madiba's condition as "consistent with his age." Lindiwe Sisulu, who in her role as defense minister oversaw the military doctors treating him, elaborated, telling the nation Madiba had undergone an investigative laparoscopy. But Mac Maharaj, now the president's spokesperson, would not disclose his whereabouts, and not even Zelda was told where he was admitted. Journalists camped out at 1 Military Hospital in Pretoria in the expectation he must be there.

Based on our previous experience, my view at the time was that when Mac said Madiba was well and that his admission was routine, we should take the opposite to be the case. I composed a new prayer, specifically for Me Graça and Zelda but also for use by other Christians who might find it helpful. The season of Lent, a time of introspection and self-denial, had just begun. I sought to use the prayer to acknowledge Madiba's failing health, pointing to the fact that toward the end of Lent, we commemorate Christ's

passion, suffering, and crucifixion, but that this is followed by
his resurrection. I released the prayer the day after Madiba was
discharged:

> *Blessed are you O Lord our God, creator of the universe;*
> *by your breath we were created,*
> *and by your will we have our being.*
>
> *You have kindled in us a fire that never dies away.*
> *In our darkest night when the flames of hope began to burn low,*
> *you raised up your servant Nelson Mandela*
> *to stoke the flames of our imagination*
> *so that we could have a foretaste of the dream of God.*
>
> *In him, the fullness of your love was pleased to dwell.*
> *You have blessed him with longevity*
> *and a resilient spirit that has allowed him to carry on his shoulders*
> *the dreams, hopes, and fears of a nation.*
>
> *We bless and praise you for all that he has meant to us,*
> *the embodiment of all that is beautiful,*
> *all that is good,*
> *all that is true,*
> *and we ask your blessing on him at this time.*
>
> *As he turns to face the setting sun,*
> *comfort and help him in his time of need,*
> *look upon him with eyes of mercy,*
> *hide him in the shadow of your wings.*
>
> *Brood over him like a mother hen broods over her chicks*
> *So that this time may be a time of rest and quietness,*
> *free from pain and anxiety.*
>
> *May he continue to lead the rest of his life*
> *in the radiance of your glory,*
> *and mark him as your own, forever.*

This we ask in the name of Jesus Christ,
Our only mediator and advocate. Amen.

I spent a lot of time in Johannesburg in early 2012, but Madiba returned to Qunu, so my contact was usually by text message with Graça and Zelda. I was in Jo'burg as a member of the Press Freedom Commission, a body appointed by the media industry under the leadership of Pius Langa, the former chief justice, to update the media's system of self-regulation. The print media were being threatened by the ANC with legislation that would have brought them under a government-created disciplinary regime, and we spent long hours holding hearings, receiving submissions, and traveling abroad to learn of other countries' systems of press self-regulation. When Madiba was president, he was sometimes critical of journalists, even attacking black journalists for allegedly taking instructions from white bosses, but he followed a policy of openness to the media. He had good relationships with many journalists and respected their independence and their right to report and comment as they saw fit. The work of the Press Freedom Commission bore fruit in the re-constitution of the mechanisms of media self-regulation and the threat of government intervention receded.

During my time on the commission, another chapter opened in my ministry. Judge Pius Langa was a fine jurist, internationally respected. As a lawyer, he had represented the underprivileged and anti-apartheid activists, and he went on to play a key role first in writing our constitution and then in developing its jurisprudence. As we got to know one another through our work on the commission, we agreed that even though he was a Methodist, I would come along and bless his new home in Johannesburg! That opened a new level of pastoral intimacy during which he disclosed a life-threatening illness to me. He steadily grew to recognize that he needed prayer and to become reconciled with meeting his Maker. He died in 2013.

As priests and pastors, we are intimately involved with milestones in people's lives: baptisms, marriages, pastoral care for the dying and funerals. For me, 2012 was a year of deaths: of Zwelakhe Sisulu, third son of Walter and Albertina and one of the country's leading journalists, at the tragically young age of 61; of Deane Yates, who with Dot had made their home a refuge for young men like me in the 1980s, a sanctuary in which we could read banned literature and have conversations not possible elsewhere; and of Duncan Buchanan, who never stopped mentoring me, even as archbishop. After Bishop Duncan retired, he would send me text messages: "Thabo, phone me!" or "Thabo, take it easy!" and remind me that "God is not in the business of rushing—slow down and take time to discern the mind of God!" I know that heaven is a livelier place for his booming laughter. Deane and Duncan were people who in my life embodied the values in one way or another of Nelson Mandela.

During that year we also saw the deaths of people not as well known to me but close to Madiba: Arthur Chaskalson, who as our first chief justice under the new constitution inaugurated an era of new respect for human rights and equality, and Jakes Gerwel, former vice-chancellor of the University of the Western Cape (of which I was by now chancellor) and, most importantly for Madiba, the civil servant who ran his presidential office and then chaired his foundation. Jakes's quiet, self-effacing personality and wise, sober counsel were invaluable to Madiba, and we sorely missed them when decisions around his treatment and welfare became contested at the end of his life.

The growing militarization of policing we saw in Ficksburg culminated in the killing of thirty-four striking miners by police armed with assault rifles at Marikana in North West Province on August 16, 2012. I was stunned and appalled by the killings, the single most deadly use of force by police since the Sharpeville massacre of 1960. At memorial services at Marikana and at the cathedral in Cape Town, my first response in the immediate aftermath of the massacre was to call on the nation to lament: "We are to cry out to God for all that has gone wrong—not just…in Marikana but for all that is wrong in our country, which contributed to this terrible, heartbreaking tragedy…" Later I stepped up my criticism of the failures in which we were all complicit:

> This is our problem: the failings of political will, of moral strength, of ethical courage. We see the injustice, we hear the cries of those who are oppressed. Even if we do not know all the answers, there is always plenty we could do. But we do not do it—and we sit back while others, in politics, government, business, and across society, do not do it.
>
> The tragedy of Marikana did not come from nowhere. It arose because we have been content to let things slide. They have slid in policy-making and implementation; in attitudes that allow economic inequalities to grow; in acceptance of high- and low-level corruption; and in ineffectual implementation of good governance and the rule of law. They have slid in the worsening trust between government and citizens, politicians and people.
>
> It is…above all a failure of leadership: in politics, but also in business, and in the cozy relationship they too often enjoy. Our leaders are the deaf, who cannot hear the loud cries of the hungry, the homeless, the needy, the oppressed. Our leaders are the blind, who cannot see what is right in front of their faces.

Around the same time as the Marikana crisis broke upon us, religious leaders of all faiths launched an anti-corruption campaign in Cape Town. Our worry at the extent of corruption had grown steadily since Anglican bishops had first given voice to it. In August 2011 I had helped launch a civil society campaign that, borrowing a soccer metaphor from the 2010 World Cup, called on South Africans to "red card" corruption. On that occasion, I said that many of us believed "that corruption—

in government and in business and in our communities—is
endemic and is eating at the very moral fiber of our nation
and its democratic values." Corruption, I added, "threatens the
dream of rooting out the residues of apartheid." At an ensuing
religious leaders' anti-corruption summit, we acknowledged
that no one could be "holier than thou" on the issue—even
religious institutions had been infiltrated. In my address about
the launch of the campaign, I pointed to statistics from the
Council of the Advancement of the South African Constitution
that showed perhaps 20 percent of our gross domestic product
was lost to corruption, robbing health, education, housing, social
development, and water and sanitation of desperately needed
investment. Corruption, I said, was "a corrosive cancer at the
heart of our nation, infecting and affecting every part of society."

Sadly, President Zuma was disinclined to follow the advice
of religious leaders and certainly not of those who, grouped
in the South African Council of Churches, led the Christian

*I visited Angola as Archbishop of Cape Town in 2012. The Anglican Church of Southern Africa
comprises twenty-nine dioceses across Angola, Namibia, Mozambique, South Africa, Leostho,
Swaziland, and the island of St. Helena.*

churches' struggle against apartheid. He instead chose to work with groupings more to his liking, sometimes led by people whose conversion to the anti-apartheid cause came late in the day as they trimmed their sails according to the prevailing winds in society. Culturally diverse Cape Town, which has a large number of adherents of a wide range of faiths, has long had a strong interfaith movement, led by the Western Cape Religious Leaders' Forum (WCRLF). The anti-corruption campaign we launched in 2012 included members of the Christian, Jewish, Muslim, Hindu, Baha'i, Brahma Kumaris, and African traditional religious communities. But when the ANC legislature convened a conference two months later purporting to strengthen the party's ties with the interfaith movement, the WCRLF was excluded.

President Zuma was the keynote speaker at the conference, and the ANC lauded him for "having worked hard to unite the religious people of South Africa." We took exception to the party's claims and, in response, said, "We do not need government to unite the religious communities of South Africa. Faith communities should strive to be an independent voice, free of government or party political interference. This is one of the most important lessons that we as religious leaders have learned from the apartheid crime against humanity, when some churches became the racist National Party at prayer." This was a reference to the way in which the white Dutch Reformed Church had compromised its witness by supporting apartheid.

In December 2012, the ANC held the every-five-year national conference at which it elected its leaders. Ahead of the conference, speculation was rife over the challenge to Zuma's leadership that was ultimately mounted by ex-president Kgalema Motlanthe, who coincidentally had attended Pholosho Senior Primary School in Alexandra, as did I.

Preaching at the journalist Zwelakhe Sisulu's funeral, I landed in
hot water with Thabo Mbeki's finance minister, Trevor Manuel.
I quoted Franklin Delano Roosevelt as saying in his second
inaugural address that the test of progress was not "whether we
add more to the abundance of those who have much; it is whether
we provide enough for those who have too little." Then I turned to
President Zuma and said if he too found himself making a second
inaugural address, "we trust that you too will make the alleviation
of poverty your first priority in your words and actions." Trevor
felt I had given the impression I was endorsing Zuma's candidacy.
I emphasized that I had said "if" the president found himself
making another inaugural address.

Early in December a group of church leaders, including Jo Seoka,
the bishop of Pretoria and president of the SACC; the Rev. Moss
Ntlha of the Evangelical Alliance; the Rev. Edwin Arrison of Kairos
South Africa, and I, decided to send a letter to the ANC ahead of
their conference, addressed through Mr. Zuma. We wrote in the
letter that some political leaders were doing their best to serve
the people: "But...too many are self-serving and arrogant," we
said. South Africa was yearning "not for a superficial change...
but for a different kind of leadership that can restore hope to the
poor." We asked: "Do you...not understand that lack of decisive
action, where waste of public resources has been revealed, leads
to a culture of impunity and immunity where the poorest again
become the main victims of bad governance? ...You cannot on
the one hand say that you are against corruption and on the other
hand clearly take part in corruption or turn a blind eye to it." We
said that if ANC leaders were not willing to take a number of steps
we spelled out, then they should "please step aside and make way
for others who are able to re-imagine what a healthy democracy in
South Africa will look like."

International media described our intervention as a "blistering
attack," and the ANC's secretary-general, Gwede Mantashe,

accused us of being "mischievous." By the time the letter was publicized, however, my mind was focused elsewhere. Madiba had been airlifted urgently from Qunu to Pretoria for medical treatment.

I was in Mozambique at the time, officiating at the wedding of Bishop Dinis Sengulane. The presidency announced Madiba's admission to hospital on the day but said nothing of the urgent circumstances. Again, they refused to disclose where he was being treated, leading to renewed controversy in the media. Again, his hospitalization made international news. It was three days before it was revealed that he was again suffering from a lung infection. I had scheduled days of prayer and fasting for the country ahead of the Day of Reconciliation on December 16, so when Me Graça sent me a text message to say his condition was serious, I added special prayers for both of them. When I went to Pretoria to speak at Day of Reconciliation commemorations at Freedom Park, the heritage site where we commemorate our heroes and celebrate our democracy, I also went to pray with them. By this time, Madiba's doctors had established that he had developed gallstones, which had to be removed after the lung infection was treated. After seeing them, it was clear that Madiba was vulnerable. He was weak and frail. Without disclosing my visit or my observations on Madiba's health, I urged South Africans to intensify their prayers for both Graça and Madiba and released for public use the prayer I had prayed with them.

At the time, we were observing Advent. In Matthew's Gospel, it is said of the coming of Jesus that "they shall name him Emmanuel, which means 'God is with us.'" In the prayer I used the concept of Emmanuel coming to release Madiba from ill health:

> *At Advent we sing and pray, O come, O come Emmanuel.*
> *We ask now, for Emmanuel, God with us, to be with Madiba*
>   *and Me Graça,*
> *Come Emmanuel and release our Madiba from the scourge of ill health;*

Come Emmanuel and offer Madiba everlasting healing;
You are a God who knows vulnerability, weakness, and frailty,
You are Lord of Lords, King of Kings, Lord of life and death,
Your power sustains us in life and death.

May your arms of love, stretched wide on the cross for us,
Now enfold Madiba, and Graça, with compassion, comfort, and
the conviction that you will never forsake them but that
you will grant Madiba eternal healing and relief from pain and suffering.

And may your blessing rest upon Madiba now and always. Amen.

Remembering the peace and tranquility of my father when I found him on his deathbed in Pimville, I began to wish that Madiba be given the space to move on and be united with his Maker in such a manner. He spent eighteen days in hospital—the longest stay he had experienced—and was released only the day after Christmas. I received a text around Epiphany (twelve days after Christmas) to say he had "recovered," but he continued to receive a high degree of medical care at home. In the wake of the long hospitalization, the vibe in the country was never the same again.

In March 2013, soon after I had been on a month-long Ignatian spiritual retreat in rural north Wales, Madiba was again in hospital overnight for a "scheduled medical check-up" and was discharged after "successful" tests. Putting "scheduled medical check-up" and "successful" in quotations reflects my skepticism of government spin in its statements. Two weeks later, he was rushed to the hospital late at night, once again for treatment of a lung infection. A buildup of fluid on his lungs had to be drained, and he spent nine days in hospital, every development covered day by day in the South African and international media. When he was released early in April, it was again to "high care" attention from a round-the-clock medical team at home in Houghton.

The next time his condition was the subject of intense public scrutiny was not because of his health as much as the behavior of politicians. The episode has never been fully explained by the ANC, but Zelda la Grange suggests it may have had its origins in inter-party competition. President Zuma had been re-elected by the ANC's national conference, and all the political parties were now looking ahead to the 2014 elections. The Democratic Alliance (DA), as the official opposition in parliament, had launched its election campaign, including a poster showing Madiba hugging the iconic liberal leader, Helen Suzman. Mamphela Ramphele, the civil society activist and academic who was also a board member of the Nelson Mandela Foundation, had just begun a bid to enter politics. During a visit to Graça, she had seen Madiba and mentioned it in a radio interview afterward.

"The DA's campaign as well as Dr. Ramphele's visit made the ANC unnecessarily nervous," suggests Zelda. "[T]hese interactions made the ANC somehow feel challenged over their 'ownership' of Madiba." Soon afterward, at the end of April, the ANC's top leaders—President Zuma, Deputy President Cyril Ramaphosa, and party chairperson Baleka Mbete—went calling on Madiba in Houghton, without any advance notice to Graça or those who controlled his schedule. Included in their party was a news crew from the SABC, the state broadcaster, but no other media. What I saw on the news that night made my stomach turn in revulsion and anger at the abuse of our national icon for political gain. As the politicians, medical team, and others laughed, joked, and posed for photographs around Madiba, he sat stiffly upright in an armchair, his face blankly staring straight ahead. Flash photography had long been banned around him as a consequence of the damage his eyes had suffered in the Robben Island quarry. But someone was using a flash, forcing him to close his eyes to avoid its blinding effect. You could see that he was either physically present but mentally in another world—or that he knew exactly what was happening and was very angry. The public had not seen any footage of him in nine months and seeing him unresponsive and ashen faced shocked viewers, leading to an outcry over the ANC's atrocious treatment of him. The episode was insensitive, uncaring, and demeaning to Madiba and his family, the behavior of desperate politicians who cared only about their own ends and ignored the means by which they were attempting to achieve them. Ironically, the images showed Madiba alienated from rather than supportive of the leaders of his party.

Six weeks later, in June, Madiba was back in hospital, driven from Johannesburg to Pretoria in an ambulance in the middle of the night after his condition deteriorated while he was being treated for yet another lung infection. The presidency announced that his condition was "serious." Members of his family flew in to visit, and journalists set up broadcast stations outside the hospital. Initially hidden from the public was the fact that there had been even more drama around his admission than first disclosed: The military ambulance taking him to hospital had broken down on the highway to Pretoria, and he and his medical team spent forty minutes stranded on a cold winter's night before a replacement came.

Madiba's medical team stabilized his condition, and all the while I kept up my texting ministry with Me Graça.

A long-planned commitment with the Anglican diocese in Perth necessitated that I travel to Australia. Stepping out of a confined, intimate space of ministry to teach at a clergy conference in a vastly different context was a trying experience. In my prayers with the church in Perth, I tried to share the anxiety that I and the country were experiencing, but I kept to myself the intensity of the prayer that was really needed. On the weekend I returned to Cape Town, Madiba took a turn for the worse. The presidency announced that his condition was now critical. I flew to Johannesburg and went to the hospital.

To avoid speculation, I tried to keep my arrival low key, wearing a black clerical shirt instead of the red shirt of a bishop in the hope I would not be recognized. By this time, Madiba had been in hospital for two weeks. A small media village camped outside, and the nation's attention was focused on his condition. Well-wishers flocked to leave flowers, messages, poems, and prayers on a makeshift wall of tribute. Schoolchildren and church groups came to sing and pray. Sangomas and African traditional healers prayed and performed their rituals, interspersed with mainstream church leaders and itinerant preachers. It was a salutary reminder that South Africa is a deeply spiritual country, that this intangible coheres us as a nation, and despite the tragedies we have lived through, Madiba has built into our genetic makeup a sense of common identity and a resilience that we don't always realize.

I slipped into the hospital grounds. Madiba's driver took me to where Madiba and Graça were being accommodated, and the police guards let me in. Madiba was in one room, and Graça had been given an adjoining room where she could sleep and had converted a hospital table into a workspace. Hooked up to machines and monitors with tubes and wires, Madiba was not responsive. It seemed to me that in many ways he was already gone, that he was being kept alive by machines and the Madiba we knew probably wasn't there anymore. The Methodists had been to pray with both of them.

Me Graça was in an excruciatingly difficult situation, and my heart went out to her. She was now the one who needed pastoral support, so I turned my attention to her. Here was a woman facing the loss of a husband in very public circumstances for the second time. As Madiba's third wife, I wondered whether she faced resistance to her role from those who had been part of his life earlier. Zelda la Grange is very critical in her book of the way in which some members of the extended family treated her. Whether correctly or not, I perceived Graça as being trapped in

the middle of a network of potentially conflicting forces: Madiba's
family from earlier marriages; the military doctors treating him;
civilian doctors; the political party to which he had dedicated his
life; the South African government; and others. As his spouse, her
sole concern was for her husband, his dignity, and his welfare.
But Madiba was bigger than a relationship, even a marriage
relationship. If it became necessary, who would make the difficult
decision, which, in our age of great medical advances, faces
an increasing number of families: What is life, and what is not
life? When do you unplug machines that are keeping someone
breathing, and when do you leave them on? Although my sense
was that Madiba needed to be released to die, who would make
such a decision and how?

Maternal and caring, as I had found her previously, Graça insisted
on offering me tea. There was a sense of tranquility and peace
as we prayed for Madiba. In his vulnerable, weak, and frail state,
I commended him to God's care and love. Then I focused on
her. As she watched and waited, she drew on her own reserves
of faith and courage to carry her. I spent two hours with her,
quietly talking, intensely aware of every movement of the nurses
next door, of the beeping of equipment, and of her anxiety when
its tone or duration changed. We talked through the spiritual
challenges Madiba must be facing and her own feelings about his
inability to reciprocate her communication with him. Without
divulging pastoral confidences, what struck me even more
strongly than before was the depth of her introspection and the
intensity of her love for and commitment to Madiba. From this
time until his death, she spent practically all her waking hours
with him, often dressed only in a tracksuit, focused solely on
caring for him. She loved him very deeply and was concerned
only for his welfare.

It was also apparent to me that she had come to accept that
Madiba was entering his last days. Death, if it does not come

in an accident, is not usually a sudden thing; it is a journey, and a pastor's job is to accompany the dying, helping them on their journey. When someone is dying, there is a psychological reality—and for a person of faith, a theological certainty—that when the final moments come, nobody is in control. When my friend and mentor, David Russell, was dying of cancer, he told me that he was going through a beautiful experience. Visiting him in the hospital, I struggled with this. "David, how do you call it beautiful?" I asked. He replied: "Thabo, you will never understand until you walk there." Seen in that light, Madiba was in a time of beauty, and Graça was not in control. All I could do was be alongside her for as long as I could to share her anxiety and to pray with her.

Before leaving the hospital, I wanted to affirm Graça as a woman of belief, of prayer, and of deep faith. In Cape Town I had looked for inspiration at the Bible readings set for the day and dictated a prayer to Sarah Rowland-Jones in which I aspired to capture both Madiba and Graça's spirituality. I had before me an image of God's loving hands, represented in the body of Jesus, his son, stretched out on the cross, and I wanted to bring that image closer to Graça, praying that God might enfold not only Madiba but also Graca with compassion and comfort and the conviction that they were not alone, even in this lonely journey. I also wanted to signal our preparedness for what was to come. The Bible readings referred to Rachel, the Old Testament figure who has come to be seen as the classic mother lamenting over her lost children, and to Jesus' friend Lazarus. This was the prayer I read in the hospital room:

Prayer for Me Graça, and all who watch and wait with Madiba

Scripture says that Rachel wept for the loss of her children and could not be consoled. Yet it also tells us that you, Lord Jesus, who wept at the death of your dear friend Lazarus, promise to be with us, and to stay with us, to the end of time.

Thank you that you who have walked the long valley of the shadow, will never forsake us, neither in life nor in death, and your everlasting arms embrace us always, in this life and the life to come.

Make your compassionate and strengthening presence known to Graça, and to all who love Madiba, at this hard time of watching and waiting.

Fill them with your holy courage and the gift of trusting faith, and take away their fear, so that they may dare to face their grief and bring it to your presence. May they know the truth of your promise that "blessed are those who mourn, for they shall be comforted."

Guide the medical staff so that they may know how to use their skills wisely and well in caring for Madiba and keeping him comfortable.

Uphold all of us with your steadfast love so that we may be filled with gratitude for all the good that he has done for us and for our nation and may we honor his legacy through our lives.

And so we bring our prayers to you:

Lord Jesus Christ, you are a God who knows vulnerability, weakness, and frailty,
You are Lord of Lords, King of Kings, Lord of life and death,
Your power sustains us in life and death.

May your arms of love, stretched wide on the cross for us,
Now enfold Madiba, and Graça, with compassion, comfort, and the conviction that you will never forsake them,

But that you will grant Madiba eternal healing and relief from pain and suffering.

And may your blessing rest upon Madiba now and always.

Grant him, we pray, a quiet night and a peaceful, perfect end.

And may the peace of God, which passes all understanding, keep your hearts and minds in the knowledge and love of God, and of his Son Jesus

Christ our Lord; and the blessing of God almighty, the Father, the Son, and the Holy Spirit, be among you and remain with you always. Amen.

By the end of the visit, Me Graça was in tears. Her voice was barely audible as she encouraged me to maintain contact with the other clergy who prayed with Madiba. It certainly seemed to me that religious leaders needed to begin to prepare South Africa for Madiba's death. Many people seemed to be in a state of denial, wanting him to live, finding the prospect of him dying unthinkable. But we had to come to terms with the fact that the father of our democracy, our icon, was starting a journey that all of us must ultimately make, a journey already taken by other icons of our struggle as well as two of his sons, Thembi, who had died in a car accident while he was in prison, and Makgatho, who had died of AIDS.

So with Graça's permission and as a means of gently guiding people to look at death in its face, I released the prayer I had used in the hospital. The phrase asking that Madiba might have "a quiet night and a peaceful, perfect end" was adapted from the service of Compline. As South Africa and indeed the world watched and waited, knowing that Madiba was critically ill, and with many, many people having difficulty in facing up to the certainty that Madiba was dying, these words caught the imagination of journalists. They flashed across the globe, from Los Angeles to London, from Nairobi to Sydney, in hundreds of news stories on the web and in print.

Chapter 11

Go Forth, Revolutionary and Loving Soul

During Madiba's last spell in hospital, regular statements from the presidency kept the public on edge. On June 27, two days after my visit, his condition had "improved during the course of the night. He remains critical but is now stable." The next five statements, into July, pronounced him remaining "critical but stable," with one—on July 4—denying a news report "that the former President is in a vegetative state." On July 22, he was still critical, "but shows sustained improvement." A month later, he was critical but stable and, "while at times his condition becomes unstable, the doctors indicate that the former President has demonstrated great resilience and his condition tends to stabilize as a result of medical interventions. Doctors are still working hard to effect a turnaround and a further improvement in his health and to keep [him]... comfortable." A week later, on August 31: "At times his condition becomes unstable, but he responds to medical interventions." The following day, he was discharged after nearly three months in hospital.

Despite Madiba's condition, said Mac Maharaj, "his team of doctors are convinced that he will receive the same level of intensive care at his Houghton home that he received in Pretoria. His home has been reconfigured to allow him to receive intensive care there. The health care personnel providing care at his home are the very same who provided care to him in hospital...We now call on all to allow the former President and his family the necessary private space, so that his continuing care can proceed with dignity and without unnecessary intrusion."

If South Africans did not already realize it, there was now little doubt in the public mind that Madiba's death was only a matter of time. At the end of my visit to the hospital in Pretoria, Graça had asked whether Lungi—whom she was by now calling "my daughter" after our visits and times of prayer—would come and spend time with her. Lungi did so and, conscious of the fact that Graça was spending a lot of her time in tracksuits, earned Graça's lasting gratitude by taking her a gown and slippers as a gift. Apart from continuing to pray for Madiba, Graça, and their family, it was time also for religious leaders to focus on how we would carry his legacy forward. Already, on his ninety-fifth birthday, on July 18, I had supported a Cape Town interfaith initiative at the invitation of the Muslim leader Imam Rashied Omar. The idea was to hold a quiet, respectful contemplation of Madiba that brought together people of all faiths and none—Muslims, Jews, Christians, and

Photo: Sayed Ridhwaan Mohamed

I joined with other faith leaders to create a human chain to commemorate our heritage.

others—in support of Madiba's values. Organized by an energetic young Cape Town photographer, Ruschka Jaffer, we resolved to form a "human chain" in which young and old, black and white, people of different classes, would line a major thoroughfare that connected the still largely segregated townships and suburbs of the city, from the most affluent to the poorest. In Cape Town's winter rain, we stood together, hand in hand and arm in arm, for sixty-seven minutes, marking the years of Madiba's activism, united in our diversity, singing and waving South African flags as a way of pledging to break down old divisions and build a new connectedness transcending the divisions of the past. (The text of the pledge we recited is at the end of the book as Appendix A.)

We repeated the exercise in the lead-up to the South African national holiday called Heritage Day. At Freedom Park in Pretoria, where we remember those who have died in the service of our country, we celebrated the values for which Madiba dedicated his life: unity, non-racialism, democracy, and a nation free from poverty. Our indigenous healers, the sangomas, started their commemoration by burning incense and performing their dances. At one time I would have avoided them, heeding my mother's warning in my childhood against their rituals, but in the spirit of the new South Africa, we accepted the importance of what different faith groups could bring in prayer to enrich our national heritage. We formed a human chain from the hilltop memorial, joined by a group of Afrikaners who came from the Voortrekker Monument, which commemorates their heritage, and then gathered in the Pretoria city center to celebrate Madiba and his message.

The next day I went to see Me Graça in Houghton. I did not see Madiba, who was effectively under quarantine in a sterile environment, but I could see and feel the tension in his nearest and dearest. After the visit, I appealed for continued prayer for Madiba and Graça, for the establishment of his legacy and for peace, and shared the prayer that I had prayed in Houghton. The day I visited was the United Nations International Day of Peace, which the World Council of Churches designates as an annual day of prayer for peace.

> *Creator God, Lord of Life and Love, you hold the whole universe*
> *in your hands*
> *and yet you also number the hairs on all our heads.*
> *You know the fates of the nations and the hopes and fears of each*
> *individual.*
> *On this, the International Day of Prayer for Peace, we pray for the*
> *peace of the world—for peace without, and for peace within.*
>
> *Jesus Christ, Prince of Peace, may your shalom touch every place of*
> *conflict, division, brokenness, or fear. May it fill our communities,*
> *families, and lives.*
>
> *From the horrors of Syria and the turmoil of South Sudan to the*
> *fractured relationships and violence in too many homes, bring your*
> *reconciling love.*
>
> *We pray also for South Africa on the eve of Heritage Day.*
> *Help us to draw on the best lessons of our past,*
> *and build on the firm foundations that, by your grace, Madiba laid for*
> *us.*
>
> *Give us courage to hold fast to his values, to follow the example of his*
> *praxis, and to share them with the world.*
>
> *We thank you that, in human chains, we can stand together for*
> *the united,*
> *non-racial, democratic nation, free from poverty, for which he strove.*
>
> *We lift our hearts, with gratitude for your loving care, giving thanks that*
> *Madiba has been able to come home. We thank you for all who have*
> *tended him, and who continue to do so, and that he now is stronger and*
> *more comfortable. We especially pray for courage and strength for Me*
> *Machel at such a time as this.*

*Hold him in the palm of your hand, surround him with your love,
and give him—and all who love him—that deep sense of assurance
    and inner peace
that we are all kept safely in your infinite merciful care that never
    lets us go.*

*Draw him ever closer to your heart, so that when your perfect time
comes, he may make that final journey home to you, without fear and
without pain.*

*Give all who love him the courage to entrust him to your never-failing
care, knowing you are doing for him things beyond all we can think or ask.*

*Come, Holy Spirit, renew the face of the earth with your breath of life,
so that even as we walk in the valley of the shadow of death,
we may know that Jesus Christ has opened for us the gates to
    everlasting life.*

This we pray in his holy, precious name. Amen.

For the last eleven weeks of his life, Nelson Mandela and his family were soaked in prayer by people at home and abroad. My text messages reflected a deepening pastoral relationship with those around him who watched and waited. In the last days of his life, I received one which shook me to my core. I no longer have the text, but as best I can remember it read: "Archbishop, hold my hand. I am weak." I read it several times and went downstairs to my chapel at Bishopscourt. I lay prostrate on the floor, feeling hot and cold. I cried, I mourned, and I wrestled with God. Lungi has an amazing ability to know when I am struggling with something, and she followed me down. "Are you okay?" she asked. "Yes, I'm okay, I'm just having a God moment." Bishopscourt, with its thick, centuries-old walls, is cold even in summer, and Lungi told me, "Let's go up." We went back upstairs, and I skirted around what was wrong, just saying, "It's about Madiba."

On the night of Thursday, December 5, 2013, I received a message from Bishop Malusi Mpumlwana. He was one of the clergy with whom Graça had asked me, in June, to keep in touch. Malusi and Madiba were very close friends, she said, and Madiba loved him. An activist alongside Steve Biko in his early life, Malusi was well-known to Anglicans, with his church, the Ethiopian Orthodox Church, having been for many decades

Nelson Mandela in 2008.

Photo: South Africa The Good News

closely associated with us as an "order" of our church. Malusi was at the home in Houghton, where he had been spending a good deal of time praying, and he was calling to say that Graça had asked him to tell me that Madiba had died.

I set about composing a new prayer. Once again, I turned to our Anglican Prayer Book and began by adapting the prayer for someone at the point of death. President Zuma went on television later that night, and I have to say that despite all the scandal that already surrounded him and continued to surround him, his handling of the announcement was impeccable: he was pastoral, he was direct, he was loving, and he ended with a message of great consolation. Once he had made his announcement, I released my prayer:

> *Go forth, revolutionary and loving soul, on your journey out of this world,*
> *In the name of God, who created you, suffered with you and liberated you.*
> *Go home, Madiba, you have selflessly done all that is good, noble, and*
> *honorable for God's people.*

We will continue where you have left off, the Lord being our helper.
We now turn to you, Lord, in this hour of darkness, sadness, pain,
and death, in tears and mourning,

We wail, yet we believe that you will console us, that you will give us the
strength to hold in our hearts and minds and the courage to enact in our
lives the values Madiba fought and stood for.

We turn to you, Lord, and entrust Madiba's soul to your eternal rest and
loving arms as he rejoins the Madiba clan, his comrades, and all the
faithful departed.

We pray particularly for his closest and dearest, for Me Graça Machel, for
his children, grandchildren, and all his relatives; may you surround them
with your loving arms, your fatherly embrace and comfort.

At this dark time of mourning, at this perfect time when you have called
him to rest and a perfect end, accept his soul and number him among the
company of the redeemed in heaven.

Console and comfort his family, South Africa, and the world.
May his long walk to freedom be enjoyed and realized in our time
by all of us.

May he rest in peace and rise in glory. Amen.

Abandoning my schedule, I joined Archbishop Tutu at his
regular Friday morning service at St. George's Cathedral in the
morning, then flew to Johannesburg to join Graça and the family
in Houghton. There I found the Rev. Vukile Mehana, the ANC
chaplain-general, leading prayers and songs with President Zuma,
members of his cabinet, and the ANC leadership. Invited to say
a few words, I declined to speak after the president but read the
prayer. Usually my public speaking voice is relatively clear but on
this occasion I struggled, trembling with emotion. Afterward, with
the party leadership gone, Lungi and I stayed on and reminisced
with Graça about our journey of the past few years. As had

become the custom, I also promised to send her a copy of the prayer.

Then began a week of constant activity as Lungi and I attended evening prayers at the Mandelas' home in Houghton and shuttled between Johannesburg, Cape Town, Pretoria, East London, and Qunu for the ceremonies leading up to Madiba's funeral and interment.

It was also a week of tension, which began when, at evening prayers, I was cornered by Cyril Ramaphosa, at the time the deputy president of the ANC, and Baleka Mbete, the party's national chairperson. They had been appointed by President Zuma to preside at the national memorial service at Soccer City, the stadium outside Johannesburg that had hosted the biggest matches of football's 2010 World Cup, on the Tuesday after Madiba's death. Apart from tens of thousands of ordinary South Africans, the service was due to be attended by scores of heads of state, ex-heads of state, European royalty, rock stars, business moguls, and others among the world's rich and powerful. Accompanied by Malusi, Cyril and Baleka told me that I had been chosen to say the Christian prayer at the service. I questioned whether I was the right choice. Surely, I asked, it should be the president of the SACC— who at the time was Jo Seoka—or Bishop Ziphozihle Siwa, the presiding bishop of Madiba's church, the Methodist Church of Southern Africa? No, I was told, the Methodists were already preaching at both the memorial service and the funeral. (Bishop Ivan Abrahams, the general secretary of the World Methodist Council and a South African, preached at the memorial service and Bishop Siwa at the funeral.)

Afterward, unhappy that Luthuli House (the ANC headquarters) was selecting who would pray, I asked Malusi what was going on. He told me that Me Machel had asked that I say the prayer at the stadium. Well, I thought, if that was the case, surely she would have asked me herself. When we buried Albertina Sisulu, an Anglican, we had followed the protocol laid down by our Anglican Prayer Book, to the extent that we refused to allow the president to speak last, which state protocol would have dictated. I couldn't understand why Luthuli House would dictate Methodist protocol. But I relented, remarking to Lungi that it was all very strange. Little did I realize what appeared to have been going on behind the scenes.

From the outset, there were difficulties over access to the various ceremonies. In Houghton, I was told that Lungi and I had to collect our accreditation at the ANC party headquarters in the Johannesburg city center. But people were being accredited at the house, so I refused to go to town, and we joined the queue. When we reached the front of the line, I was told, no, the clergy had to be accredited at Wits University. I stood my ground, and we eventually received our accreditation. As events unfolded over the ensuing week, I learned that we weren't the only people who struggled to be accredited. All week, all manner of people, including foreign guests, were pushed from pillar to post, traveling from one venue to another to secure accreditation. Some prominent friends of Madiba never received it.

On the Sunday after Madiba died, I was scheduled to make my first visit to one of Cape Town's most important parishes in a black residential area, Holy Cross Church in Nyanga. So I returned from Johannesburg and in Nyanga, I had my opportunity to pay tribute to Madiba and to reflect on his life. (My homily is at the end of the book as Appendix B.) From there it was back to Johannesburg for the memorial service at Soccer City, where Madiba was last seen in public as he greeted the spectators at the final of the World Cup. I joined other faith leaders—Jewish, Hindu, and Muslim—in opening the service with prayer. I completed my contribution with the words I had used the previous week, urging Madiba to "Go forth, revolutionary and loving soul, on your journey out of this world..." (The Soccer City prayer is included as Appendix C.) A lineup of other speakers followed, including members of the Mandela family and world leaders. Among these were the presidents of Brazil, Cuba, India, Namibia, and the United States and the vice-president of China. Barack Obama was given a rapturous reception and his eulogy was really moving. Both he and Ban Ki-moon, the secretary-general of the United Nations, attracted more applause than President Zuma, whose image on the stadium screens was repeatedly booed until those controlling the broadcast were instructed to stop showing him. It was very sad; it would have been disappointing for Madiba, who would have found the behavior undisciplined and undignified. I was moved by how solicitous Bongekile Ngema-Zuma, the president's fourth wife and a member of the Anglican Women's Fellowship, was for us religious leaders. It was pouring with rain, and when I began to get wet, she anxiously tried to keep me protected from the downpour.

Over the ensuing days, Lungi and I kept in touch with Graça by phone and text message and visited and prayed with her for strength on the day we all went to the Union Buildings in Pretoria to view Madiba as he lay in state. Following Thabo Mbeki and his wife, Zanele, past the soldiers and sailors arrayed alongside his coffin, Lungi and I paused at Madiba's side as I prayed, "May your soul rest in peace and rise in glory."

Madiba's body was to be flown to the Eastern Cape on Saturday for the funeral in Qunu on Sunday, and I was asked to stay on in Johannesburg to accompany the chaplains in a military aircraft. Dating back to the days of apartheid, I have an unease about the military and as a church leader I prefer to keep a distance from them and their weapons as a matter of conscience. So I declined the request on the grounds that I needed to get back to Cape Town to fetch changes of clothing and to gather my church vestments for the funeral.

I arrived in Qunu on Friday in time to be asked by Lindiwe Sisulu to say prayers at a low-key service held in a marquee outside Madiba's home for the handful of people already preparing for the next two days. Tensions were apparent between government, party, and family about who was to go where and who was to do what, and one of those at the service told me, "Bishop, don't ask how we are. We will do the funeral, and then come back to you so you can pray for our healing." The next morning I was asked to be at the airport to meet the military aircraft carrying Madiba's body. A few smaller planes arrived ahead of it, and Graça, Winnie Madikizela-Mandela, and other members of the family joined us. Then the Hercules C-130 transport aircraft arrived, accompanied by two fighter jets. Despite my opposition to shows of military might, I still shiver as I recall the strength of my emotions—and the sense that this was right—as a guard of honor in ceremonial dress lined up, a military band struck up a solemn rendition of the national anthem, and the flag-draped coffin was loaded into a hearse. Motorcycle outriders then led the cortège through the streets of the nearby town of Mthatha, lined with people waving and crying, and to Qunu.

In Qunu, I read the prayers as the coffin was taken from the hearse and handed over to the leaders of abeThembu, Madiba's grouping of the Xhosa nation. On the coffin lay a small branch, the significance of which I was unaware. Asking a Thembu leader about it, I learned that it had been broken off a tree, called *umPhafa* or *umLahlankosi*, in Johannesburg. The belief was that when someone died, the person's soul found rest in the tree and that to bring the person's spirit home, a branch had to be brought with the body—rich symbolism indeed. The leaders removed the branch and covered Madiba's remains with a leopard skin, indicating his right to the status of a chief and a member of the Thembu royal household. They performed their traditional rites, reciting phrases and ululating in isiXhosa, bringing him and his soul back to Qunu, and handed the coffin back to the clergy. Reciting Christian prayers, we escorted it into Madiba's home, where it was taken up to his bedroom to lie overnight in accordance with African tradition.

I had been asked by Me Graça to lead a private valedictory service in the home early on the Sunday morning before the funeral. I constructed the service on the basis of the Anglican Prayer Book, using a mixture of those prayers with the one I had prayed with her and Madiba. The structure of our prayer book, with its roots in the English Reformation nearly five centuries ago, is wonderful in allowing us to be creative in designing services that both speak to the situation in which we find ourselves and to respect the theology and the beauty and aesthetics of its language.

In a brief homily, I asked for God to comfort and strengthen Graça, Winnie, and all those who mourned, and pleaded that we should never forget the price that he and his companions paid for love of their country. In the prayers I gave thanks for all those who had nurtured and supported Madiba through his life, trying to name some of those whose roles had not been acknowledged in the ten days since his death: from those who brought him up in nearby Mvezo, where he was born, to fellow prisoners, chaplains, lawyers, lobbyists, artists, church leaders, Zelda la Grange, and Graça, "who brought him happiness in the last years and kept faithful vigil to the end." (The text of the service is included as Appendix D.) Then we handed his body over to the military for the public funeral service and burial.

One of the church leaders I had named in the prayers was Archbishop Tutu, whose treatment by the ANC had cast a pall over proceedings. I learned only after it happened that he had been accredited to attend the Soccer City memorial service not as a member of the clergy but only because he chaired "The Elders," the global leaders' group founded by Madiba to work for peace and human rights. Consequently, he was seated not with his fellow South Africans but with international guests in the Elders group such as former United Nations Secretary-General Kofi Annan, former American President Jimmy Carter, former Irish President Mary Robinson, and former Norwegian Prime Minister Gro Harlem Brundtland. As an afterthought (Tutu was not on the program), he was asked during the service to say a concluding blessing. This was after the boisterous crowd had booed President Zuma, and in true Tutu tradition, he scolded them for failing to respect the dignity of the occasion and called for discipline. He managed to silence the crowd but it was a fraction of what it had been; people had long begun streaming out of the stadium, heading for home.

Then on Saturday, while in Qunu, I was tipped off by a member of my staff that Archbishop Tutu, unable to get accreditation to the funeral, had announced that he would not be attending. "Much as I would have loved to attend...to say a final farewell to someone I loved and cherished," he said, "it would have been disrespectful to Tata to gate-crash what was billed as a private family funeral." I was thus prepared when Nathi Mthethwa, the police minister, asked to speak to me urgently about the issue. He reassured me that Archbishop Desmond would not need accreditation and that the police would allow him to enter the area—this came at the same time another government minister was telling journalists he was accredited. In a last-minute dash, Trevor Manuel, by now the planning minister in the presidency, arranged a private plane to get Archbishop Desmond there on Sunday morning.

Looking back, I believe that a clandestine decision was taken to sideline the archbishop. Whatever its origins, this explained the insistence of party officials on dictating what role which religious leaders would play at both the memorial and the funeral. Although confusion or inefficiency may have been responsible for some people's difficulties in getting accreditation, this was an unlikely explanation for the archbishop. But it is not certain what motivated the attempts to exclude him. Archbishop Desmond had criticized the extended Mandela family a few months earlier, saying that feuding among the children when Madiba lay gravely ill in hospital was "almost like spitting in Madiba's face." He had also been a strong critic of Mr. Zuma even before he became president, and in 2011 he had lashed out at the government when they failed to grant the Dalai Lama a visa to visit South Africa; he said the government did not represent him and angrily threatened to start praying for the ANC's downfall. The ANC would have wanted the funeral to be a platform on which the party would shine by sharing their founding father with the world. If Archbishop Desmond had spoken, he might well have embarrassed them with the truth and asked deeply theological questions about our life as a nation, the values Madiba lived by, and whether the practice of cronyism and corruption lived up to those values.

During the funeral service, I received a message from Cyril Ramaphosa asking me to come up to the podium to single out Archbishop Desmond and to assure him that he was welcome. In essence, my response was: "Why should I do that? He's bigger than to need that. There was a debacle over his accreditation, and I don't know what you guys were up to. It will only irritate him." Later, before Bishop Siwa began his sermon, there was another appeal. "Shall we call you on stage?" I was asked. "To do what?" I replied. I wasn't prepared to be dragged into a mess of their own making. In hindsight, I think the ANC chaplain should have quietly asked Bishop Siwa to invite Archbishop Desmond to play a part. Perhaps I could have been more alert to what was happening and brought more pressure to bear, although if any of us had acted publicly we could have worsened the situation by taking the focus of events away from Madiba and his life.

At the end of the funeral, we all processed to the graveside for the interment. The burial program did not name the officiants, so in a quick consultation, Bishop Siwa, Malusi Mpumlwana, the former SACC General Secretary Frank Chikane, and I decided to ask Archbishop Desmond to pray a blessing over the tombstone.

But I don't want to conclude my account of Madiba's send-off with what went wrong. For five years, I had the enormous privilege of being one of the pastors who walked alongside both him and Graça in their time of need. In retrospect, I realize that she had in effect asked me to help Madiba face death. Now that he had been released from his suffering, I had an abiding concern for her spiritual welfare. The past ten days, not to speak of the past six months, had been grueling for her. I am reluctant to speak of what I do know of her private thoughts or to speculate on what I don't know, but we have the benefit of what she shared with the world six months later, in her first interview at the end of the period of mourning she observed after Madiba's death. She told David Smith of *The Guardian:*

> Because Madiba was sick for a long time, his passing was not a surprise, but believe me, there's no such thing as saying I saw it coming. No. When the moment comes, it's there and you start the journey absolutely as one, two, three, five minutes until you get the days. There's nothing which prepares you even if you know your beloved one is sick. Nothing prepares you for the pain of seeing him passing.

She also described her happiest memories of their time together:

> Ever since you have seen me with Madiba, we always walked hand in hand. There hasn't been any moment where we were together we wouldn't hold each other's hand...Whether it was in privacy, whether it was publicly, it was that kind of connection of communication which we had together...When we were

relaxed, whether it's in public or whatever, there was always a broad smile on his face. And that's the comforting thing: that we were there together. We shared so many moments of laughter and that human connection was very special.

Of his love for children:

His heart was of the age of 95 if you like, but the inner him, the person he is, remained a child. He remained a child to the end.. when he sees another child his face would light up, and a big smile would come, he forgot about everything else and his attention would be on that child.

And of her sense of loss:

If you can imagine how millions of people felt this sense of loss, then you can imagine what it means for me. That huge presence, filling every detail of my life, every detail of my life full of him. And now it's pain, it's emptiness, actually it's searching now, who I am now after this experience? It's like something has changed inside you as well...[W]hat next? What am I going to do, how am I going to be part of the thousands of millions of people who are trying to work for a better world?"[118]

Well, Graça is doing magnificent work through the Graça Machel Trust, a pan-African advocacy organization based in Johannesburg that works to improve child health and nutrition, education, women's economic and social empowerment, leadership, and governance. But that is another story, one for her to tell.

---

118 *The Guardian*, London, 27 June 2014; 18 July 2014 (podcast)

Chapter 12

Madiba's Legacy

How should we remember Nelson Mandela? His vision was for
a free, democratic, non-racial world in which we are all afforded
equal opportunities and are freed from poverty, marginalization,
and disempowerment. Is this vision realizable and, if so, how?
What is his spiritual legacy for South Africans and the world? Is
his a legacy worth emulating, or are we romanticizing him and
his achievements in a way that leaves us ill-equipped to meet the
challenges of times very different from those in which he lived?
What does it mean to live with faith and courage in South Africa
and the world today?

The good that Mandela stood for and did is unparalleled in our
lifetime. He was extraordinary, an icon of peace and reconciliation
who appealed to a sense of common humanity among all people.
But he was a human being like all of us, vulnerable and fallible.
He smiled, he joked, he was funny, he was jealous, he frowned,
he got angry. He feared death and obscurity. He doubted, he
coerced, he outmaneuvered. Developing wisdom, strength,
and grace in the face of adversity, while he was no saint in the
traditional Christian sense, he was a symbol of holiness. By that I
mean one who is set apart but is able to hold oneself and others
accountable to a greater Being, able to draw people together based
on a vision for the common good. In pursuance of this common
good, Madiba worked so that, as John's Gospel expresses it in

one of my favorite biblical passages, all "may have life, and have it abundantly."[119]

Although he was not a regular churchgoer, Madiba held onto the Christian beliefs imbued in his childhood. He was not dogmatic about them but rather looked at which of the values proclaimed by the Kingdom of God could be used to unite people. We have established a secular state in South Africa, but we have absorbed personal religious values into the organization of our societal life. The values of our constitution reflect the influence of Madiba's spirituality and the spiritual values of the oppressed, who time and again during the struggle against apartheid would hear biblical passages that reflected their suffering, their hopes, and aspirations: the passages in Amos and Exodus in

Preaching during an evening prayer service at St. George's Cathedral in Cape Town in December 2015 on the second anniversary of Madiba's death.

119 John 10:10.

what we Christians call the Old Testament that speak of justice
and liberation and the passage in Saint Paul's letter to the
Philippians, which speaks of seeking that which is honorable. In
acknowledging the sins of our past and vowing never to go there
again, the preamble to the U.S. Constitution speaks to an almost
Christian process of repenting of our sins, in resolving to do good
once we have been absolved, in order that we may enjoy equality,
justice, and peace.

On the day Lungi and I watched Madiba interacting with the
Afrikaner family who had suffered unspeakable loss, we saw him
as Madiba the caring human being, Madiba the healer, Madiba
the sage, the father, the one who understood pain and the special
agony of having to be forgiven. I saw in him the constancy and
zeal that I aspire to in my calling and vocation, practicing it
naturally across race, gender, age, and socio-economic status.
As one link in the chain formed by the many people who were
touched by Madiba, I feel privileged to have lived in this time
and honored to have had the experience of ministering to him.
Perhaps the only adequate response—even more important than
telling the story in this book—would be to go on my knees, to
fall silent and weep tears of gratitude, joy, and disbelief, tears
that would make me recommit, in however feeble a way, to be a
conduit for justice, for peace, for reconciliation and forgiveness
for as long as I have the opportunity to serve as archbishop and
beyond.

Of course, seeking the Christian way of dealing with these
concepts does not mean shying away from raising injustices and
trying to gloss over things that divide us. It does not mean turning
a blind eye to the fact that our constitution does not allow for
restitution of much of the land that we, the Makgobas, and others
lost under colonialism. Nor does it mean running away from the
pain caused by the use of Swazi troops in the nineteenth century
to suppress us and others, an issue I raised briefly with the

current monarch of the Swazi people, King Mswati III of eSwatini, on a visit to his kingdom some years ago. (He probably doesn't remember this, since it was overshadowed by Lungi's insistence, against traditional protocol, on giving him a hug when she greeted him!) We need to talk about the abscesses of our history, not to pull anyone down or stoke conflict but to say they must be pierced because just naming the facts brings catharsis.

When I was a newly consecrated bishop in Komani, David Russell quoted Desmond Tutu so powerfully that it has remained with me ever since. We had gone to the place of King Sandile of amaRharhabe to offer the apology to which I referred in chapter 6. The church had collaborated in the jailing of Sandile's famous forebear on Robben Island and accepted the family's children in

Zonnebloem College to be educated in Western ways. How do you say, "Sorry, please forgive me," when you have forced your will on a people in this way; when you have rewritten their place in history and made them poor and uneducated in the country of their birth? David told

Presenting the Archbishop's Award for Peace with Justice to Archbishop Emeritus Desmond and Mrs. Leah Tutu in April 2016.

Desmond Tutu's bicycle story: of how you can't steal someone's bicycle, then ride it to the person's home to say, "Forgive me for stealing it," then ride it back home. You have to make restitution, give the bicycle back first, then ask for forgiveness for stealing it. Showing redemptive attitudes and taking redemptive action involve the equivalent of returning the bicycle. They heal both the wronged and the wrongdoer. They create a space for *indaba*, for humble listening, for two hearts to hear the same pulse, for one to get to know the other's story, leading to the full realization of Jesus' power to heal the divisions we have created.

We also need to take a bigger, broader view in assessing the impact of colonial dispossession and collaboration on the development of the identities of South Africans. During the writing of this book, I visited Rwanda with a group of archbishops from elsewhere in Africa and was able to slip away and hop on a local motorbike taxi to visit the Kigali Genocide Memorial. Viewing the skulls of hundreds of Rwandans who died in the 1994 genocide, I both despaired of ever finding my great-grandfather Kgoši Makgoba's skull and was reminded of other genocides about which I had learned in my youth, from that of the Herero people of Namibia a century ago to those in Cambodia and the Balkans more recently. I could not but be overwhelmed by the memorial but was also disturbed by my experience of Kigali. It is impressively clean, effectively policed, and works well as a city, but I got the distinct impression that the efficiency I experienced could be the result of an obsession to run away from the country's dreadful past.

The values for which Madiba lived and was prepared to die recognized the reality that, left to itself, humanity is capable of wiping itself off the face of the earth. Yes, we need to confront squarely what keeps us apart, to give voice to the injustices of the past, just as Madiba did. But if the human race is to survive, we also need to recognize the complexity of our history and to reach out, as Madiba never stopped doing, across the barriers that divide us to find one another.

In this situation, what is my responsibility, as a priest, a religious leader, and a South African? At one level, it is to engage other leaders in society to promote biblical values, which are at their heart similar to the values promoted by all faiths. In the chapter of a book based on an interview with me early on in my time as archbishop, the authors described my role—and I daresay that of other faith leaders—as being that of "pastor to the nation."[120] In that capacity I see my pastoral responsibility to minister to all on a non-partisan basis: to cry with those who are crying, to laugh with those who are laughing, and, when it comes to the powerful, both to love and to confront those in positions of authority. I try

to fulfill that calling in encounters with national leaders, from presidents of southern African countries to cabinet ministers—on planes, at funerals, in their offices, and at Bishopscourt. In my capacity as Prince Mangosuthu Buthelezi's archbishop—he is an Anglican—I have traveled to Ulundi to unveil a statue of

Showing Archbishop of Canterbury Justin Welby around Alexandra during a visit in 2014. At right is Bishop Steve Moreo of Johannesburg.

him. I have overcome reservations about interacting with a one-time believer in apartheid to appear on a platform with former president F.W. de Klerk to commemorate the anniversary of his 1990 speech announcing Madiba's release. I even engage with kings, from the Zulu monarch, King Goodwill Zwelithini, to King Mswati, King Sandile, and King Letsie III of Lesotho, with whom I enjoy a particularly good relationship.

However, we who are ordained as clergy also have a more profound, deeper duty than this. At my first ordination, when I was made a deacon, more than twenty-five years ago, I was

120 Charles Villa-Vicencio and Mills Soko (2012). *Conversations in Transition: Leading South African Voices.* Cape Town: David Philip, 219-229.

charged with a special ministry. In the words of the prayer book,
I was told by my bishop that: "In the name of Jesus Christ, you
are to serve all people, and to seek out particularly the poor, the
weak, the sick, and the lonely." My later ordination as a priest, my
consecration as a bishop, and my installation as an archbishop
have not changed
that. I remain a
deacon, as all priests
do, so my task
remains to seek out
the poor and needy,
to seek out those who
need God's healing
love and touch, and to
be especially worried
about those who are
suffering.

*On a "Walk of Witness" after a fire swept a shack
settlement near Cape Town, accompanied by community
and chapelry leaders and Canon Delene Mark of HOPE
Africa.*

This is why I visited Ficksburg after the death of Andries Tatane,
Marikana after the massacre there, and Cape Town townships
with inadequate sanitation. This is why after eruptions of
xenophobic violence, I led a walk of witness in Alexandra and
visited migrants chased out of their homes in the Western
Cape. It is also why, to the bemusement of many, I visited the
divided community of Ventersdorp in North West Province for
the funeral of the white supremacist Eugene Terre'Blanche after
he was murdered by a farm worker. My vocation as a deacon
also underpins my passion for restoring the church's role in
promoting good, affordable education across Southern Africa. It
also fueled my anger at the appalling conditions in the mud-brick
schools of the Eastern Cape, which I visited in the company of a
delegation of prominent South Africans to find disgusting toilets,
no hand basins, broken windows, holes in classroom floors, and
too few teachers. This vocation is why, as chancellor of a local
university, the University of the Western Cape, I reached out

to negotiate with students during protests against their tuition fees, and why I identified with our son, Nyakallo, when he was arrested with them. It is why I have hosted a series of what we call "Courageous Conversations," which pull together people from mining communities in South Africa, executives, unions, NGOs, faith leaders, and the legal professionals involved in Marikana, to seek to reposition the sector as a partner for long-term sustainable development.

A deacon's concern for the poor and the needy is also why I and my fellow leaders in the Western Cape Religious Leaders' Forum decided to act when, three months after Madiba's death, our country's "public protector" or ombudsman, Thuli Madonsela, published her report on the use of more than R200 million in state funds (U.S. $20 million at the time) to upgrade President Zuma's private rural estate at Nkandla in KwaZulu-Natal. Coming against the backdrop of report after report by the government's own auditor-general, disclosing billions of rands in unauthorized,

On Holy Saturday in 2014, the interfaith community—including Christian, Jewish, and Muslim leaders—marched to South Africa's parliament to protest government corruption. Archbishop Emeritus Desmond Tutu, on my right, came out of retirement to support the cause.

irregular, fruitless, and wasteful spending, followed by little or no
remedial action, the public protector's report was devastating. Yet
the responses from within the ANC ranged from barely concealed
hostility to the report to open attacks on Thuli Madonsela and
her colleagues. In an echo of the church's activism in the 1980s
and in particular that of Archbishop Tutu in Cape Town, our first
response was to hold a prayer vigil on the steps of St. George's
Cathedral, including present and past Anglican bishops, among
them Garth Counsell, the Bishop of Table Bay, Geoff Quinlan,
one of the Tutu-era suffragan bishops, and Archbishop Desmond
himself. Holding flowers and posters, we declared our solidarity
with the public protector under the banner "A Flower for Thuli,
A Message for the President." I was also joined by Lungi and our
daughter Paballo, who in Standard 10 at school, was taking part
in her first public protest.

Then the city's religious leaders met and resolved, in a decision
which deliberately evoked the spirit of the 1980s, to march to
parliament on Holy Saturday, the day before Easter. We called our
action a "Procession of Witness" and based it on an appeal for our
political leaders to account for their behavior and live up to the
national values established by the constitution. We invoked the
spirit of Madiba: One his greatest characteristics, we said, "was his
ability to revisit his positions and decisions and to change course
when it seemed right to do so, not in his own personal interests
but in the interests of building and holding the nation together."
We eschewed party political objectives, insisting that marchers
should not carry party banners and that we, and not political
leaders, would lead the march. We challenged the politicians to
"reset their moral compasses" and to follow Mandela's example.

The march drew supporters from the full spectrum of the inter-
faith community, from the Muslim Judicial Council and the
Union of Orthodox Synagogues to the Methodist Church, the
Dutch Reformed Church, the Uniting Reformed Church, and the

Uniting Presbyterian Church. In my speech outside parliament, I said the collapse of standards and values among those serving in government had turned from a trickle to a flood, and I challenged President Zuma with a series of questions on his

Photo: John Allen

Speaking at an anti-corruption march in Cape Town in 2015.

silence in response to the public protector's report: "Unfortunately those advising him have forgotten the admonition: Silence screams the truth." (The full text is appended as Appendix E.)

After that march and another anti-corruption march on parliament eighteen months later, it became apparent that the Nkandla scandal was the tip of an iceberg. When I joined an SACC delegation to urge President Zuma to admit that he had benefited from state resources at Nkandla and told him that people were coming to us to share other stories of corruption, he refused to budge and said he didn't know of any corruption. A few months later, the deputy finance minister, Mcebesi Jonas, reported that Zuma's friends, the Gupta family of Johannesburg, had offered him a multi-million rand bribe, prompting others to reveal their experiences of the Guptas' attempts to swing state business their way. The ANC resolved to call on them and others to report their experiences. Believing—correctly, as it turned out—that few people would go to the ANC, the SACC established an "unburdening panel" and encouraged church members and others to come forward.

The result was the publication of an alarming report, backed up soon afterward by leaked emails from within the Gupta businesses. It said the evidence pointed to "observable trends of inappropriate control of State systems through a power-elite that is pivoted around the President of the Republic that is systematically siphoning the assets of the State." This elite, the report said, was "capturing" state-owned companies by weakening their governance and operational structures, weeding skilled professionals out of the civil service, taking control over the management of the country's finances, securing the loyalty of the state's intelligence and security apparatus, and creating parallel governance and decision-making structures that undermine the executive. Frighteningly, those who came to the SACC wanted only to speak to a priest, not to lawyers, because they feared for their and their families' lives.[121]

We had to accept, rationally and emotionally, that after twenty years of democracy we were living under a deeply corrupt regime. In the months that followed, revelation after revelation revealed the depth of the rot, eventually leading to President Zuma's removal from office by his party early in 2018, less than four years into his second five-year term. As his successor, Cyril Ramaphosa, took over the reins of power, it became clear that cleaning up will be an enormous task. The network of patronage and control extends so deeply into government—including the agencies responsible for law enforcement, prosecutions, communications, and infrastructure development—that it will take a concerted campaign of the whole of society to root it out and to replace it with strong systems and institutions, served by a non-partisan civil service that cannot be undermined by one person or party's whim.

South Africa is not irretrievably broken, nor do our recent difficulties discount what we have achieved since our political

---

121 SACC Report to the Church Public On the Unburdening Panel Process: http://allafrica.com/stories/201705280179.html [Accessed June 11, 2017]

liberation in 1994. We are firmly grounded within a constitutional order, and many institutions—the judiciary as a pre-eminent example—are in good working order. We have hundreds and thousands of new houses and many new clinics. In areas where we have replaced mud schools, the new buildings are first class. We have water, sanitation, and electricity where we never had it before. Millions of people have been rescued from destitution by social grants. We showed the world what we are capable of when we hosted the 2010 World Cup: the new stadiums, the upgraded airports, and the improved roads. Great changes have brought significant improvements to the lives of millions and rebuilt social, cultural, political, economic, and faith paradigms.

However, those very achievements, in showing what is possible, highlight where we have failed to live up to our potential. Despite the changes, despite the talk, despite the policies we advocate, levels of inequality in our society remain shocking. There are huge differences between the development of the wealthy parts of our cities and that of nearly everywhere else. We have failed to eliminate the desperate conditions in which many of our people live, creating potential for an explosion of anger. Many of us operate in separate spheres, held apart from one another in the silos in which we lived and worked before 1994. We live with massive disparities of income, largely based on race but increasingly based on whether you have made it into the middle class. Government programs to empower black South Africans economically meant to close the gap between the rich and the poor instead often contribute to inequality, with the children of the rich likely to enjoy a good education and thus good lives, and the children of the poor often condemned to failing schools and a self-perpetuating cycle of poverty. It sometimes feels as if some of our leaders stopped their struggle for a new South Africa at the point at which they joined the ranks of those who corruptly and immorally amassed wealth in the previous dispensation.

Every day we read about pervasive inequality in the delivery
of government services. We are failing the unemployed and
underemployed. Despite the promise of equal treatment in the
South African constitution, gay and lesbian people are persecuted,
even subjected to physical abuse—a result of attitudes that
are often tolerated within religious communities. Women are
disrespected and abused because of the inequalities that plague
their lives, with domestic abuse at the hands of spouses running
at shocking levels.

But the greatest inequality in South African society today is
the inequality of opportunity. Access to basic services such as
education, including early childhood development, health care,
running water, sanitation, and electricity provides an individual,
irrespective of background, the opportunity to advance and reach
her or his unique human potential. But that access, an important
predictor of future outcomes, is not the same for everyone.

The solution to our problems does not lie simply in replacing one
leader with another or one party in government with another.
The challenges we confront demand a comprehensive campaign
joined by churches, temples, mosques, synagogues, and the
rest of civil society. Such a campaign needs to be based on an
overarching vision, a vision of biblical scope and proportions, that
roots it in the sure belief that although we may be going through
bumpy turbulence in our national life now, we can realize the
values embedded in our constitution—that we can indeed build
a united, democratic nation in which we heal the divisions of the
past and establish a society based on democratic values, social
justice, and fundamental human rights, a society that improves
the quality of life of all citizens and, by establishing equality of
opportunity, will free the God-given potential of each person.

I call such a campaign "the new struggle" in South Africa. The
new struggle, as opposed to the old struggle, the great struggle

against apartheid, acknowledges that in many ways we stand where we stood before the advent of democracy. The new struggle repudiates the values that underpinned colonialism and apartheid: narrow self-interest, callous selfishness, and the pursuit of personal gain, of power, status, and material wealth, regardless of the consequences for other people or our planet. The new struggle is for a new society, a more equal society, a society of equality of opportunity in which the wealth that comes from new economic growth is shared equitably among all.

At the level of fundamental human values, the new struggle is about replacing "me" with "we" in our thinking about the nature and future of our society. Sadly, we have to acknowledge that we live in a society of "me." Over the past two decades, we have lost many of our traditional values, and our culture now tends to organize itself around and reward the "me." In our consumer culture, "we" isn't popular. We are slipping away from the values of ubuntu. In a "me" society, we ask: What are "my" and my family's and friends' needs and aspirations, not what are "our" needs and aspirations. When Madiba died, the topmost leaders of one of our cities diverted money meant for arrangements for his funeral to their friends and for their own personal gain. That reflected the values of people who are living in a society of "me."

For South Africa to flourish, we need to move from "me" to "we," asking not what *I* can do, but what *we* can do, together, to meet not my needs or those of my immediate circle but our needs, to work together for the common good. We-focused societies bring out the best in their citizens. We-centered leaders are characterized by caring, courage, and vision. Environments that foster we-centered behaviors encourage diversity of thought and expression of feeling. They encourage risk taking and tolerate "failure." We cultures support sharing. They are dedicated to fairness and the achievement of the full potential within everyone. They open opportunity.

To pursue the new struggle, we need a new, inclusive process of negotiation, including capital, labor, government, and civil society, to rethink our policies on the economy and land. As I said when preaching at Easter Vigil at St. George's Cathedral in 2017, we need to overcome the skewed racial ordering of our economy and the obscene inequality it produces, not by indulging the rapacious greed of a few politically connected individuals but by building a new, fairer society that distributes wealth more equitably for all. That is not to say I support the seizure of assets or of land that is being used productively nor the expropriation of land without due process. Our constitution allows for mechanisms of orderly restitution, and I am aware from our experience in Makgoba's Kloof of the difficulties of taking over land and using it effectively. But the Mandela and Mbeki administrations showed that if government convenes representatives of different interest groups, we can find rational, workable solutions to our most difficult problems. (The full text of the Easter sermon is Appendix F.)

We in the churches and the wider faith community have a role as bridge-builders in helping to address the challenges South Africa faces. In saying this, I acknowledge that although we are institutions inspired by the divine, we are led by mortal, frail human beings. In some scandalous instances publicized recently, some among our number have discredited us by making their followers eat grass or drink gasoline. When it comes to the promotion of human rights, we have an uneven record. While the Anglican Church unanimously condemns the ill-treatment of people on the grounds of their sexual orientation, we are divided on the issue of blessing single-sex marriages. My own belief is that we have not yet shown adequate respect for the integrity of committed, loving relationships between gay and lesbian couples. We have done better in recognizing the untapped potential of women; I am proud that dioceses in Swaziland and the Western Cape were the first in Africa to elect women bishops. And we

Dedicating a plaque at Bishopscourt that honors the first day Nelson Mandela woke up as a free man after being imprisoned for twenty-seven years.

have made an important contribution to the worldwide Anglican Communion by introducing just the kind of bridge-building dialogue I am proposing for South Africa. When the communion was beset with conflicting views on ministry to gay and lesbian Christians, we told our fellow Anglicans in other countries that God understands isiZulu too, and we could take a page out of African tradition by dealing with our differences through a process of *indaba* or dialogue based on an African model. Freed from past colonial constraints, empowered by our cultural and linguistic richness, we are able to draw on our indigenous tradition and propose a new form of leadership, one in which we listen to one another carefully and seek solutions based on consensus. (More on this in the next chapter.)

We have to acknowledge that the new struggle will not be easy. If we are to wage it effectively and realize Madiba's vision for South Africa and the world, both white and black South Africans need to emulate the courage that his faith gave him; the courage that made him prepared to sacrifice the interests of his family and his liberty and to risk his life to pursue his vision. It was courage that ignited the old struggle and kept it burning until we emerged from the darkness of apartheid. Thousands laid down their lives or sacrificed their liberty so their families and their communities could reap the benefits of democracy. My ministry to Madiba reminded me, to paraphrase one of his best-known sayings, that courage is not the absence of fear but the capacity to triumph over it.

I am concerned that except for a few white clerics in the churches, white South African leaders— particularly in business—have lost the confidence to speak their minds and criticize. They have been made to feel excessively guilty and scared, as if they are second-class citizens in South Africa, and they have recoiled into a fear reminiscent of the apartheid years. In a few years they may be saying, just as they did after apartheid, that "we did not know." When whites keep silent for fear of being branded racists, they fail to contribute to solving our problems. Likewise, when black South Africans keep quiet for fear of being penalized in some way—or because they worry that white racists will exploit differences between blacks—they, too, fail to help solve our problems. Our future lies in the ability of both black and white South Africans to be critical and vocal and to work alongside the poor and speak boldly to power.

It also worries me that some young black South Africans in the universities cannot be bothered with non-racialism. South Africa has a core of good, able people, both black and white, rich and poor, who can help resolve our problems, and apart from the important issue of principle involved, at a practical level we cannot afford to trash the contributions of anyone.

We face, and we will face for some years to come, a crisis in governance and the economy. Most of our political leaders, embroiled in intra-party and inter-party squabbling, don't seem to have a vision or any sense of destiny, let alone practical plans of action they are truly committed to implementing. But we need not despair. Our people showed enormous resilience against much greater odds during the old struggle. From them, from Madiba, from generations past, I have learned never to lose hope. I am not speaking of hope in the sense of an anesthetic administered to dull the throbbing pain of the everyday reality of inequality and indifference to suffering. As the eminent South African feminist theologian Denise Ackermann says, hope "is not that blithe sense that all will end well...because human progress is guaranteed." No, hope is a determination, a conviction that seeks to name our problems and highlight our differences, precisely in order to mobilize people to overcome them. As Denise adds: "To live out my hope is to try to make that which I hope for come about— sooner rather than later." It is "never to surrender our power to imagine a better world." We must not only remain hopeful but take it upon ourselves to take action to resolve our challenges.

The crisis South Africa is experiencing is one of those epochs in our nation's history that will mark a significant turning point. Whether the turn is for good or for ill will depend on us, on our beliefs and actions. Human progress is never guaranteed unless there is struggle. Every step we take toward the goal of ending inequality requires sacrifice, suffering, and most of all struggle. If there is no struggle, there is no progress. Madiba and his compatriots in the struggle for freedom and justice may have not been overt in declaring their creeds, but they had a mature faith, one that exuded the kind of hope that, requiring patience and endurance, confronts wrong and the abuse of power. On top of that, they had a child-like courage that overcame fear and refused to be trapped in preconceived stereotypes of who people are and what can and cannot be achieved. Their faith and courage provided them with the resilience and resources they needed to point others to places they had not been. They can point us now to where we want to take our country and our world.

Afterword

A Young Palestinian on a Donkey

Reconciliation in Church and Society: Reflections for the Anglican Communion

On a visit to New York recently, I could not but help reflect on how closely the Anglican Communion's history across the globe is bound up with the spread of European colonialism and its effects on the indigenous peoples who were subjugated by British and other settlers as they took over their land.

I was staying in downtown Manhattan with Lungi and Paballo, courtesy of Trinity Church Wall Street, in a guest apartment near the East River, and we decided to visit the New York branch of the National Museum of the American Indian. Part of the famed Smithsonian Institution, the museum is a few minutes' walk down Broadway, past Trinity. My wife and daughter, being more creative, were fascinated by the fine artwork, clothing, and artifacts on display from peoples in different parts of the Americas. I was captured by the ceremonial rituals and dance depicted on a screen and found some of the movements interestingly similar to those of the rural baPedi at home. Also similar was the way in which European missionaries had conflated Western culture with the gospel, outlawing the traditional cultural practices of indigenous peoples after branding them as "dancing with the devil." But what finished me completely was moving on to another exhibition space, where I read afresh of how the indigenous people of the Americas were "extinguished" not so long ago. Just as settlers from another continent had progressively fought and dispossessed, group by group, the original inhabitants of Southern Africa during the eighteenth and nineteenth centuries, so had they done the same in the United States. In South Africa, my people, baTlou, had been among the last to be defeated, ending with the killing and decapitation of my great-grandfather, Mamphoku, in 1895. In the United States, what historians have called "the last 'frontier' war" took place only five years earlier, when somewhere between 150 and 300 men, women and children of the Lakota people of the Sioux nation were massacred in the Battle of Wounded Knee, the event which is said to have marked "the symbolic end of Indian freedom."[123]

The day after visiting the Indian museum, I went out again to learn about another aspect of American history. This time I went on my own, walking north up Broadway to the African Burial Ground National Monument. The monument has been built on part of what was called the "Negroes Buriel (sic) Ground" in the seventeenth and eighteenth centuries. The graves lay forgotten for up to two hundred years, until 1991 when they were rediscovered thirty feet below street level during the construction of a new government office tower. Work was stopped, and the remains of hundreds of enslaved and free Africans were exhumed and taken to Howard University in Washington for research. In 2003 the skeletal remains of 419 people were ceremoniously returned to New York in hand-carved coffins. As the cortège processed

123 Howard Lamar and Leonard Thompson (1981). *The Frontier in History: North America and Southern Africa Compared* (New Haven: Yale University Press), 32, 208.

up Wall Street from the East River and turned the corner into Broadway, Trinity—the only community institution that had existed when the Africans in the coffins had been alive—tolled its bells to commemorate their reburial. At the Burial Ground, the coffins were re-interred in seven crypts that were lowered into the ground. They are now marked by re-burial mounds.[124]

Compared to the Genocide Memorial I visited in Rwanda, where the exhibits include piles of skulls and bones of victims, the New York monument is sanitized. There are photos of the remains as they were exhumed, but I wished that at least one bare bone or exhumed grave had been left visible. However, what did touch me was how the researchers at Howard had been able to assign some identity to individuals by analyzing their DNA and studying their bones and teeth, finding indications of where they came from, whether they died at the same time because of disease, and how old they were (most lived at most to the age of about fifty-five).

At the museum and going online afterwards, the similarities between the South African and the American experiences of colonialism and slavery became clear. When the Englishman Henry Hudson arrived to explore the channels around present-day New York in 1609, he was employed by the Dutch East India Company, and fifteen years later it was the Dutch West India Company that first colonized the island. Thirty years after that, the Dutch East India Company colonized what is now Cape Town. The main source of enslaved Africans shipped into New York by the Dutch was what is now the west African country of

124 Gwynned Cannan (2003). Unearthing Our Past, in Trinity News, Vol. 50, No. 4, Winter 2003 (New York: Parish of Trinity Church), 12; Website of the African Burial Ground, National Park Service: https://www.nps.gov/afbg/learn/historyculture/reinterment.htm [Accessed July 30, 2018]

Angola (now part of our Anglican Province in southern Africa). After the British took over the colony and renamed it New York, the slaving net was spread to incorporate West Africa and, at one stage, Madagascar.[125] Under Dutch rule, Cape Town initially received shipments of enslaved people from Angola and West Africa; later they came from Madagascar, the East African coast, India, and the Indonesian archipelago.[126]

Closer to home for the Anglican Communion, the church was deeply complicit in the evil of slavery. Before the middle of the eighteenth century, the system was viewed as a fact of life in England, and the Church of England was stained by its involvement in it, especially in the Caribbean.[127] In the United States many Episcopal churches were built using enslaved labor, and Episcopalians, including George Washington, were slave holders.[128] In Southern Africa the Anglican church escaped complicity in slavery perhaps only because we were established after its abolition, but the nineteenth-century missionaries suppressed African culture and often behaved as the religious arm of British colonial oppression.

Recently I learned firsthand of how even in South America, which was not colonized by the British, Anglicans are as ambivalent as we are in Africa about the influence of missionaries. In 2018, I visited Chile as part of a delegation looking into the request of the

125 Edna Greene Medford, Ed. (2009). *Historical Perspectives of the African Burial Ground: New York Blacks and the Diaspora*. (Washington D.C.: Howard University Press), 9, 25.
126 Richard Elphick and Herman Giliomee, eds. (1989). *The Shaping of South African Society, 1652-1840*. (Cape Town: Maskew Miller Longman), 109-121.
127 James Walvin (2008). *Slavery, the Slave Trade and the Churches*, Quaker Studies: Vol. 12: Iss. 2, Article 3. Available at: http://digitalcommons.georgefox.edu/quakerstudies/vol12/iss2/
128 Episcopal News Service, February 20, 2017: https://www.episcopalnewsservice. org/2017/02/20/national-cathedral-continues-to-debate-the-lee-jackson-windows/ [Accessed August 5, 2018]; George Washington's Mount Vernon: https://www.mountvernon.org/george-washington/slavery/ten-facts-about-washington-slavery/ [Accessed August 5, 2018]

church there to form its own province in the Communion.[129] I was part of a group that visited an area in which the Mapuche people, Chile's largest indigenous ethnic group, are well-represented in the church. Just as in South Africa, the church in Chile has helped since the nineteenth century to bring education and healthcare to the Mapuche, but also as in South Africa, they feel to some extent that in the process they lost their language and their land. So now they are fighting to reclaim both the language and the land.

When discussing what I was going to say in this chapter, I was asked: Given the history of your own people, given the suffering inflicted on the original inhabitants of Africa, Asia, and the Americas by interlopers who proclaimed themselves Christian, why would you choose to be a Christian?

It's a profound question but one with a simple answer: I am a Christian, and I remain a Christian because I remember that our faith begins with a young Palestinian on a donkey. I draw this phrase, and some of my reflections on it, from the memoir written by Denise Ackermann entitled *Surprised by the Man on the Borrowed Donkey*.[130] The image conjured up by Denise's title tells me that since Roman times, we have perverted the Word and the mission of Jesus Christ and its message about what God is up to in our world. Over the centuries, we've allowed ourselves to be pointed to imperial agendas. Christ's message has been attached to national flags, to military might, and to the AK-47. But that is not the gospel. Christianity is not imperialism. Christianity is not colonialism. Christianity is loving our neighbors as ourselves. The man who links us to God is he who enters Jerusalem a nonentity, riding a borrowed donkey. He is humble, and he is marginalized,

---

129 Anglican Communion News Service, August 15, 2018: http://www.anglicannews.org/news/2018/08/anglican-consultative-council-chair-expresses-hope-of-provincial-status-for-chile.aspx
130 Denise Ackermann (2014). *Surprised by the Man on the Borrowed Donkey: Ordinary Blessings.* (Cape Town: Lux Verbi).

but his message of love and simplicity is powerful; powerful enough to challenge the perversion of common humanity that empire engenders. It tells the Roman Empire that God's kingdom is not about creating an economic system that crushes an agrarian people. The Christian identity I aspire to is one of equality, harmony, reconciliation, truth, and, indeed, one of turning the other cheek. For me, that is more persuasive and forceful than the values of those who hold secular power.

Moreover, the fact that Christianity was introduced to our part of Africa by people with mixed motives does not determine who we are as people of faith today. Many of the early church fathers—Athanasius of Alexandria, Augustine of Hippo, Cyprian of Carthage, Origen and Tertullian—were African. Farther south on the continent, the churches in Nubia and Aksum were not the product of Western evangelization; they were there before Augustine of Canterbury was enthroned.[131]

So I consider myself a proudly African Christian. That being the case, how do I and other African Christians join with those in other continents today as we seek to promote the kingdom of God in church and society? To return to the questions I asked in the first chapter, can there really be closure for us all? How do the original inhabitants of colonized continents deal with the pain we feel when we see the descendants of settlers prospering on our land? More specifically, what do we as Anglicans have to offer in promoting reconciliation in and between our nations and within the Anglican Communion?

In South Africa, we began to address these questions under the leadership of Nelson Mandela by adopting a new constitution that enshrined some key fundamentals: We explicitly recognized the injustices and resolved not to repeat the atrocities of the

---

131 Bengt Sundkler and Christopher Steed (2000). *The History of the Church in Africa.* (Cambridge: Cambridge University Press), 30-37.

past; we committed ourselves to democratic freedoms and respect for human dignity; and we said we wanted equality for all. In one of the first steps we took, we established a Truth and Reconciliation Commission to investigate the human rights abuses of the apartheid era and to grant amnesty to perpetrators who came forward to confess to their crimes. The process had its weaknesses, and the commission is criticized in the country today, but I give thanks for its work and for the role of Desmond Tutu in presiding over it. It was very important in entrenching the values of our constitution right from the beginning of our democracy. Thousands of survivors and victims came forward to report what happened to them. Many hundreds had the opportunity to give evidence in public hearings covered extensively on radio and television. The telling of those stories had a cathartic effect that cannot be nullified; one can't even quantify the immense difference that those hearings made in the healing of our country.

We have been remiss, however, in not pursuing the process of reconciliation adequately since the commission delivered its report. The generation of young people who have not had the opportunity to listen to the testimony and to learn where our society comes from is becoming impatient about our lack of progress toward real equality of opportunity. We need to commemorate the stories of our past, to tell them again and again, to broadcast them on radio and make them available on apps for mobile phones—not to lull the young into a sense of complacency about our progress but to understand how far we have come and why we should not respond to our current challenges by repeating the mistakes of the past. Above all, we should not underestimate the threat to true reconciliation posed by the gap between rich and poor. I have said that we cannot witness to Christ's saving, forgiving, and reconciling love for all people without being concerned by the stubborn persistence of what I call inter-generational inequality in South Africa, in which those who are likely to flourish in our society are the sons and daughters of the elite, while the children of the poor struggle to break out of a vicious cycle of poverty and are condemned to getting the crumbs that fall from the tables of the wealthy.

It is up to readers living in other countries to discern what is needed to build reconciliation within your societies and to engage in dialogue with those in other countries on how to effect reconciliation between nations. But a crucial first step is having the courage to name the past and to own the pain that has been caused by treating others as being less than human. The Church of England used the opportunity of the 200th anniversary of the abolition of the slavery trade in 1807 to apologize for its role.[132] The Episcopal Church followed in 2008, when it put on record its "profound regret that the...Church lent the institution of slavery its support and justification based on Scripture." At the same time, then-Presiding Bishop Katharine Jefferts Schori acknowledged that Americans were not adequately teaching their children about "the sins of this nation: enslavement of Native Americans by early colonists; northern involvement in the African slave trade; the wretched excesses of plantation slavery; or the institutionalized criminalization of black life in the south after the Civil War."[133]

More recently, Episcopal parishes and institutions have joined the debate in the American South and beyond over the commemoration of leaders of the Confederate states that fought in the Civil War of 1861 to 1865 in defense of the right of states to retain slavery.[134] Washington National Cathedral removed portrayals of the Confederate battle flag in stained glass

132 Jeremy M. Bergen (2011). *Ecclesial Repentance: The Churches Confront Their Sinful Past.* (New York: T&T Clark), 78-79.
133 Episcopal News Service, October 4, 2008: http://archive.episcopalchurch.org/79425_101324_ENG_HTM.htm; Homily at Service of Repentance, St. Thomas, Philadelphia, 4 October 2008: http://archive.episcopalchurch.org/documents/Sermon_by_KJS_10-4.pdf [Accessed August 5, 2018]
134 Episcopal News Service, August 25, 2017: https://www.episcopalnewsservice.org/2017/08/25/pressure-mounts-to-remove-confederate-symbols-from-episcopal-institutions/ [Accessed August 5, 2018]

windows commemorating Confederate generals, then decided
to do away with the windows themselves.[135] In Cincinnati,
Christ Church Cathedral initiated a process reminiscent of
that at our cathedral in Makhanda over the memorial to John
Graham; in Cincinnati, the vestry decided to replace a stained
glass window depicting Confederate General Robert E. Lee and
a plaque honoring Leonidas Polk, an Episcopal bishop who also
served as a Confederate general. In their stead will be images of
abolitionists Harriet Tubman and Frederick Douglass. Trinity Wall
Street has documented its interactions with enslaved Africans,
from enlisting slave labor in the building of its first church
to providing catechism classes and at times to implementing
segregation in parish churchyards, probably reinforcing the need
for the development of the separate African Burial Ground.[136]
Of this period in the parish's history, Trinity's current rector, Bill
Lupfer, has observed that "it's important for us to be honest about
our past. We were comfortable making a distinction between
pastoral care and social advocacy, and so we cared for people who
were slaves pastorally, but we didn't do the tough work of social
advocacy to abolish slavery...We need to acknowledge that Trinity
was involved in slavery...that we benefited from that brokenness,
and that we have work to do...to help heal that brokenness. There
are no excuses."[137]

During my visit to New York, I read one of the seminal texts of
the American civil rights struggle, Martin Luther King Jr.'s "Letter
from a Birmingham Jail."[138] The 1963 letter is a reply to a public
statement by eight liberal Alabama religious leaders, headed

---

135 Episcopal News Service, September 6, 2017: https://www.episcopalnewsservice.
org/2017/09/06/46437/ [Accessed August 5, 2018]
136 Cannan (2004), 14-15.
137 *The Shadow of Slavery,* January 19, 2016. Trinity Video production for Sacred Conversations
for Racial Justice, Trinity Institute 2016. Available at: https://www.trinitywallstreet.org/video/
shadow-slavery
138 Martin Luther King, Jr. (1992). *I Have a Dream: Writings and Speeches That Changed the World.*
Edited by James M. Washington. (San Francisco: HarperSanFrancisco), 86-100.

by the Episcopal bishop of Alabama, opposing demonstrations against racism in Birmingham, Alabama, and urging local black leaders to repudiate outsiders such as King and instead to rely on court action and local negotiations to achieve desegregation. King's response, defending non-violent direct action and voicing his disappointment with "the white moderate," pierced my soul, mirroring as it did our experiences in the Anglican and other churches under apartheid. Recalling our disappointment with liberals, the pain caused by their inaction, and the betrayal by an established church of the cause of the poor, I felt strongly for King and his sadness. His letter will stay with me for years, saying as it does that the key to overcoming injustice and becoming a tool for reconciliation is to summon up the faith and courage to overcome inaction and fear in the face of division and suspicion.

Whether we live in Africa, South America, the United Kingdom, the United States, or elsewhere, the painful truths of our past have to be shared for healing and thus reconciliation to happen. When we say hello to someone in South Africa's most widely used language, isiZulu, we say "Sawobona!" Literally translated, we are saying, "I see you!" The reply is also "Sawobona!" "And I see you!" Reaching across the barriers that divide us within and between our societies involves saying to one another, "I see you!" During the General Convention of the Episcopal Church in Texas in 2018, which I attended with a number of other archbishops in the communion, a group went to a small town nearby to hold a service in support of women locked up in a detention center for allegedly entering the U.S. illegally. I tagged along as a small group of singing and praying protesters went as close to the center as the police would allow. I wondered whether the detainees were even aware of our presence until someone inside held up what appeared to be a sheet of white paper behind the slits in the wall; in response to our message saying, "We see you!" she was responding, "And I see you!"

The false narratives of the past can be corrected only if we share with others our own understanding of it. Also while in New York, I listened to a National Public Radio podcast of a program that, surprisingly to me, suggested that Americans are lagging behind the Germans in commemorating the darker parts of their history.[139] In Germany, I heard, concrete swastikas were destroyed and some buildings were blown up, just as statues are being pulled down and windows and plaques removed in the United States. But in Berlin and other cities, there has also been a focus on creating new memorials; for example, the enormous Memorial to the Murdered Jews of Europe and the Stolpersteine or "stumbling stones" scattered across cities outside the former homes of Nazi victims, concrete cubes carrying brass plates inscribed with their names. Now, in Montgomery, Alabama, a city that was for a time the capital of the Confederacy, an organization called the Equal Justice Initiative has recently remedied what it sees as a gap in the commemoration of American history by establishing The Legacy Museum and The National Memorial for Peace and Justice.[140] The museum and the memorial aim to "motivate people to say never again to this history of enslavement and lynching and segregation."[141]

Creating cultural spaces such as the Apartheid Museum in Johannesburg, the Genocide Memorial in Kigali, the African Burial Ground monument in New York, and the memorial in Montgomery can be a powerful way of owning and making visible our history, teaching society how ideologies based on the dehumanization of one group of God's children by another lead to terrible practices that poison human relations for generations

---

139 *The Worst Thing We've Ever Done,* On the Media, June 1, 2018: https://www.wnycstudios.org/story/on-the-media-2018-06-01/ [Accessed June 21, 2018]

140 Website: https://museumandmemorial.eji.org/

141 Bryan Stevenson, founder of the Equal Justice Initiative, in "The Worst Thing We've Ever Done," *On the Media,* June 1, 2018.

to come. And who is better placed than the Church to shine a light into the dark recesses of our history, to promote discussion and discernment of how to bring about healing, and to find mechanisms for moving forward? Our work should not be limited to memorials and exhibitions: We can lobby for place and street names to be changed to reflect the contributions of past generations who were extinguished or displaced, we can campaign for the restoration of land and for reparations, even if they are token, and we can work for the more equitable sharing of resources to bring about justice for those who were previously persecuted and discriminated against.

However, the Anglican Communion is not at present setting a good example to the world about how to achieve reconciliation. Our continuing differences over human sexuality detract from the credibility of our efforts in wider society, and if we are to overcome them, Anglicans in Africa need to take the lead. As African Christians who belong to a global family, we really need to have the confidence in our vocation to become bridge-builders for the Communion, not by lording it over others but by rejecting the trappings and glitter of power and rekindling the identity assumed by that young Palestinian fellow on a donkey.

When I became Archbishop of Cape Town in 2008, Anglicans in Southern Africa, and especially in South Africa, were seen as not quite African by our brothers and sisters elsewhere on the continent. That was partly our fault as South Africans; isolated and prohibited from traveling to liberated nations during apartheid, we tended to see them as part of a different world and were insensitive to the nature of the struggles of their citizens. The mobilization of resources against apartheid in the West did not help: The assistance we were given, as well as Desmond Tutu's popularity, led to other Africans feeling they were going unrecognized and not being taken seriously. But the insensitivity cut both ways. We felt isolated by attitudes toward us: that we spoke English "like it's coming out of your nostrils," as I was once told; that we had imbibed English mannerisms; and that we were less African because our skin color was brown, white, or a lighter hue of black than that of people farther to the north.

At times I found attitudes toward us hurtful, and there may have been times when I hurt others. But when I took office, I resolved that just as I have visited places in the West that were uncomfortable for me as an African, I will visit places in Africa that are uncomfortable for me as a South African. I decided that I would bring who I am, warts and all, created by God as a child of God, to other provinces of the Communion on the continent. As a result I have taken a personal interest in the proceedings of the Council of Anglican Provinces of Africa (CAPA). And as primates in other provinces have reached retirement age, as the senior primate on the continent, I have attended as many enthronements of their successors as my schedule has allowed.

On recent trips to the installations of new primates in the Democratic Republic of Congo, in South Sudan, and in Rwanda, I have begun to wonder whether we as African Anglicans are adequately reflecting African values. At all the services, we've had representatives from different strands of thought and organization among the world's Anglicans: bishops who have attended or will attend the Lambeth Conference; bishops who have boycotted Lambeth but attended sessions of the Global Anglican Future Conference (GAFCON, whose mission is "to retain and restore the Bible to the heart of the Anglican Communion"); bishops who have attended both; and bishops from churches such as the Anglican Church in North America (ACNA), who are not recognized by the Archbishop of Canterbury as part of the Anglican Communion at all. As we have mingled at the services, the dinners, and the receptions, negotiating the sensitivities of a divided Communion, I have wondered: Surely we are missing opportunities if we don't engage each other. Does GAFCON

242   Faith & Courage

have to be treated as an organization outside the structure of the
Communion? Should we be deciding who is "in" and who is
"out" on the basis of rules? Aren't we wanting to over-legislate?
Has GAFCON a role to play representing the views of substantial
numbers of like-thinking Anglicans? In relation to Rwanda, have
we ever really considered the implications of the horrific genocide
in Rwanda, of the pain of being excluded from humanity as the
world looked the other way? Are we serious about reconciliation,
or do we hope the groups that represent points of view different
from ours will wither away and die? Where do I stand amidst
this mess?

In Africa we say in isiZulu, Umuntu Ngumuntu Ngabantu, which
can be translated variously as "A person is a person because of
other persons," or "I am because we are." This means that I cannot
be fully human unless your humanity is fully recognized. As
Africans, we aspire to organize ourselves as human beings on the
basis of relationship rather than structure or legislation. We need
legislation, yes, but it doesn't win friendship. Jesus said: "Do not
think that I have come to abolish the law or the prophets; I have
come not to abolish but to fulfill" (Matthew 5:17). And how does
Jesus tell me, Thabo, to fulfill the law? Not primarily by following
rules. Rather by loving God with all my heart and all my soul and
all my mind, and by loving my neighbor as myself. "On these two
commandments hang all the law and the prophets" (Matthew
22:37-40). Since I was a child I have been challenged by another
biblical example of the importance of relationship: When I bring
my gift to the altar, I cannot offer it to God unless I have made
amends with a brother or sister with whom I have a disagreement
(Matthew 5:23-24). That is radical. Even the religious practice
of worshiping God is secondary to walking with and being
reconciled to my fellow Christian.

The story of how Cleopas and his companion recognized Jesus
after his resurrection resonates powerfully for me as an African.

When they met him on the road to Emmaus, they walked and talked with him for ages before realizing who he was—and when they did so, it was only when they sat down to a meal together. Back in Jerusalem, they declared to the disciples "how he had been made known to them in the breaking of the bread" (Luke 24: 30-35). In Africa, food is at the center of human interaction. When you are making a pastoral visit and are offered food, you can't say no—even if you have just been well fed at a big reception nearby. You might have to explain why you are just nibbling, but you can't decline the offer. By eating their food, you are showing you respect them, that even if they cannot afford an elaborate meal, you are honoring them by recognizing their hospitality. As you converse, you might be told how the meal was prepared, perhaps that it is the first meal after the harvest and what has gone into bringing it to table. In the breaking of the bread together in the home, we gain deeper knowledge about one another, and we fulfill the biblical mandate of the presence of communion. We've made communion so structured and formal that we often forget that it is about *koinonia*—it's about fellowship. The fellowship we enjoy when we break bread together during worship is at the heart of the sacrament of Holy Eucharist. So when archbishops say the fabric of the Communion is broken, and therefore they are going to boycott the eucharist, I find it mindboggling.

If we are to bring African values to the Communion, surely we should maintain ties of fellowship, using those attributes that come naturally to us: forming relationships, wrestling with one another, not running away from one another. Can we not just move forward through this mess, not looking for instant solutions but doing the best we can, step by step? Growing up in the appalling conditions of Alexandra, where you might come upon a corpse in the mud on the way to church on a Sunday morning, has probably affected not only my faith and my spirituality but also how I do theology. The experience of getting up in the morning and being able to put on a clean white shirt and walk past a dead body on the way to worship has enabled me to say: *I'm not perfect, my surroundings and the world are not perfect, but can we just get on with the business of living, of enabling God's people and affirming those we can affirm?* Surely we can find a way of saying, "Can we walk together even if we don't agree?" Before I began to attend CAPA meetings regularly, I was anxious at the prospect, but when I went and shared meals with my colleagues, as we shared bread together and shared worship together, I formed relationships which, in spite of our differences on some issues, have become strong.

Instead of being divisive and rigid, as Africans we should build bridges and challenge those who want to organize themselves on the basis of excluding others. That is the currency truly needed in the Anglican Communion. The provinces of Africa constitute a substantial part of the Anglican world; surely Burundi, Central Africa, Congo, the Indian Ocean, Kenya, Nigeria, Rwanda, Southern Africa, South Sudan, Sudan, Tanzania, Uganda, West Africa, and now possibly the Horn of Africa can bring our gift of friendship to the Communion and elevate the wider body to a higher level of *koinonia*, even on issues on which we don't agree such as human sexuality. Building bridges doesn't take away the core of who we are in Christ.

I see no prospect of bridging our differences over human sexuality if we continue on our current path, on which partisans on both sides are saying to the other: You are not wanting to listen to our story and hear of our pain. We need to change course: We are sent to go and make disciples and to baptize people in the name of the Father, the Son, and the Holy Spirit, not to put them in a particular box. Wherever we stand on the spectrum about our views on sexuality, our principal obligation is to bring God's love and care to others in our own missional context, without spending inordinate amounts of time trying to shift the views of others who have a completely different context in which to minister and who are not interested in shifting. I don't think that is being good stewards of our time and resources.

We have to acknowledge on the one hand that most provinces of the Communion are of a common mind on their canons on marriage: They have no desire to change them, and therefore there is no prospect of getting agreement across the Communion to change the position that marriage is the union only of a man and a woman. On the other hand, we need to accept that other provinces minister in a context in which same-sex unions are accepted and even recognized in civil law. Among the members of congregations in those provinces are couples of the same sex who seek the pastoral care of the church, not as sinners but as people created by God the way they are. My mind struggles to understand how I can refuse pastoral ministry to a baptized child of God living in a faithful, monogamous relationship with his or her partner who seeks God's blessing on that relationship.

I believe there is a consensus building across most provinces of the Communion that we need to break away from being bogged down in the debate over human sexuality and focus instead on the critical issues of mission and ministry that we face in our different contexts. We need to respect our differences—and we can't do that if we put one another in boxes and become entrenched in them. We can do this by adopting a new Anglican *via media*, a middle way that bridges the divide. We can agree to disagree by treating same-sex unions not as a church-dividing matter but as one of pastoral accommodation to the needs of each individual province. The majority will say there is no pressure from within to change their position or even to think about it; they have other, much bigger priorities. But those provinces for which ministry to the gay and lesbian community is a high priority should be able to minister to that community as they see fit.

What is at the heart of reconciliation? In its essence, it can be summed up in three "Rs": remedying brokenness, removing tensions, and righting wrongs. Once we realize that something is not going well in a community, whether in society or the church, we need to deal with the brokenness and address both the tensions that caused it and the further tensions to which it led. We can't just say, "Let's vote. Are you in or out?" That is not taking the theological concept of atonement seriously. From the beginning, when God created us and then we strayed away from God, we see repeatedly in the Old Testament how God called us back again and again. At the same time we also need to right the wrongs that we may have committed. I have to ask, how do I as Thabo, for whom Christ died, deal with my part in creating the brokenness and the tension? I need to acknowledge my role, admit that I have wronged others and broken relationship. For the sake of the community, I and all those who have contributed to the brokenness need to confess our part in it and ask for the forgiveness of others and of God. Then, not out of guilt but in the spirit of wanting to build this community for God, we need to accept the forgiveness and move on. We need to seek the roads we can build together so that we can move forward.

Reconciliation is not easy. Achieving it will involve being hurt and feeling rejected at times. But it is urgent that we ask: What is our part in responding to God's love for us, demonstrated in giving his Son, Jesus Christ, to call us from our lostness? And as we respond, there is no need to be anxious, for in the final analysis, reconciliation is not really our process—it is God's process, it is grace, and it is offered to us, as Christ prays in John 17 his high priestly prayer, that we should become one as he is one with God.

Appendix A

Mandela Day Pledge at the Human Chain

Cape Town, July 18, 2013

I, one link in this human chain, pledge to do all I can to build an undivided South Africa free from poverty as envisioned by Nelson Mandela.

I will observe and study his conduct and seek to emulate his actions that have helped to bring peace to our country.

A simple smile, a handshake, kindness, a listening ear, encouragement, spreading hope, giving a helping hand, taking action, not tearing down another—that is the Madiba way.

I reject anything or anyone who seeks to demean or to divide us and place our focus only on the ugliness that forms part of our lives.

Instead of focusing on ugliness and hatred, I choose to focus on beauty and love.

By doing this, I will have the strength to deal with the difficult challenges that I face to make Madiba's dream a reality.

I am committed to being the best person I can possibly be. The stronger I am the more I can help heal my family and my neighborhood.

I am committed to the values of our constitution, which says that our country belongs to all who live in it.

We have in Madiba one of the world's greatest leaders. It is not always in the life of a people that they are so blessed with inspirational and visionary leadership.

Madiba's maternal side is Khoisan, the earliest people who lived at the Cape, at least 2,000 years ago. His paternal side is Xhosa, whose people intermingled with the Khoisan over many centuries.

The merging of these two strong human strands has given us a leader who has not flinched in his resolve to set us free.

I commit to encourage all of those whom I come into contact with to study and emulate his conduct so that we draw on the positive example he has set for us, and never forget that our fragile psyches need nurturing and tenderness to bring healing to our tortured nation.

I am proud of how far we have journeyed on the road to self-determination as a people and will continue always to be inspired by his example.

Appendix B

Celebrating Madiba's Legacy and Its Lasting Impact around the Globe

Cape Town, December 8, 2013

A homily delivered on the Day of Prayer and Reflection for Nelson Mandela

May I speak in the name of God who created us; whose righteousness recreates us and his presence sustains us. Amen.

People of Holy Cross, what a joy to be with you this morning on this the second Sunday in Advent. On January 1, 2014, it will be my seventh year as archbishop, but I am still doing things for the first time. This is my first parish visit to you and when we planned it, little did I know that it will coincide with a call for prayer and reflection following Madiba's death. Yes, we pray and reflect every Sunday and don't need to be reminded, but the call is to soak the country in prayers following Madiba's death. So in my homily and message today, forgive me if I read my message and address both to the nation and Madiba's family instead of preaching and reflecting on local needs and challenges. You are part of the clan, part of the bigger picture, and together are the human family.

In this spirit, I have given my homily the theme: "Celebrating Madiba's legacy and its lasting impact around the globe."

The Bible passages read this morning are apt for this day of reflection and prayer celebrating Madiba's legacy. The Old Testament passage, Isaiah (11:1-10), imagines a time, context, and world of righteousness and faithfulness, harmony, unity, and respect for difference and creation, a safe world where none shall be hurt or destroyed; a utopia, yes, but God says this world is possible, and Madiba's life and sayings too held forth this Isaiah vision and dream. The passage in Matthew's Gospel (3:1-12) through the lips of John evaluates an oppressive Roman administration and also urges people to have this holy imagination, to pursue it by "making a way for the Lord, make his path straight"—not the ways of crooked leaders nor of self-righteous religious leaders, but the way of the Lord Jesus and God's kingdom. The passage from Paul's Letter to the Romans (15:4-13) offers one practical example of imagining and creating this dream that God has in store for us.

Paul suggests radical hospitality: "Welcome one another, therefore, just as Christ has welcomed you, for the glory of God." Is this hospitality—where there is no greed, corruption, insecurity, or inequality—possible? Have we lost the plot as individuals and societies that, as Matthew says, we can be gathered as chaff and burnt with unquenchable fire? The answer is no. God created us for good; we need to work out this good for ourselves and not let it be drowned by evil and bad. The answer is, yes, if in spite of the good in us, we continue to maim, kill, and refuse to be built up for all that brings peace and hope.

Madiba held this hope that we can do better as human beings. Allow me then to paint a picture of this as I pay tribute to this great man.

On the international stage, the name Nelson Mandela is synonymous with the universal struggle for human rights, freedom, and the fight for democracy, issues that resonate just as strongly today as they did when he walked free from prison twenty-three years ago. Today, this Nobel Peace laureate is revered around the world as an inspirational symbol of peace and forgiveness. He acts as a powerful and continuing reminder that individuals do have the power to make change happen in the world, no matter how mighty the obstacles might be: the vision of hope I am talking about from the Romans and Isaiah's passage read today.

So, how do we celebrate Madiba's lasting legacy to the world? To some, he is one of the world's most revered statesmen, who has inspired generations of global citizens through his leadership in the struggle to replace the apartheid regime of South Africa with a multi-racial democracy. This legacy will undoubtedly be one of continuing inspiration. To many, Nelson Mandela is regarded as the greatest statesman in the world. His political leadership steered South Africa through the most difficult time in its history, all the while never succumbing to political pressure, never compromising his ideals or principles, and never pandering to the world's media. He will go down in history as one of the world's greatest leaders because of the impact he had, not just on the lives of South Africans, but on the lives of countless people around the world. He has made an irreversible difference to the global fight for democracy and human rights—or, put differently, for the values of the kingdom or the radical hospitality that today's Bible lessons say we must usher in during our time, in the likeness of Christ for God's glory and for the good of his people and creation.

Since leaving public office, Nelson Mandela has continued to be an inspirational advocate and champion for peace and social justice, both in South Africa and around the world, inspiring change where conflict and human rights abuses still exist. His establishment of highly respected and influential organizations such as the Nelson Mandela Foundation and The Elders, an independent group of public figures committed to addressing global problems and easing human suffering, continue to make a difference. Perhaps one of his greatest legacies to both South Africa and the world is his vocal advocacy of AIDS awareness. As far back as 2002, Mandela became a highly vocal campaigner for AIDS awareness and treatment programs in the country, confronting a culture where the epidemic had for many years been fueled by a combination of stigma and ignorance. On a personal level, the impact of HIV/AIDS was deeply felt as the disease later claimed the life of his son Makgatho in 2005, just as it did the lives of thousands of South African citizens during that period. His inspirational and passionate voice on the subject of AIDS awareness contributed to the change in attitudes and behaviors being experienced today as South Africa sets its sights on working for an AIDS-free generation.

Over the years, Nelson Mandela's contribution to the betterment of the world and humanity as a whole has been recognized through the highest accolades, awards, and recognition being bestowed upon him, the legacy of which continues today. He was awarded the Nobel Peace Prize for his efforts on behalf of his country and his people, sharing the 1993 prize with F.W. de Klerk, the last president of the apartheid era, who worked with Mandela to end the scourge of apartheid. He was the recipient of the prestigious
US Presidential Medal of Freedom and the Order of Canada, becoming the first living person to be made an honorary Canadian citizen. Nelson Mandela is also the last person to have been awarded the rare Lenin Peace Prize from the Soviet Union and the Bailiff Grand Cross of the Order of St. John and the Order of Merit, awarded to him by Britain's Elizabeth II. There

are many more prestigious awards that would take too much time to mention during this service; we are grateful to God that the human family saw it fit to bestow these honors upon this son of our soil, Madiba.

Perhaps his greatest legacy can be summed up in the continued inspiration he has provided as the one leader who has worked tirelessly to make change happen by appealing to people's common humanity, and by leading by example to many other leaders around the world who are still trying to achieve such change in their own political and social environments. Former US President Bill Clinton has said of the impact Madiba has had on him personally over the years: "More than any human being, Madiba has been the great inspiration for the life I lead and the work I do, especially in the area of HIV/AIDS... In return for everything Madiba has taught us, we each owe it to him to support his work and legacy by doing and living our own as best we can...throughout our entire lives."

President Barack Obama recognizes the impact that Nelson Mandela has had on the world, calling him an inspiration who has given everything to his people. Speaking on Nelson Mandela International Day on July 18 last year, he said: "Madiba continues to be a beacon for the global community, and for all who work for democracy, justice, and reconciliation. On behalf of the people of the United States, we congratulate Nelson Mandela and honor his vision for a better world."

Ultimately, Mandela's legacy exemplifies wisdom, strength, and grace in the face of adversity and great challenge. It demonstrates to all citizens of the world that there is a viable path to follow towards achieving justice, reconciliation, and democracy, and that change can happen through individual and collective acts of service. Through his example, he has set the standard for service to country and mankind worldwide, whether we are individual citizens, cabinet ministers, or presidents, and continues to call on us all to better serve our fellow human beings and contribute to the betterment of our communities.

Today, Madiba is thought of as Father or Tata to all South Africans, but to the rest of the world he is undoubtedly thought of as one of the outstanding heroes of the last century, alongside other inspirational global leaders such as Martin Luther King Jr. and Mahatma Gandhi. Each of these individuals was committed to the global struggle for human dignity, equality, and democracy, and Madiba remains a beacon of hope and an inspiration for those around the world who are still fighting for their freedom and for justice. As we look back and learn from Nelson Mandela's own long walk to freedom and reflect on his lifelong dedication to instilling the values of ubuntu, integrity, and learning, his legacy is an inspiring one. It will continue to inspire generations of people to come who themselves want to change the world and make it a better place in which all citizens can live and thrive.

May Madiba's soul rest in peace. May his nearest and dearest be comforted and consoled, and may we continue where he has left off, the Lord being our helper. And may this account of this one fallible man, not a saint but a hopeful and whole person, a loving person and, dare I say, a holy man, inspire us to serve God in others and God's creation until we too are called to God's rest and are given a perfect end.

May the God of hope fill you with all joy and peace even at this time of mourning so that by the power of the Holy Spirit you may abound in hope. *Amen.*

Appendix C

Prayer at the National Memorial Service for Nelson Mandela

Soccer City, Johannesburg, December 10, 2013

Let us pray;
Masithandaze;
Are rapeleng;
Laat ons bid.

Creator God, Lord of Life and Love,
You hold the whole universe in your hands and
Yet you also number the hairs on all our heads,
You know the fates of the nations and
The hopes and fears of each individual.

On this day of Madiba's memorial service
We pray for the peace of the world—
for peace without and for peace within.

Jesus Christ, Prince of Peace,
May your Shalom touch every place of conflict, division,
            brokenness, or fear,
May it fill our communities, families, and lives.

From the horrors and turmoil of nations in conflict,
to the fractured relationships and violence of too many homes,
bring your reconciling love.

Lord, we pray for South Africa in particular on this Memorial Day.
Help us to draw on the best lessons of our past
And to build on the firm foundation that, by your grace,
        Madiba laid for us.

Give us courage to hold fast to his values,
to follow the example of his praxis and to share them with
        the world.

We lift our hearts with gratitude for your loving care
that you have now called Madiba home to his eternal rest,
where pain and suffering are no more.

We commend his soul to your merciful keeping
And his family to your loving embrace,

And we say to Madiba:

Go forth, revolutionary and loving soul, on your journey out
        of this world,
In the name of God, who created you, suffered with you,
        and liberated you.

Go home, Madiba, you have selflessly done all that is good,
        noble, and honorable for God's people.

We will continue where you have left off, the Lord being
        our helper.

We now turn to you, Lord, in this hour of darkness, sadness,
        pain, and death, in tears and mourning,

We wail, yet we believe that you will console us, that you will give us the strength to hold in our hearts and minds, and the courage to enact in our lives, the values Madiba fought and stood for.

We turn to you, Lord, and entrust Madiba's soul to your eternal rest and loving arms as he rejoins the Madiba clan, his comrades, and all the faithful departed.

We pray particularly for his closest and dearest, for Me Graça Machel, for his children, grandchildren, great-grandchildren, and all his relatives;

May you surround them with your loving arms, your fatherly embrace and comfort.

At this dark time of mourning, at this perfect time when you have called him to rest and a perfect end, accept his soul and number him among the company of the redeemed in heaven.

Console and comfort his family, South Africa, and the world.

May his long walk to freedom be enjoyed and realized in our time by all of us.

May he rest in peace and rise in glory. *Amen.*

Appendix D

Valedictory Service at the Home of Nelson Rolihlahla Mandela

Qunu, December 15, 2013

The liturgy used for a service conducted before Madiba's remains were handed over to the military for his funeral

Silence

The steadfast love of The Lord never ceases,
His mercies never come to an end,
They are new every morning.

The Kyrie (isiXhosa)

Nkosi, senzele inceba.
(*Lord, have mercy*)
Kristu, senzele inceba.
(*Christ, have mercy*)
Nkosi, senzele inceba.

The Lord's Prayer

Collect for the Day

Almighty God, neither death, nor life can separate us from your love: with the whole company of the redeemed in heaven and earth; we praise and magnify your glorious Name, Father, Son and Holy Spirit, one God, blessed for ever.

Matthew 5: 3-10

Blessed are the poor in spirit, for theirs is the Kingdom of Heaven
Blessed are those who mourn, for they will be comforted
Blessed are those who hunger and thirst for righteousness,
        for they will be filled
Blessed are the merciful, for they will receive mercy
Blessed are the pure in heart, for they will see God
Blessed are the peacemakers, for they will be children of God
Blessed are those who are persecuted for righteousness sake,
        for theirs is the Kingdom of Heaven

Homily

Madiba is dead.

Bathembu, Mr. President and Deputy, and all gathered in this center of Madiba's home, the gospel passage we have just heard assures us that "you are there" when you mourn, for God will comfort you. So I ask God's comfort and strength upon you all as you grieve the death of Madiba even as we gather for this family valedictory service to celebrate this remarkable man.

Many profound tributes have been paid to this outstanding man, who dedicated his life to the service of humanity, the cause of justice, and care of creation.

Using today's gospel passage, he thirsted and hungered for righteousness and he is now fulfilled.

Bathembu, Masimkhulule, (*Let us release him*) to the merciful keeping of God—let us forgive each other where we have erred, or where the nation and world have erred.

Masimkhulule, by pursuing all that makes for peace. Let us never forget the price that he and his friends paid for peace and to get South Africa and the world to be where we are.

He remains a symbol of blessedness, hope, peace, admiration, wisdom, love, and goodness. How do we or will we measure up to these qualities?

Ma Graça, Bathembu, and all gathered here, may God fill you with his warmth and consolation, may he hold you together and sow love in you. May he strengthen you to grieve and mourn Madiba.

God bless you, Ma Machel, Ma Winnie, and all gathered here as we move to the final service for Madiba's burial. God bless South Africa and Africa. *Amen.*

Prayers

Let us now pray before the military takes over.

We give thanks for those who nurtured Madiba, including his father, his mother, the people of Mvezo, and the people of this community of Qunu, including the boys and girls with whom he ran through this beautiful countryside;

We give thanks for those who helped form him in his early days in Johannesburg, for his mentor, Walter Sisulu, and Albertina, for OR Tambo and Adelaide, for the attorneys who gave him his first job in the law, and those who studied with him, such as George Bizos, going on to become lifelong friends;

We give thanks for those, not all of whom shared his politics, who supported him and the cause of liberation while he was on trial and then incarcerated on Robben Island and in Pollsmoor Prison;

The list, Lord, is too long to name all the names, but in a representative capacity we give thanks for:

- The chaplains from the churches who visited him and those with him in prison

- The chaplains and clergy, present here and not, who prayed for the family and Madiba throughout his life

- The lawyers, such as Arthur Chaskalson, Issy Maisels, and Duma Nokwe, who defended the leaders of his generation

- Those such as Helen Suzman and Jacques Moreillon of the International Committee of the Red Cross, who campaigned to ameliorate conditions for him and his fellow prisoners

- The artists, such as Nadine Gordimer, Hugh Masekela, Caiphas Simenya, Letta Mbulu, Jonas Gwangwa, and others, who used their international reputations to support him and our struggle

- The church leaders who held the torch high while our leaders were imprisoned—people such as Trevor Huddleston, Beyers Naudé, Stanley Mogoba, and Archbishop Desmond Tutu

- His friends from the Rivonia Trial to his last days, such as Ahmed Kathrada, Andrew Mlangeni, and Denis Goldberg

- For those who cared for him in his last years: the medical professionals, the bodyguards, the drivers, the household staff, and the staff of the Nelson Mandela Foundation, from Jakes Gerwel to his dedicated assistant Zelda la Grange

- Those in the planning committee for this mourning and funeral service, family members, government, and others unknown to us, you know them, Lord

- For all the members of his family, who loved and cared for him, for his spouses, their children, grandchildren, and great-grandchildren: for his first wife, Evelyn; for Winnie— whose defiance constituted an anti-apartheid struggle all of its own; and for Graça, who brought him happiness in his last years and kept faithful vigil to the end.

Finally,

O Lord, support us all the day long of this troubled life,
    until the shadows lengthen,
And the evening comes, and the busy world is hushed,
    the fever of life is over,
And our work is done.
Then, Lord, in your mercy grant us safe lodging, a holy rest,
And peace at the last, through Jesus Christ our Lord.

We now hand over to the military, Bathembu, in the peace of Christ.

Amen.

Appendix E

Address to a "Procession of Witness" to Parliament

Cape Town, April 19, 2014

Today is a day we're issuing to all South Africans a "Call to Witness." What does this mean? For me, I'm asking all South Africans to turn themselves inside out and expose their sense of moral consciousness to the sun. Why? Because, the sun is God's disinfectant.

Because of the ethical state of the nation, we need to be morally disinfected...morally disinfected so that we can recapture the dream of South Africa. Over the last six months, you have no idea how many thousands of South Africans have said to me, "Your Grace, I'm so very tired of seeing the moral pollution. I am so tired of seeing the pervasive unethical contamination. It is so painful to see the inequality." They ask. They plead: "Archbishop, we should be joyfully celebrating the twentieth year of democracy and liberation, but I've never felt so depressed by the crisis of distrust in our country's government." They ask, "Where do we go from here?"

Well, where do we go from here?

The welter of emotions our situation unleashes demands prophets for a time such as this. My hope, and the hope of my fellow

religious leaders, is that in the next few days—over and above
demanding explanations, which seem not to be coming—you will
start a national conversation around three essential questions.

Firstly, "How long must South Africa live out its daily existence
suffering from such a lack of transparency?" Real transparency
is an essential ingredient for trust...the absence of transparency
results in a withering, pervasive weight of distrust taking over.

And one might follow up the first question by asking, "Is the
distrust we feel for today's leadership more or less than the
distrust we felt during the days of apartheid?" The cost of the lack
of trust we are experiencing is incalculable. Elsewhere, I have
spoken of the need for a Renaissance of Trust and Responsibility.
When you disarm the people of our communities of their trust
in our leaders, you not only offend them, but more seriously, you
show our communities that you distrust them. You are either
afraid of their values or distrust their values. You are afraid of their
ability to make informed, values-based decisions or you distrust
our constitutional values. You are afraid of their opinion or do not
trust them to exercise their choices responsibly. You are afraid of
their judgment or do not trust them to apply their judgment. Or,
most seriously, you are afraid to let them question your actions
and motivations or do not trust them to understand your actions.

So question three becomes, "How did we here in South Africa
find ourselves in such a void of morality?" The collapse in trust
didn't happen all at once. I recall the Ernest Hemingway dialogue
in *The Sun Also Rises*. When a man asks another, "How did you
go bankrupt?" the other answers, "Two ways. Gradually, then
suddenly." So it is with the collapse of standards and values. What
started as a trickle is now a flood. The wave of distrust is wiping
out the incremental progress we have made on accountability,
democratic choice, and the rule of law.

In the face of the nation's questions to our President on the international embarrassment we call "the Nkandla question," he has opted for silence. Unfortunately, those advising him have forgotten the admonition: Silence screams the truth.

This is not what our country wants from our President. It is not what our country needs from our President. And it is not what we voted for when we asked our President to take responsibility for our country's navigation. I, like many, want to believe our President when he said that he didn't rob our nation's treasury. But if he didn't, did he hold the stepladder? If he did, sadly he's as guilty as the person who climbed through your window.

All this leads us to some questions:

1. Mr. President, how much longer do the citizens of South Africa have to wait for you to explain how you came to make the decisions you made on Nkandla?

2. Mr. President, which of our constitutional values did you use in making your decisions about the R234 million spent at Nkandla?

3. Mr. President, what is your plan for responding to the historic levels of distrust that permeate every discussion about our national government?

4. Mr. President, what is your plan for beginning a national conversation about our national values before the election so that every South African can vote their conscience?

Mr. President, our country deserves better. Our country's communities deserve better. Our families deserve better. Our children deserve better. You were elected to provide a moral compass for our nation. You were elected to be a model of a

leader who makes values-based decisions. You were our hope.
That's a huge responsibility. We need to hear the voice of
responsibility speak.

We're facing an historic opportunity, and it's not the celebration
of our twentieth year of democracy and liberation. It is how
you decide our destiny. It's in your moments of decision or
indecision that our destiny is shaped. Mr. President, how you are
remembered in history, your legacy, is going to be determined by
how you speak to the nation about how you made the decisions
you have made.

All the nation wants is a leader who sets an example by
taking responsibility. A leader who is transparent. A leader
who acknowledges imperfection and who in acknowledging
imperfection, commits to a life as a values-based leader. Nothing
short of that will be enough.

Mr. President and all of us listening today, now wearing my cap
as an archbishop and of course a Christian leader: Easter assures
us that it is at such heights of pain, despair, hollowness, and
distrust, that the risen Lord, the Christ, bursts anew into our lives
to restore and transform them. Easter is a time of rebirth. Christ
forgives the penitent, he heals the broken and gives hope to the
hopeless. Easter is a time also for renewal. We are strengthened
to offer ourselves in service of the common good, following the
example our savior set for us.

May our walk today establish God's shalom, his salaam, his peace.
May we now courageously look inwards, disinfect ourselves of all
that is not values-based, and proclaim a vision of the resurrected
Christ who has overcome death. Let us pursue all that leads
to trust, accountability, and transparency. I want to end with a
prayer, before we receive the final blessing. Let us pray:

God bless South Africa
Heal her present wounds and of the past,
Guide her with values-based leadership
Lead her into the way of truth,
Rekindle her levels of trust,
Until all shall be equal
And all shall flourish.
For Christ's sake, Amen.

Appendix F

Sermon for the Easter Vigil at St. George's Cathedral

Cape Town, April 15, 2017

Christ is risen, He is risen indeed! Alleluia! Happy Easter to you all.

We come to this Easter Sunday, to this open tomb, with the dark reality of our country very much at the forefront of our minds. Over these Lenten days we have come to the lowest point in our political life. Like many, I feel that the dream of South Africa sometimes feels more like a nightmare, a prolonged Passiontide, so to speak. Personal interests, corruption, private gain, entitlement, a vicious contempt for the poor and the common good, a culture of blatant lies, and cronyism—and possibly worse—dominate our public landscape.

This past week, the nightmare got worse as the full impact of the President's recent actions unfolded. They have devastated our hopes for the kind of foreign investment, which we desperately need to grow our economy and create new jobs. Their impact on consumer confidence and trust is immeasurable. Tens of thousands of jobs are directly affected by just a 10 percent drop in consumer confidence. If we cannot turn the situation around, at the end of the road we are now on, we face the prospect of employees fired; shops shuttering; malls closing; the poor unable to afford bread, paraffin, electricity, and the cost of burials; possible hyperinflation—it is as if we are entering the Zimbabwe moment.

In this hour we grieve because the words of GK Chesterton, used to such effect by Trevor Huddleston as apartheid's grip intensified in the 1950s, are again apt now:

> *I tell you naught for your comfort,*
> *Yea, naught for your desire,*
> *Save that the sky grows darker yet*
> *And the sea rises higher.*

Many of us over the past days have felt a deep resonance with the gospel observation [in John 13:30] that when Judas left the room in which the disciples shared the Last Supper with Jesus, we are told "it was night." Every time anyone turns their back on love, betrays the bonds of fellowship, and steals from others, it is night! This is true for us in South Africa and indeed in so many, far too many, other parts of the world.

Our nightmare is similar to that under which the ancient Hebrews lived in tonight's reading. In our case, while we aren't being disadvantaged by colonial slavery any longer—and no matter what anyone says, colonialism was for most of us a form of slavery—while colonialism and apartheid are over, some of our institutions, part of our economy and some among our leaders have become slaves to a new form of colonial oppression. It is a moral and economic oppression that manifests itself in the form of one family's capture of our country, and a President whose integrity, soul, and heart have been compromised.

Yet, even as we survey this and the litany of other social pathologies that afflict our country and our world, we have in faith to say that even though it is absolutely true that darkness overwhelms us, the events at the tomb of Jesus on Easter Day signal a greater victory, a more abundant truth. At the heart of the message of the resurrection of Jesus is the stubborn insistence that nothing is irrevocable. No betrayal is final. There is no loss that cannot be redeemed. It is never too late to start again. As John Shea reminds us: "What the resurrection teaches us is not how to live but how to live again and again!"

The promise of Easter can be likened to what I call the new struggle in South Africa. In that struggle, the realization of the promise of Easter is measured not only by how soon we replace the current administration but also by how well we ready ourselves for what comes next. How do we prepare ourselves for the future after the end of a deeply corrupt regime? After President Zuma has fallen, will those who benefit from his patronage fall too? Because if we change leaders but the patronage system that the current leadership has produced doesn't change, if state-owned enterprises, the prosecution, and law enforcement agencies remain captured by corrupt interests, we are no better off.

The resurrection doesn't only recall the fact that God raised the body of Jesus from the dead. It certainly means that, but it also means that that power raises us from the multiple tombs that hold us in captivity. In one of the last days leading up to the Passion, we read that wonderful story, that precursor of Easter Sunday, when Jesus, having wept at the tomb of Lazarus, also called him out of the tomb. He challenged him to leave the places of death and to walk away from its shadows.

Over the past days, as we have recalled how Jesus called Lazarus to leave an environment that offered him no future, hundreds of thousands of South Africans have issued the same challenge to those in public life. Ordinary South Africans, in their places of work, in their places of worship, and tens of thousands of them on the streets, have issued a call to our political leaders. They have called on them to come out from the places that hold them in bondage to the death of greed, in bondage to the lust for and the seduction of power, in bondage to the shadow of moral corruption that has enveloped South Africa.

Ordinary South Africans have called to their leaders, just as Jesus did to Lazarus: Come out! Come out of the tomb! To those who are economically, socially, and morally deaf; to those who ignore the crisis of distrust that has cast the longest and darkest shadow our great country has ever seen in the democratic era, ordinary South Africans have said:

- Don't stay in places that will pull us all into a culture that wounds or kills us

- Don't be overtaken by the culture into which our President and some of our elected officials have descended

- Don't ignore the pleas, cries, and profound sense of pain and suffering that plague our wonderful and beautiful nation

If resurrection is about the fact that good will triumph over evil, justice over injustice, hope over despair, then part of that resurrection dynamic means, for us, that we call out the dead and those who deal in death, that we remind them that their destiny is to be in the Upper Room, that place where new life emerges, where the power to restore is released, and where joy is glimpsed amidst even the residual sadness. Resurrection means that we can start again, that life is a story of multiple beginnings but that it challenges us to call the dead out of the tomb as a first step.

What does being obedient to Jesus and following in his footsteps entail this Easter? What does it mean for us to imitate his voice

in our own Lazarus moment? What are our obligations as
citizens, all of us with equal rights and responsibilities under the
constitution? You've heard me say this before: Our destiny is not a
matter of chance. It is a matter of choice. Your choice. My choice.
Our choice. To all gathered here on this most holy night: If there
was ever a time we needed to rise up and take ownership of our
future, it is now.

South Africa needs real leaders who must be ready to sacrifice
all to ensure dignity, equality, opportunity, and freedom for all of
our people. We cannot and should not ever be afraid to raise our
voices for honesty, truth, and compassion, and against injustice
and lying and greed. It is time to take sides. Silence encourages
the tormentor, never the tormented. Nothing strengthens
authority as much as silence. Neutrality helps the oppressor,
never the victim. As Archbishop Emeritus Desmond has said, "If
an elephant has its foot on the tail of a mouse and you say that
you are neutral, the mouse will not appreciate your neutrality."
We need to rise up, to stand up and speak up for our rights, our
children's rights, and our grandchildren's rights.

Let us acknowledge that the old order, the economic system that
makes us one of the most unequal societies on earth, must go.
Let us challenge the narrative of the corrupt, who use that old
order as a fig leaf behind which they hide their greed. As I have
said before, we need to overcome the skewed racial ordering of
our economy and the obscene inequality that it produces, not
by indulging the rapacious greed of a few politically connected
individuals but by building a new, fairer society that distributes
wealth more equitably for all.

We are God's engineers and everything of meaning and
importance that we have accomplished in the past twenty-four
years has been the result of refusing to be stopped by the walls

that divide us and demonstrating our ability to be exceptional bridge builders. Let the different interest groups and elements of our society that are committed to these ideals—whether rich or poor, whether black, white, colored, or Indian, whether Christian, Communist, Muslim, Hindu, or Jew—let us all find one another in a powerful, united coalition that puts first the interests of the poor and thereby the interests of all of us.

While the Mandela and Mbeki administrations made mistakes—among them, shutting down dissent from within the ANC's parliamentary caucus—their record shows that if government pulls together representatives of different interest groups, we can find rational, workable solutions to our most difficult problems. In that spirit, let us turn this moment of crisis into a moment of opportunity and convene a land Codesa to negotiate a solution to this emotional issue and, in the light of the downgrades of our credit ratings, an economic Codesa too.

In this new struggle, let us reject the participation of white racists who don't believe that black people are capable of running a country or an economy. They are not welcome on marches and protests. Let us also not be distracted by hurtful and anachronistic comments on colonialism. Let us also reject those who want an unequal, tribal, sexist, and racialized South Africa, who exploit the views of a minority of racists to portray their opponents as stooges and to threaten white compatriots for exercising their civic rights.

To all politicians—Mr. President, honorable Members of Parliament, Madam Premier—we appeal to all of you to rise above your petty everyday squabbles and obsessions and to recognize this as a turning point in our history. My father once gave me a very important lesson: You can, he said, if you think you can. It's just a matter of removing the apostrophe and the "t" from can't. I want to issue a special challenge to our MPs tonight: when you are called upon to decide on whether you have confidence in our President, vote for the country's future and not for your own pockets. You should know that:

> South Africa will be watching.
> The world will be watching.
> Vote your conscience.

There is something particularly poignant in Matthew's account of the resurrection. The greatest news in all history, the turning point in human affairs, the testimony to the relentless love of God so much stronger than even death, is entrusted to Mary Magdalene and the other Mary. It is entrusted to two women, to people who in the first place had the courage to confront the power of death by going to the tomb and, as it were, taking on that seemingly immutable power. The Good News of the Gospel was announced to those who in the culture of the time were marginalized and often discriminated against, the victims of abuse, poor, and unnecessarily burdened.

Resurrection narratives are entrusted to those who do not shrink before the challenges of history and are not cowed by what seems insurmountable, strong, and unchanging. It is often the poor, the discriminated against, the victims of oppression, who slowly tire of death and begin to live differently, to live resurrection lives and so announce a new moment in history. It is often that bottom billion of the world who through their testimonies of resistance and fearlessness offer us moments of hope and therefore of resurrection. To them, as indeed to us, is entrusted the good news that life is changed now, not ended, and that every moment of life is caught up in new possibilities.

At this moment in our history, where we are faced with hard choices that take us out of our comfort zones, we need to hear Jesus' resurrection words: "Be not afraid, go and tell."

In closing, let me share with each of you a very personal message, from my heart to yours: God loves you, and so do I. God bless you, God bless your family, and God bless South Africa. May it be so at this challenging Easter time. Alleluia!

Acknowledgments

I am deeply indebted to a number of people for their role, wittingly or unwittingly, in the writing of this book, and to no one more than Me Graça Machel, who generously invited me to join a spiritual journey with her and Madiba for nearly five years and who just as generously wrote the Foreword.

I have no words for Lungi, Nyakallo, and Paballo. Thank you Lungi for your critical eye and unwavering support, and thank you all for bearing with me as I carry out my many tasks.

My thanks go also to Nkosi Mandla Mandela, Madiba's grandson, for encouraging me to record my experiences with his grandfather, and to Zelda la Grange, Madiba's ever-present personal assistant, who sacrificed half of her adult life to serve him and our country and who was always both warm and efficient in welcoming me to Madiba's home.

Special thanks to Lynn Franklin in New York, formerly Archbishop Desmond Tutu's literary agent, who urged me to expand a short account of my ministry to Madiba into a longer memoir incorporating my heritage and experiences. She also generously connected me with my publishers. At Tafelberg, my warm thanks to editors Gill Moodie and Alison Lowry for their skills and publishing know-how.

In Britain, my profound thanks to Richard Burridge, Dean of King's College, London, and to the Rev. Canon Jim Rosenthal, formerly Director of Communications for the Anglican Communion Office, for linking me to my British and American publishers respectively. Warm thanks also to Alison Barr at SPCK in London and to Richelle Thompson and the Rev. Canon Scott Gunn at Forward Movement in Cincinnati.

I am grateful to Lesley Magoro for helping me recount my "activism" in Alexandra, to Wendy Sheen and Liz Allen, for transcribing many hours of my dictation, to the Rev. Canon Dr. Sarah Rowland-Jones, researcher and staff member during my ministry to Madiba, for all her insights, and to Paulina Mapheto and Henriette Le Cointre-Potgieter of Polokwane, who were wonderful in helping to trace historic photos of Makgoba's Kloof and the campaign against the Makgoba clan. A special thanks to the Trustees of the Archbishop Thabo Makgoba Development Trust for their support too.

John Allen was there for me from the beginning, from connecting me with Lynn to doing research and, metaphorically speaking, translating my Sepedi into English. He visited Makgoba's Kloof, accompanied me to Alexandra and Soweto, spent hours interviewing me then used his skills as a reporter to edit my dictated reminiscences and the interviews into a narrative.

About Forward Movement

Forward Movement is committed to inspiring disciples and empowering evangelists. Our ministry is lived out by creating resources such as books, small-group studies, apps, and conferences.

Our daily devotional, *Forward Day by Day*, is also available in Spanish (*Adelante Día a Día*) and Braille, online, as a podcast, and as an app for smartphones or tablets. It is mailed to more than fifty countries, and we donate nearly 30,000 copies each quarter to prisons, hospitals, and nursing homes.

We actively seek partners across the church and look for ways to provide resources that inspire and challenge. A ministry of the Episcopal Church for over eighty years, Forward Movement is a nonprofit organization funded by sales of resources and by gifts from generous donors.

To learn more about Forward Movement and our resources, visit www.ForwardMovement.org. We are delighted to be doing this work and invite your prayers and support.